Praise for *More Energy, More You!*

'It is an absolute pleasure for me to recommend to you the work of Dr. Sally Rundle. The first time I met Sally I knew we were kindred spirits – always with laughter and a sense of fun she has given of her wisdom and honesty to me at times when I needed perspective and clarity.

We have a shared passion and curiosity for learning and how we can bring that knowledge into making a difference – both in our own lives and the lives of those we touch. When we get so busy 'doing' that we forget to 'be' – Sally has a way of letting you know what's important and how you can apply that to living well.

And so *dear reader,* without hesitation I pass the baton onto you so that you may tap into the loving guidance and support that Sally will give to you in her new book *More Energy, More You!*'

Anne Templeman-Jones, Non-Executive Director, EMBA

'In her book *More Energy, More You!* Sally takes us on an important journey – into the physical, emotional, mental and spiritual energies that make up the whole of who we are as human beings. When we come to realise and understand that we are out of alignment in any of these areas we can then positively approach change so we can recalibrate to improve ourselves. Sally shows us that our intentional awareness can bring intentional change and this is the most essential ingredient to well-being – important at any stage of life and especially as we age. I highly recommend *More Energy, More You!* a resource you will want to read and re-read on your journey to live your best life.'

Julianne Parkinson, Chief Executive Officer, Global Centre for Modern Ageing

'I love the idea of being able to find uncomplicated and easy-to-use approaches that can instantly improve a person's energy and well-being. As an intuitive healer I am so aware of how people show up and the way their energy can impact upon their health and well-being. Sally's book is filled with an abundance of knowledge on the ways that our energy can become drained, how to know what's happening and what to do about it and she does this in her always engaging and delightful manner – a must read!'

Keryn Armfield, Medical Intuitive and Healer

'Sally offers a unique blend of depth and breadth of knowledge, combined with a gifted intuitive 'knowing.' Her life-long curiosity for learning, vision and commitment to living a spirited life, inspire and positively impact all with whom she works.

Whether working with Sally professionally, privately or merely having a conversation with this dynamic woman, you will experience powerful shifts. Sally's book offers a masterful collation of inspiring wisdom, easy to access strategies to take care of ourselves and generate more 'verve' in our busy lives. This is an essential resource for both the younger generation who are living and working at an ever-increasing pace, as well as those people who value living life to the full.'

Shelley Owen, Creative Coach and Mentor; Coach Supervisor (IECL)

MORE ENERGY, MORE YOU!

Practical Approaches to Restore and
Balance your Mind, Body and Spirit

SALLY J RUNDLE Ph.D.

BALBOA.
PRESS

A DIVISION OF HAY HOUSE

For Jessie and Jae, my tomorrow's hope.
I love you both.

Tell me, what you are going to do with this one wild and precious life?
Mary Oliver, Poet

CONTENTS

FOREWORD

We are aware when we feel fully of energy – we feel great. We are aware when we are lacking energy – it affects our whole world view. Our energy is very powerful indeed and yet many of us spend very little time bringing a conscious awareness to enhance it.

When we have positive energy others around us can sense our vitality and inner glow. We all know this: when you smile, the world smiles back.

The ebbs and flows our energy takes is dependent on so many things that affect us; both internal and external. The wonderful thing is we can all take charge and responsibility for how we feel. We can change our personal energy for the better with daily activities and practices.

Energy comes in many forms which affects all spheres of our lives – our emotional well-being, sound mental health, physical robustness and our spiritual life and connection. It's possible with practice, time, awareness and intention to engage in each area to learn and modify how your energy affects you and the people around you.

This book acts as a big toolbox. You can duck in and out of it to pick out real gems that speak to what you need right at this time. Some of it is pretty 'out there' but all of it opens our eyes to what may be possible.

The physical strategies cover how to boost recovery, reduce pain and promote balance and prevent illness so you can give your body the day-to-day energy nourishment it needs as it moves through eating, sleeping, playing, moving, pausing and stopping. This is where Dr. Sally Rundle brings in successful strategies in the fields of energy management, nutritional science and exercise physiology for optimum health.

For mental well-being there are concepts to help gain clarity and to release mental blocks; whilst emotional strategies seek to improve resilience and to release trauma.

Spiritually, astute wisdom and guidance will help to restore and re-connect you to your own intuition, purpose and presence.

Sally delivers a plethora of options with an extensive list of people and connections to explore. Some, maybe all, will appeal to you at this moment. What I am sure of is that the depth of options and actions presented is so rich in content that you will come back time and again to delve into the resources offered on these pages. This is a recipe book which I delighted in reading and learned much.

Sally is a lifelong explorer. I have watched in awe as she has traversed the 'road less travelled.' Sally has a way of weaving science, knowledge and ancient wisdom together in a distinctive and perceptive style as she brings you to know yourself and how unique each of us truly are.

In my life there are very few people I have met who have had the curiosity, drive for learning and such capacity for integration of knowledge into a working whole that Sally has. Over the 25 years I have known Sally this process has been a constant and I have been lucky enough to have been the recipient of her astonishing breadth and depth of knowledge and her generously shared wisdom.

She walks the talk. Sally has beautiful energy.

As a Yoga practitioner, and as an influencer and advocate for positive change in this world, I am sure that *More Energy, More You!* will take you on a journey of self-discovery so you can fully participate in all aspects of your energy and your true being can shine.

Karen Mahlab AM, Founder and Chief Executive Officer, Pro Bono Australia

Energy Medicine is not just a set of ideas somewhere out in the ethers. It is designed to empower you to make better choices for your health and strengthen the connection to your daily life.

Donna Eden
Energy Medicine Pioneer

PREFACE

My inspiration for this book comes from individuals I have been fortunate to meet and who have astounded me in how they approach and live a spirited life. Most of them have worked through major life challenges or have overcome personal tragedies. Each has risen above the daily version of themselves and lived from the truest expression of their spirited selves. From them I have drawn a heart-felt appreciation for the human spirit. Every one of them reminds me that we are far more capable than we realise especially when asked or have a need to do more. These powerful reminders have supported my own journey, a lifelong pursuit of mastery of my own energy, its boundless potential and elegant dance. I feel that I am honouring them by living my uniqueness.

On my life's path, I have discovered my own verve. This is what I call energy that shows up in the way of a buzzy zest when I go out into the world, exploring beyond my edge of comfort. A delight for self-discovery has been the driver that has enabled me to gain the most from each encounter. In the second half of life's lessons, I have learned from others the gentler side of living, this being a softer sway. To stop and 'smell the roses' eases my restlessness for wanting more and invites me into just savouring each timeless moment.

I have spent my life researching and modelling individuals who in their own unique way are living a spirited life. I have been deeply curious about how they manage their energy and sensitivity and what gives them the capacity to be their authentic selves in the world.

I am intrigued with quirky individuals who choose to go against the flow and have found ways to get on their own orbit and live a lifestyle that works for their energy. They range from leaders in organisations, entrepreneurs creating their own businesses, change agents and pioneers in the field of energy medicine. This book shares some of the strategies that they use. They are practical, simple techniques and tools which I know work. I have constantly re-applied them in my own life whenever I am seeking an inner balance and strength.

My aim is to provide a set of resources where you, the reader, can find at least one strategy that could make a difference in your life. Sometimes all it takes is doing one thing differently and this can make a significant impact in the amount and quality of your energy.

ACKNOWLEDGEMENT

Gary Yardley, my friend and colleague, thank you for your wise guidance, creative thinking and support in shaping and bringing together my ideas within this book. Your mentoring was a key to unlocking the potential of this book and bringing it to life.

Adi Shakti, my deep appreciation for your thoughtful proofing and adding quality to my words and expression.

Bridget Ransome, a huge heartfelt thank you for your skilful editing, book coaching and meticulous passion for seeing me achieve the dream of bringing this book into the world.

My beautiful 'soul sisters,' Shelley, Karen, Keryn, Anne, Julianne, Trina, Judy, Maureen, Deb, Jan and Buffy you have been loving and encouraging in helping me stay the course and believe in myself. I am grateful for our wonderful connection.

Emma Watson my supervisor and energy psychology coach, thank you for supporting me to hold steady through this journey and to uncover my confidence to be my best self.

My energy teachers and mentors, Jan Smith, Donna Eden, Mali Burgess, Cyndi Dale, Steve Wells, Dr. David Lake and Wanda Zumallen you opened me to a new world of energy medicine, intuition, healing and transformational change.

My darling mother, Jannie, your love and unwavering belief gives me spirited energy. My sister, Martha, brother Dave and the rest of the family tribe, thank you for your support, sense of fun and desire to live life to the full. I love you all.

Jessie, my creative and talented niece, thank you for your captivating images; your artistic abilities amaze and inspire me. Jae, my curious nephew and 'truth seeker,' – your questions about life's mysteries intrigue and enliven me. I enjoy our conversations and look forward to more of them.

Finally, thank you to the team at Balboa Press.

INTRODUCTION

Everyone in my Dad's life was given a special nickname that reflected their attitude and approach to life. Mine was *The Buzzer*. I was given this tag because from the moment I could walk, I was into everything with an insatiable curiosity for learning. I loved learning new things in class and on my own from the world around me. I thrived in school – reading and chatting with strangers. Anywhere and everywhere there was an opportunity for learning. I was like a buzzy bee, going from flower to flower, always on the move, seeking out the next place to land and to discover a different nectar.

My mother tells the story that at two years of age, somehow, I escaped from the house and wandered down towards the local railway station. There I helped myself to a sandwich from a workman's lunchbox. She found me walking home munching on the sandwich and accompanied by three local dogs who were probably taking care of me. Seeing her, I said boldly, *Here I are!*

For my brother and sister, being *The Buzzer* meant I created events for entertaining them and having every imaginable adventure. This ranged from doing nativity plays at Christmas-time for the neighbourhood, performing skits in front of our parents' friends to make them laugh, singing in our concerts, exploring the creeks of Adelaide and selling sticky toffees at our stall erected on the footpath outside our family home, to name a few. We were the adventure siblings and it gave me a wonderful place to express the buzzer energy.

I turned up in this life-time with an attitude and energy signature that was social, bubbly, active and extroverted and this has empowered me to connect and engage with people and activities. It has been very helpful in my work, social life, when I moved to different cities and countries and, of course, helped me to connect with wonderful friends. The buzzy vibration picks up my energy, focuses my next learning and takes me out into the world.

I moved through my twenties and thirties gliding on the flow of this energy, passionate for the next learning challenge, and thriving being in the world, full of my own verve. With four degrees and an international Ph.D. and running my own company, I found myself with all the trappings of learning and a successful career. My verve had delivered a string of achievements, yet there was still a restlessness to seek more.

Then, in my mid-forties something changed. I felt a yearning that had not been there before. It was coming from deep within me – a desire to be more relaxed, open and at ease. My natural up-beat rhythm was signalling change. Suddenly, and inexplicably, I was having trouble with picking up my energy; a needed lift to take me back out into the world. In a nut-shell, my natural extroverted nature could not sustain itself so easily anymore. I needed more of an equilibrium with being out in the world and in being still.

Coupled with this inner change, I was coping with a significant external change. My dad suffered a massive stroke. I was in New York working when it happened and received the phone call no-one wants to get when miles from home. The flight back to Australia was one of the loneliest and emptiest times I have experienced. I spent the whole flight reflecting on my life with him, and everything he meant to me. I knew he was going, if only he would hold on until I got there.

Making it back to Adelaide, Dad was in a coma for ten days. One minute he was with us, the next gone. Together with my brother and sister we tried to make sense of this trauma. For me, he was my sounding board and mentor, always there with encouragement when I was taking risks, being out in the world and creating new opportunities. He had always believed in me and loved my buzzy spirit. My life changed forever.

I missed him terribly and I felt I was drowning in the grief. The result being, my verve crashed and while I could pull myself up, the lift was temporary. It took some time for the sadness to lighten.

At the time it was confusing. What was happening? This juncture was a turning point in my life. I was becoming aware of another subtler energy wanting to express itself. It was so different from the personality energy of the bubbly, vivacious extrovert. My first inkling was of a stiller, lighter energy that enveloped me; a quietness that flowed and moved gently. When I finally connected with this energy I felt a natural ease, an effortlessness and serenity of spirit. It felt so very good being stilled on the surface yet moving strongly from within. I wanted this to stay with me.

I later came to learn that my journey in this life was about moving between these two predominant energies of being buzzy and a deeper current of stillness, my new-found 'sway.' These two wondrous states of **verve** and **sway** allowed me to gain a greater mastery over my energy. This didn't mean being in control or all knowing, it meant more of being conscious with how I use the two halves of my unique energy signature – the vivacious and the still – Sally's verve and sway!

At this time, I discovered something quite extraordinary; a whole new field of endeavour opened before me, something which altered my life course, for I intuitively knew I must walk this different path. This new course was the way of the subtle energy dimension. This is not something widely discussed in the business world and is often dismissed as lacking any readily accepted business case studies about energy medicine and intuition in the work-place.

This field of energy medicine and metaphysics focuses on the energy we do not normally perceive with our five senses because it mainly vibrates at a higher frequency. Our subtle energy body has been shown to affect our well-being, thinking and emotional health.

At last I had found an outlet for my sway a playful enjoyment, leaving my verve to pursue the potential of others in the business world. It was such a joy walking these two paths side-by-side, opening a different future of discovery.

My journey of awakening my energy and intuition afforded me the opportunity to engage with the emergent field of energy medicine and the healing power of the mind-body-spirit connection. I have travelled world-wide meeting and learning from experts in the fields of medical intuition, shamanism, human performance, meditation, sound and light therapy, mindfulness, consciousness and energy healing.

Our Personal Energy Challenge in Today's World

In our fast-paced modern world of increased demands and stretched resources, it is becoming more and more difficult to find time to look after and nurture ourselves. There are just so many things we must do and expectations placed upon us for living the 'perfect life.' While we are busy, these distractions sometimes detract from who we are and our desire to fulfil all our dreams.

Healthy energy is what we all seek and wish for as this is the first noticeable indicator of well-being. We all know when someone appears healthy because we can perceive it in their actions, they are aglow with vitality and vibrancy. Even with age we can still perceive this in others, with how they expend their energy and grace. They appear at ease within themselves and have enough for doing what they wish.

Your energy is precious, without it life becomes a drudge and listless because there is no charge to ignite your endeavours. The reverse is easily noticed by those around you, they know when you are slightly off, and not humming with your usual animation.

The majority of people today, are crammed into living in fast-paced, densely populated cities. For many of us, this style of living takes its toll on our bodies and can result in a constant state of external stressors that trigger a 'flight or fight' response. Being dynamic requires a vast expenditure of energy and then recovery.

Perpetual stress is an unnatural state and is perceived by the mind and body as a threat. Whether it be physical, social, or relationship based, it will cause a stress reaction, instantly sending the body into a cascading process of hormones and chemicals to deal with any pressured demand. Without a restful retreat we are at the mercy of these chemical responses, and lack any ability to turn them off and in time we create a sense of deep weariness.

Being able to combat this 'full-on' state of hypervigilance is vital to our health and success. Physician and best-selling author, Dr. Lissa Rankin, reminds us that a key to our capacity for well-being and happiness is to turn on the body's natural self-repair and healing mechanism. She prompts us to recognise that 'The body is equipped with natural self-repair mechanisms that can be flipped on or off with thoughts, beliefs, and feelings that originate in the mind.'

This self-healing and energy restoration only occur during what is coined 'the relaxation response.' It is during this time when the body shifts from a state of arousal back towards normal functioning and carries out its preventative maintenance, mending and rejuvenation. Yet, sadly, within a time poor environment of constant pressures the time we have left to just sit, to pause and relax is drastically reduced and can become the first casualty of stress.

The reality is that the two responses, stress and self-healing, cannot coincide together or work side-by-side. It is either one or the other. When the body is in a state of stress, it is less likely to conduct effective maintenance functions or access elevated emotions such as joy, love and contentment. Multi-tasking and catching fleeting moments are, invariably, not enough to sustain the body's need for relief. What it needs is a frequent and tranquil reprieve from massive over stimulation.

If you are someone who wants to self-manage your health, vitality and resilience, this book is for you. If you seek to make a change in how you take care of your energy but are not sure where to start, this book provides you with practical solutions. If you are a coach looking for new ways to help your clients, this book will give you a range of resources to meet your clients' needs. You may also be someone who already knows about energy management and are looking for some new techniques to add to your repertoire.

Just for a moment stop and consider the following questions as a gauge to your current energy state:

How is your energy right now?

Are you feeling stretched, depleted and wondering how you can keep going?

Are you waking up tired in the morning with a long 'to-do' list and feeling driven into high different gear so you can get through your day's tasks?

Are you finding it hard to capture 'you time' so you can have experiences that will raise your spirits and energy?

Do you have a sense that there is something missing from your life?

Are you feeling that you are not expressing all of who you are, or could be?

If you said 'yes' to some of these questions you are not alone. Research is revealing that as a society we are experiencing lower levels of well-being and higher levels of stress, depression and anxiety.

In this book, you will find over seventy strategies useful for inducing a relaxation response in your body and mind which will turn on your innate ability to self-heal. You also will learn more effective ways to take care of your energy, reduce being fully wired and strung taut with tension and gain more ease in life.

There are four distinct areas to take care of your energy so you can live a full and spirited life with a truer expression of yourself. Daily life impacts upon and draws down your four energy streams: physical, cognitive, emotional and spiritual.

1. **Physical Energy:** bounces back after its resting state and wears thin as the day progresses. Physical weariness and exhaustion is a sign that your body is seeking rejuvenation.

2. **Cognitive or Mindful Energy**: focused on the task of making sense of your surrounds, needs and priorities. Your mind can keep processing with little pause until depleted. Loss of clarity and mental heaviness is a sign that your mind is seeking freshness.

3. **Emotional Energy:** which seeks out pleasurable and comforting moments. Your emotional reserves can become taxed by unnecessary worries, demands and dramas. Increased anxiety, agitation and overwhelm is a sign that your emotional centre seeks relief.

4. **Spiritual Energy:** a desire for a connection and life purpose. Your spirited self can be easily waylaid by distractions and repetitions that want your immediate attention. A yearning to find ease is a sign that your spiritual self wants to find a greater sense of connection beyond yourself.

All four types of energy require a distinct form of energy management. In this book, I have collated the techniques and approaches from successful and vibrant individuals and then blended this knowledge with an ancient wisdom.

This collective know-how offers the simple promise to make a profound difference to your daily energetic flow. It will also help you re-discover or enhance your joy for living. Most of these energetic strategies are evidence-based which means they have been shown to create positive measurable results within the body, its energy production and performance. They also offer a beneficial side-effect to create mental resilience and emotional agility. Within my practice, I have utilised these effective techniques to add a source of richness for my clients and as a way for ensuring vibrancy in daily life.

These four areas of energy management are methods that we can learn to use to better cope and adapt to a stressful life of competing wants and needy demands. If used for harnessing energy, we can expand our tolerance, give ourselves more time, extend our resources and shift from reaction to responsiveness in the choices we make. These strategies are designed to restore choice in our daily lives and in turn will help us to find more productive and dynamic ways to engage with others.

Pioneer in the field of positive psychology, Professor Martin Seligman, is clear on the benefits of taking care of our energy and the positive effects it has on our relationships, health and communities:

'A vital person is someone whose aliveness and spirit are expressed not only in personal productivity and activity - such individuals often infectiously energize those with whom they come into contact.'

(Character Strengths and Virtues)

When you spend time looking after yourself you are being kind, considerate and caring of you and these moments will have resounding long-term benefits for your holistic well-being.

You can delay or put off making self-care a priority, however, the research on ageing well shows this to be detrimental. Living in constant stress catches up and ages your being before its time and diminishes vitality. If you lack the energy and time for healing yourself, then caring for another's health and welfare also becomes more taxing.

Energy is a finite and dwindling resource when not replenished and leaves you drained and disinterested when tackling something new. It becomes a subtracting force which can take you away from what you wish and hope for - to live a healthy life with positive, vibrant relationships.

CHAPTER ONE

Flowing Energies – Verve and Sway

The threads that run through our life – one pulling us into the world to achieve and make things happen, the other pulling us back from the world to nourish and replenish ourselves – can seem at odds, but in fact they reinforce each other.

Arianna Huffington, *The Sleep Revolution*

Have you ever noticed that your energy ebbs and flows? To what extent are you aware of how this daily flux impacts how you interact fully with life?

For each of us there is a frequency that radiates around, through and within us, affecting how we show up and how we move towards our hopes and dreams. This unique configuration of how we flow shapes how our energy works for, or against us. I use the energy concept of your passionate *Verve* and your gentler *Sway* as a way to describe daily, weekly and yearly peaks and troughs of energy. In between these ebbs and flows sits a range of different energies that allow us a daily equilibrium, an optimal resting state. The younger we are, the more verve we have at hand with the body growing into its power. In contrast, the older we are, we seek more of a gentler sway for sustaining our lessening energy.

Verve is the energy that comes from within, picks us up and takes us into the world. In comparison with sway, its flow is more powerful. It gives voice to your internal passion, the charge you have for being alive and contributing in the world.

Verve is like the bow of the ship that surges forward, lifting and dropping with the rise and fall of the waves, yet unwavering in its focus. Its force happens when you pick up your energy and go into the world focused and knowing what you are seeking. Verve momentum is your natural drive that converts your dreams, visions and aspirations into actions. It says, 'I'm here, I can do it. Isn't this fun, awesome and great?' With verve comes confidence and tenacity in taking on the world. It is a powerful vibrancy and vitality that charges you with a readiness to tackle your day.

There is what I call a 'Verve Index,' which means that some people come with more verve than others. They have more inherent drive, passion and resolve to produce and create their dreams. For some it is strong early and fades later. While others seem to have an unrelenting source of verve for life.

In contrast, Sway is a natural relaxed state, your rhythm and natural ease. It comes into being when you lean back or move forth in a stylised and graceful way. With sway comes a lack of awkwardness, stiffness or self-consciousness. It is a gentler energy for engaging with the external world of people and nature. This enables how we can warmly and openly respond towards another's energy configuration and frequency.

Sway offers a kinder and warmer approach which is caressing in its invitation to engage and exchange. Sway is soft and powerful in its quietude which feels like a sensual soothing ease, a smooth velvet energy. It embraces all our senses and gives us a light-heartedness of being and helps us to ride the ups and downs of life. With this vibration we connect with our generosity of spirit and compassion to tolerate, accommodate, forgive and forgo the angst of life's transgressions.

There are, of course, a range of energies that sit between your passionate verve and kinder sway. You may have already noticed that you had a stronger sense of verve than sway when you were younger. The vibrant and flourishing verve that gave you an abundant energy combined with wholehearted enthusiasm when you approached demanding situations and challenges head on. It helped you to stay firm with your purpose and bounce back from set-backs. It fuelled your desire to explore and discover a curiosity with any given subject or activity. For some, it may have fired off sudden outbursts of vigour or even a fiery anger that needed a direction and outlet to burn off its intensity.

Consideration of your own time and maturity of responses ensures a sensitive approach for living life. A key aspect is to know and to learn when there are more productive times in going with the flow rather than swimming against the endless tide in order to prove your worth and value.

Sway is a recalibration of the inevitable 'let down of energy' that comes when we lean back and release our verve. It is an opportunity to measure your energy expenditure and to move towards the creation of a 'sustainable self.' Accessing more of your sway is a way to be at ease with yourself. It stems from an acceptance of the beauty found within; and an appreciation for living life's moments with a gentler pace, affording you a deeper intimacy with self, others and nature.

We each will have a preferred energy style, sliding the spectrum between both *verve* and *sway* to find our own unique resting state. This style will have been shaped by life's experiences, cultural influences and our families. Choosing how we want to live into our promise and spirited life, may require a shift in how our energy works. The concept of energetic intelligence says that those with the greatest range and deftness to reach each state will be the most dynamic and adaptable within their surrounds, able to fit in with or to take charge of a shared ambience when required or wanted.

In this book I delight in showing you simpler ways to harness your personal *Verve* and *Sway*, to become a more vital, vibrant you.

What research states about building and sustaining energy

Within social interactions and relationships, engagement and co-operation become the most effective way to manage one's energy resources and to harness more from shared effort or synergy. When teams collaborate and work at their full potential they are more productive in their use of energy; the sum of the parts is greater than those involved and it is more fun to share in success.

The dynamic interaction to share speaks more about one's style to either 'force a push of wills' or 'invite a pull of delight' so as to contribute and develop relationships. In share contexts, going with the flow or sway is more about enjoying the journey, whereas driving a passionate verve ensures a destination is reached. In today's world of high performance demands where everything is goal orientated, we demand more of one at the detriment of the other. Verve and sway are complementary in order to thrive as a dynamic being - where you can't have one without the other without experiencing burnout or an indifference to life.

Tony Schwartz, CEO of the *Energy Project* is passionate about re-inventing and rejuvenating the workplace in a demanding world of rising complexity. He states:

> 'Human beings are not computers. We're not meant to run at high speeds, continuously, for long periods of time. Science tells us we're at our best when we move rhythmically between spending and renewing energy — which is what we need if we are to fuel sustainable engagement and high performance. The solution is that we are at our best when we move between expending energy and intermittently renewing our energy.' (The Human Era @ Work)

In partnership with *Harvard Business Review*, The Energy Project assessed the factors that influence how people feel at work and how they perform as a result. What emerged from this 'Quality of Life Study' of twenty-thousand employees across the globe in multiple industries makes common sense. Schwartz says, that the better people's needs are met, the more healthy, happy, engaged, productive and loyal they become. By taking care of people, they will in turn take care of the business.

The results of the study found that employees have four predictable core needs at work: physically to rest and renew; emotionally feeling cared for and valued; mentally being empowered with boundaries that help to focus attention in absorbing ways; and spiritually, desiring a sense of meaning and purpose in their work.

While this study was specifically directed towards employees and the workplace, other research from positive psychology, neuroscience and mindfulness suggest there is an alignment between these core needs and how we can live a fulfilling, healthy and spirited life.

In the *Physical dimension* it is about how we find balance between intense effort and real renewal and replenishment. Our ultimate aim is to find a balance of energy expenditure so we can enjoy more throughout our work days, weekends and holiday periods.

What would it be like to wake up each morning with vitality and to take this through your day? This physical energy is persuasive, either use it or lose it; it cannot be saved for a rainy day. This energy wants to be expended and, sadly, batteries don't exist to store it, even though we often talk about getting away and recharging our batteries! The physical is a process of daily renewal, rather than a depletion begging a re-start after being burnt out. To start up from a place of exhaustion or inertia requires more energy to constantly re-boot, compared with sustaining a steadier life pace.

Compelling knowledge from biological science suggests that our body only goes into cellular repair when it is in a state of coherence. In other words, it is relaxed - not stressed. In this dimension the focus is about how we eat, sleep, play, move, pause and stop. There are many popular topics in this area. I will draw upon successful performance strategies from the emerging fields of energy management, nutritional science and exercise physiology.

In the *Mental dimension* it is about how we strengthen our focus, clarity and cognitive agility. Confusion and lack of coherence are the major distractions and pull on our mental priorities. What would it be like to get your best ideas and then have flashes of insight to convey simpler solutions? Pressures and stressors of the mind come from our need to problem-solve and to find answers to the challenges we face. The lack of rigour to sustain focus and then manage the many distractions that captivate the mind's imagination can drain its ability to perform.

Fundamentally, our mind's capacity is that of an interactive organ designed for making sense of the world around us, exploring both sequential logic and abstract concepts. For doing the latter, we must access more of what William Duggan calls 'strategic intuition.' This form of intuition is clear thought and knowing that happens when we must figure out what we can do in a new and unfamiliar situation. It comes from being able to lean back, slow down our thinking and quieten the mind sufficiently enough to germinate new and different thoughts. In the cognitive section of this book, I will be drawing upon the emerging fields of neuroscience, consciousness, hypnosis and mindfulness.

In the *Emotional dimension* it is about how we fuel our emotional energy. We will explore what is involved in being optimistic and positive and what it takes for us to be engaged with our lives. What do we need to feel satisfied, respected and valued? The research from the field of positive psychology, neuroscience and contemplative science is proving that well-being is a skill and elevated emotions such as love, gratitude, kindness and self-compassion are keys that fuel our emotional energy and health. Equally important is how we tackle difficult and uncomfortable emotions such as anxiety, fear, resentment, anger, shame and blame. These emotions can deplete our energy. Learning skills to embrace what Dr. Todd Kashdan refers to as, 'the upside of our dark side' are important for increasing emotional agility.

To accept the inevitability found within uncomfortable states is important for self-development and so we can optimise our energy as dynamic beings, warts and all! In the emotional section of the book, I will draw upon the latest tools and techniques from the fields of psychotherapy, positive psychology and emotional intelligence.

In the *Spirited dimension*, the extent with which we have a sense of purpose, significance and self-worth in our lives will affect our energy. Our desire to constantly seek out meaning and relevance draws us out-wards in the pursuit of truths, and in the desire to create viable reality, one based in some semblance of fact so as to tackle the larger questions of science. This speaks to our inner turmoil in an attempt to make sense of our life's purpose and our reason to exist. How clear you are about your own personal code of ethics and values will provide a set of guiding principles to live by. Feeling lost and less than your strengths is debilitating to your potential energy. Finding your joy for what you love doing and what lifts you up in the world feeds spirited growth.

There is also the larger question of your connection with the universe – a Divine Spirit. This may come in the form of your faith, religion or collective consciousness. In the spiritual section of the book, I will draw upon the great philosophers, the arts, and the fields of metaphysics, subtle energy and intuitive healing.

What is Energy Medicine?

In 2007, Dr. Mehmet Oz, as a guest on *The Oprah Show* proposed:

> 'We're beginning now to understand things that we know in our hearts were true but could not measure. As we get better at understanding how little we know about the body, we begin to realise that the next big frontier in medicine is energy medicine. It's not the mechanistic parts of the joints moving. It's not the chemistry of our bodies. It's understanding, for the first time, how energy influences how we feel.' (Dr. Mehmet Oz, November 20, 2007, *The Oprah Show*)

Energy Medicine is a broad concept which includes the use of subtle energy techniques which are not yet fully measured by conventional medicine and science. It is a system of self-care and self-management. There are simple and effective techniques that you can learn to keep your energy humming and in balance.

Working with your subtle energy involves sensing your energy fields, finding energy blockages and then transmitting energy to yourself for re-ordering harmony and energy flows within the body. It also involves becoming aware of and working with external energies which surround you every day. These are a natural set of unseen rhythms from our immediate surrounds, nature and other energetic entities. More than likely, at an unconscious level you already benefit from these subtle nuances. What is exciting is that given guidance you can tap into these natural forces and sustain your own health and balance.

Together we will explore how to enhance and refresh your physical, emotional, mental and spiritual well-being. We will also examine what depletes your energy and causes you to push or drag through life, a drudgery, rather than moving with verve and sway.

This book is my invitation to you, one offering you a lifetime discovery of new and unusual ways to engage with your energy signature and to find your joy.

It is my wish that you will treasure and cherish your journey travelled so far with fondness. Ground yourself to find balance and calmness each day. Feel energised, excited and exuberant about tomorrow's possibilities. Nurture a source of vitality – one that fuels your capacity to live your dreams, grow your abilities, develop your talent and flourish with your own unknown and yet to be discovered. Modern dancer and choreographer, Martha Graham, expresses the invitation to you, to be your exceptional self, 'There is a vitality, a life force, an energy, a quickening, that is translated through you into action, and because there is only one of you in all time, this expression is unique. If you block it, it will never exist through any other medium and will be lost.'

May you harness more of your own energy, so you can become more of you!

How to Use This Book

This is a resource book designed to offer strategies and techniques which empower your energy to thrive so you can be the best version of you. The four key areas of this book are body, mind, emotion and spiritual energy. They are far from being distinct, rather they each have an overlap and operate as an inter-dependent system. Each of these four energies is offered as a starting point for calibrating and better understanding your available resources. The strategies will help you to harness your ability to sustain personal growth and development. You will grow older with days passing, that is a given. How you engage in and what condition you arrive at each developmental stage, will determine your enjoyment for a life well-lived. This vitality for living will be shaped by your energetic consumption and its subsequent renewal.

Each of these four energy streams contributes to your overall flourishing, and for most one of the four will be or become the dominant energy source at various stages of your development. For example, physical energy is clearly the exuberance of youth, the force, the punch and passion which becomes less strident as we grow older. Some less generous souls would say that this drive and ambition is often wasted upon the young when compared with maturity, which implies that when you have gained enough life wisdom only then can you fully appreciate a boundless energetic verve with a balanced sway.

Stressful and Unfulfilling Energy

Generally, our energy levels and needs are more readily noticed when there is a lack felt or when they occur in less than pleasurable ways, far from our desired outcomes or feelings. There are some common forms of energy depletion that we all wish to reduce from our daily lives.

Your physical body is depleted if you are experiencing: sluggish energy, a lack of vibrancy and vigour, a lowered vitality that is quickly depleted and drained and that leaves you feeling tired, irritable and prickly and wanting sleepful rest.

Your mind is weary if you are having: restless energy, constant churning thoughts, an agitated and stirred up inner state, doubts and fears holding your attention, and leaves you unable to settle or find peace of mind.

Your emotions are flat if you are feeling: stodgy energy, slow, sluggish, you are easily distracted and disjointed, which leaves you feeling despondent, disappointed and fragile and with life's vulnerable impatience of wanting it all.

Your spirited self is worn down if you are being: reactive, unconscious, unconnected and lonely rather than having or being offered a considered choice in life, which leaves you at the mercy of being a victim or passive with a fated life laid out before you.

Using the Seventy-Two Strategies Provided

In using this book as a resource, I recommend you:

1. Start with your primary stressed or unfulfilled energy or area of depletion. Focus on the one energy domain that would add the most to your daily energy.

2. Review the list of strategies and then decide which aspect of your imbalance of energy requires your attention and rejuvenation. Read and follow the designated strategy. You may find that you have to repeat this to gain full benefits.

3. Then, find one strategy from each of the other three domains that, when used in conjunction with your primary strategy, will enhance its positive effects.

Remember that each of your four energy domains are at times independent sources of energy. They each have different sources for being refreshed and renewed and also ways of being depleted. They do work separately, yet they are interactive on and with the other domains which make up your whole vibrational signature. Physical rest may not be enough for an exhausted spirit or a doubting mind … this is where you may need more than one and even up to four strategies. If this is you, take one from each of the four energies to re-harmonize your frequency.

Alternatively, you could start with the energy you most feel likely to move towards to create a more satisfying flow and harmonic vibration.

The Energy Boost Assessment

One way to determine what your body needs is by an 'Energy Boost Assessment.' Mark out what you want to boost and lift. This will indicate which of the four areas you will most likely benefit from an energy boost.

If You Need a Physical Energy Boost

Of the body – a vibrant energy: where you feel your body come alive, lighten its step, whisper its charge and quicken its pulse. There is a boundless feeling of lightness and a desire to engage with a physical aspect of your day and night's rest.

Physical Functions and Considerations:

Body Mobility: Flexing your core strength and posture which influences how you stand, sit and ultimately move through your day.

Energetic Daily Routines: Ways for strengthening and uplifting your tone by balancing your energies. Taking a pause, a rest and relaxation.

Flows: Keeping circulation of fluids, nutrients and essences optimal for sustaining your capacity for aliveness and health.

Work and Play: Balancing between intense focus, effort and comfort cycles to ensure consistent performance, enjoyment and living life to the full.

If You Need a Cognitive Energy Boost

Of the mind – an agile energy: This is where your ideas can easily crystalize and thought patterns extend your realm of what is possible. There is an inner knowing and clarity, quickly making links with new and complex issues and offering you peace of mind.

Cognitive Functions and Considerations:

Creativity and Inventiveness: Having originality of thought and using your imagination to create different ideas and solutions.

Challenge Your Life Patterns: Confront and question habits, rituals and approaches that no longer serve you and your best interests.

Critical Discernments: Make important judgements with sensitivity and astuteness. Allow calculated risks with life i.e. the less travelled path.

Clarity of Mind: Have openness, discernment and be non- judgemental of yourself and others. Sound recall of memories that offer relevancy in any given moment.

If You Need an Emotional Energy Boost

Of the emotion - attracting energy: This is where you can draw towards you those things you wish to connect with and desire to give a pleasant sensation. There is an inner grace which is comfortably open and vulnerable to seek out beautiful synergies.

Emotional Functions and Considerations:

Emotional intelligence: Choose and have a say in how you respond to others and life's challenges. You have the emotional availability to change your state and to grow from the moment.

Enriching dynamic connections: Engage with differences of routine and people. Stimulate and embrace change as a progressive pathway to grow and expand your perspective.

Healthy relationships: Being open and honest about your feelings and allowing others the same, creating mutual respect. Seek out a shared intimacy by offering of self and inviting others in.

Caring and nurturing: Freely giving kindness, compassion and tenderness with those who need emotional support or altering the atmosphere of your surroundings and increasing a higher vibration of goodwill.

If You Need a Spirited Energy Boost

Of the spirit – awakening energy: This is where you rise above self and daily concerns and tap into the larger human condition. There is freedom from being duty-bound, an effortless part of something larger than life.

Consciousness: An awareness that transcends your physical reality and five senses. The brain is not the producer of consciousness, but it functions as the receiver to filter and monitors what is allowed in.

Will and Willingness: Living your uniqueness and promise, what you are disposed or inclined towards; expressing more of who you are. Aspects of will are a soulful energy, adding a generosity of spirit and hope.

Faith in the unknown: An openness with the unexplained and unrevealed nature of life and all that which cannot be explained. Having belief in another or a concept without having or needing evidence.

Intuitive or '6th sense:' An extra-sensory ability to bring in unconscious information without using the five senses through an inkling, or intuitive knowing of something more than just a conscious awareness of something tangible.

For optimising the resources in this book, my personal advice to you is to be discerning with your take-out. Focus on finding eight or less strategies from the overall seventy-two strategies, that best suits your present needs. Rather than trying them all on at once, select those that will make a real difference to you right now.

Remember just one from the right area can be enough of a change you need to better manage your energy. You can repeat this process in six months time, adding as you grow into the better you.

Be mindful of your preferred energy strength or what you are immediately drawn towards. It is more likely that you will find more of an expansive energy by exploring those domains you have least ability with.

These energy domains of least attraction of activity may at first appear confusing and less relevant to your needs. Please be patient and allow you unconscious mind to stay with the intent of the strategies, as your own thinking style might not readily comprehend its hidden energetic value to the future you.

I invite you to enjoy and delight in all the strategies; some will be
pertinent to you and others you can share with others.

Sally J. Rundle Ph.D.

Your Physical Energy

CHAPTER TWO
Physical Nourishers

In today's knowledge-driven economy, the best measure of productivity is how much energy people bring to their work and lives. The challenge is how we free, fuel and inspire ourselves to engage more of our strengths and potential to our daily lives.

Tony Schwartz, CEO, *The Energy Project*

Your *Physical You,* is about your body and its ability to generate energy. Keeping the physical body flexible and viable is essential for personal well-being as this gives you the energy to remain active and vital in how you engage with your world. Taking care of this amazing energy system is worth the investment. Without the body operating at its optimal capacity, it can become a barrier for you to perform at your best and to live the life you want.

Remaining physically vibrant is about sustained energy and endurance as you pass through different stages of your development and growth. The energy you have in your twenties is different from the energy in your forties and fifties. Research today is showing that the way we exercise and are active is very different in our twenties than in our forties and beyond. In fact, strenuous activity can be a stressor on the body rather than an enhancer. Speaking from my own personal experience, it is easy to take the body for granted by pushing and then demanding more from it without providing sufficient rest and recovery. Sometimes, I would forget I had a body, pushing it to exhaustion with tiredness pulling me up short. My focus was more my mind and will, with my body just coming along for the ride. I have learned the hard way that if I continue pushing, my physical health would eventually put the brakes on and I would find myself slowing down either with a simple ailment or generalised fatigue.

Holistic health expert, Dr. Deepak Chopra says:

> 'If you consciously let your body take care of you, it will become your greatest ally and trusted partner.' (2015. Twitter. *@ Deepak Chopra*)

Being in partnership with your own body means listening fully to its wisdom and intelligence. Its health message is unique for you and will easily guide you towards its needs and the support you can give to maintain a healthier state of well-being. The physical body is a system that is primarily about life-giving flows such as circulation, lymph, nutrition, absorption and exchange. As you work with this highly intelligent complex system it will provide you with an environment to sustain you to give your body the energy it needs for an optimal outcome.

Physical energy imbalance: there are five common effects when lacking healthy vibrant energy:

1. Restlessness and agitation

2. Tiredness and weakness

3. Depletion or imbalances of hormones

4. Ailments and accidents

5. Allergies and intolerances.

An ideal physical body is one that gives you a range in function and motion. The old saying, 'If you don't use it, you lose it,' bodes well for physical performance. If you stop using particular muscle groups, you can lose muscle mass and strength. For example, if you are a runner you use and train a specific group of muscles. If you get on a bike and go for a substantial ride, you are using a different group of muscles and you will generally experience faster muscle fatigue.

My chiropractor, Dr. Frank Marcellino, focuses on three basic components for good health and fitness in his patients, these are: strength, flexibility and vitality. He sees that the natural consequence of strength, flexibility and vitality leads to true relaxation and better healing. Muscular strength builds muscle mass and lean body mass. Flexibility increases the range of movement and mobility, particularly in our joints. It also supports balance and posture. Vitality (vigour and zest) comes from being physically active on a daily basis. It improves quality of life and gives the impetus for getting up and living each day to the fullest.

The body readily responds to changing environmental conditions both externally and internally. It is a remarkable system. It can quickly acclimatise to daily needs and then readily make significant adjustments to cope with even extreme demands. For example, have you ever trained for a distance running event, big hike, trek or started a new weights routine at the gym? The art of this training is to achieve a progressive overload; to take the body towards 70-80% of its capacity so it will force an adaption to a new level of demand. As you increase the intensity of training, your body generates increases in cardiac output, haemoglobin (carry more oxygen) and aerobic enzymes and capillary mass in your legs. This all assists to cope with the new environmental pressures which are self-induced!

The body is constantly shifting and adjusting to where you are, what you are doing, eating and experiencing. It does this through natural flows. The challenge is do you go with these natural flows or do you push and pull against them? Discomfort is a signal that you are going against your own flow. It is the body's way of demanding your attention. Physically, it is probably signalling you to either move, rest, sleep, nourish or stretch as a way of re-charging or discharging energy. When I go against these natural flows, my body will let me know by triggering tension spots, and will reduce my vitality as there is not enough fuel left in my tank, this drops my blood sugar levels, or makes my eye-lids really heavy. These signs let me know it is time to close my eyes, rest and lie down.

A few years ago, I was fortunate to meet Dr. Tal Ben Shahar, an expert in Positive Psychology at Harvard University when he was in Melbourne giving a two-day seminar on the Mind-Body Connection. He asked:

'How many of you believe you need more will-power?'

About 80% of the audience raised their hands. His next comment was surprising, and it has stayed with me, 'What you have, is what you have. Wishing an increased will-power, will not make much difference. What we all need are rituals for supporting our lifestyle or way and these come from creating habits.'

Regarding routines, I am not talking about rigid structures or rules where you are completely governed by your beliefs and rituals. Living a rich and meaningful life is allowing yourself a stylish flow with the rhythm of your energy and your body's rhythms. Each day is different and therefore your rituals are important to create a context of renewal on an on-going basis so you can be a better you. This is about flowing through your day, week, month and year, finding and harnessing, as you go, sufficient essential variety to draw on different tools and resources as you need them. The purpose of this approach is to offer useful ways to renew, replenish and restore your energy and preferred nourishment; rather than just dragging your body along for the ride.

With your physical energy the starting point is to obtain a greater understanding of your own body and what it needs to function at an optimal level. Everyone has a unique configuration and what works for someone else, may not be useful for you. In this section you will find eighteen dedicated strategies which offer you *Physical Nourishers*, as a way of caring for the body. Nourishment and nourishing your body form the essence of physical energy; both will ensure you optimise and then sustain your energetic verve and gentler sway.

The Physical Realm seeks a daily nourishment of the following:

Body Mobility	Your physical structure, core strength and posture which influences how you stand, sit and, ultimately move.
Energetic Daily Routines	Ways to strengthen, uplift, tone and then balance your energies.
Channels and Flows	Keeping circulation of fluids, nutrients and essences optimal to sustain your capacity for aliveness and health.
Energy Expended	Pacing your verve and sway, the energy shifts in between these states, and understanding your default with stress.
Hygiene	Using home cleaning products, space clearing techniques and personal care products to create a clean space.
Libido	Taking pause and connecting with the sexual drive, activating the body's intimate need for release.
Work and Play	Balancing between intense focus, effort and rest cycles to sustain performance, enjoyment and balance.
Pastimes	Being in nature, indoor creative pursuits, outdoor hobbies, gardening, self-expression and volunteering.

Living intuitively within the physical realm requires a trust in your inner wisdom in relation to your own body and its needs. In many of our cultures, we have lost this connection because of modern day perfected rules, media and marketing. Take a moment and just observe young children, noticing how they flow with their intuition with what to eat, how they play and when to rest. Sometimes they become over-tired – an awful clashing state – with their desire for doing more, yet unable to continue onwards due to their body's need for rest. What if we were to listen fully to our body's needs and then capture its rejuvenated flow? Pioneer and CEO of body positive movement 'Fit Bottomed Girls,' Jennipher Walters says:

> 'Eat when you're hungry. Stop when you're full. Don't see food as either "good" or "bad." Eat what you want, when you want. It kind of sounds like the best "diet" out there, right? Except, it's not actually a diet. It's truly a way of sustaining you — an intuitive eating way of life.' (*Life Wellness*, Huffington Post)

Most of us have been exposed to years of different diets, to seek a healthy solution for longevity and thriving in life. The vast amount of information available can often be contradictory and confusing. For example, rules such as it is imperative to eat breakfast, eat five small meals a day, fast for two days each week, or eat right for your blood type. To attempt to follow these different methodologies can cause an underlying feeling of guilt or inadequacy when the results don't instantly occur or match their supposed hype.

Being attuned to our bodies can guide us to eat when we are hungry, notice how we feel during and after we eat and can ensure we pay attention to unusual cravings as they are often indicators of something missing. The body knows what it wants and needs for optimum operation – the challenge is to hear and feel the messages it sends.

The eighteen physical nourishers provide resources and strategies to assist you with the following questions:

How do you manage a healthy body shape for each developmental stage?

How do you effectively replenish your energetic needs?

How do you optimise your energy output through a daily cycle?

How aware are you of the body's required nutrients and trace elements?

This part of the book focuses on the physical aspect of becoming a better you. It offers effective strategies to increase your physical energy, vitality and resilience. These techniques will help you pause and recover so you can fully replenish your energy.

Physical Nourisher Strategies

The following eighteen strategies are useful in coping with either stressful moments or when faced with significant life hurdles. They nourish your natural verve and sway.

Physical Verve: a push energy, a strenuous activity, a charged burst of endeavour or a focused strength. Each of these are high demand upon the body's energy and resources.

Physical Sway: a pull energy, a momentary lull, a quiet resting, a meditation, a mini nap. Each of these are a lower demand of energy and rebalancing of the body's homeostasis.

These nourishers are the substance of what successful individuals use when they need to optimise their physical output and daily performance. They thrive in enjoying a gentler sway and lean into their passionate verve for living a vibrant life.

Nourisher	Description
1. Breath of Fresh Air	Using diverse types of focused deep, slow breathing to relieve physical tension and create relaxation which can bring the body to a more contemplative state.
2. Re-aligning your Posture	Change your body posture to shift your mental state. Take charge of how your body expresses itself positively and to ease stress.
3. Fragrant Pauses	Take brief and regular 'pauses' to sustain your physical energy, engagement and mental concentration to overcome fatigue.
4. Touching Moments	Use physical touch and sensuality to release powerful 'feel good' hormones in your body and to enhance your emotional state.
5. Softly Sleeping	Have restful sleep by using a blend of the body's natural rhythms; and herbs for settling self and sink down into a deep state.

6. Sultry Siestas	Optimise daily rest and recovery cycles to be more focused, productive and energised. Use micro-rest moments to replenish.
7. Fluid Movement	Increase your fitness by exercising with intermittent cycles, sit less and move more to increase your vigour and pep for life.
8. Chi of Life	Approach food as medicine by eating whole foods, locally grown fruits and vegetables. Enhance the body's natural intuitive healing.
9. Stomach Everything	Take care of your gut health, improve your body's capacity to digest, absorb and optimise nourishment and ease physical discomfort.
10. Refresh Raw	Use the power of live raw foods, rich in phyto-nutrients and enzymes to give your digestion a 'spark of life' and to improve vitality.
11. Sweet and Sour	Re-program your body by reducing refined sugar and carbohydrates to gain more balance in your body's blood sugar levels.
12. Perfumed Pleasures	Use essential oils and flower essences to increase anti-oxidants in the body, promote relaxation and enhance positive moods.
13. Verdant Green	Being within nature and bathe in natural energies, shift your own energy and access a state of calmness and relaxation and clear the mind.
14. Essence of You	Boost super minerals to support your body's metabolism and the different methods it uses for getting them into your system.
15. Grounding Delights	Ground your body's rhythm with the earth's energy, create a magnetic balance and stability within your own bio-electrical system.
16. Refresh your Space	Use space clearing techniques and devices to shift energy in your home and work environments to keep it fresh and vibrant.
17. Detox your World	Choose low toxicity environments in your home and garden by reducing the chemical load and disruption to your hormones.
18. Keep your Vibration High	Apply simple approaches for when you are feeling sluggish or tired and pick up your energy to feel uplifted and refreshed.

If we could give every individual the right amount of nourishment, exercise, not too little and not too much, we would have the safest way to health.

Hippocrates

1. Breath of Fresh Air

A strategy designed to reduce stress and tension.

Useful for: becoming more open and present.

Future proofing: 'How can I fully enjoy more ease?'

Breathing is the most natural process we do, it's always with us. Slow-paced, deep breathing can be a useful technique to restore balance in the mind, body and energy system. Consciously using your 'breath' is a simple, easy and accessible way to influence your physiology and maintain healthy body balance.

How this strategy offers you an alternate coping approach

Slow, deep breathing is an effective way for reversing the symptoms of the 'flight-fight-and-freeze' response that occurs when you perceive some form of threat to your safety. Under stress, your brain activates your sympathetic nervous system. This is the 'accelerator' response. Instantly you go into a high state of alert. Your heart beats faster and pumps more blood and your body releases a surge of cascading hormones. The result is your breathing becomes shallow which brings in more oxygen, all in readiness for your response to the perceived threat.

Deep breathing activates your parasympathetic nervous system, the 'brake response,' allows your body to reverse the accumulated stress symptoms. Deep, slow breathing stimulates the main nerve in the parasympathetic nervous system, the Vagus nerve. Research is discovering the power of this important cranial nerve. It runs from the brain right through into the gut and has a significant impact on our body's balance. When activated by slow, deep breathing, the Vagus nerve slows down your heart rate and creates a calming effect in your body, and, conversely, your mind.

The physical benefits of a regular practice of simple deep breathing is well documented. This includes increased energy levels, muscle relaxation, improved sleep, happier gut health and decreased feelings of stress.

This is how you can delight and enjoy its benefits

An easy practice to start with is called 'Breath 4-2-5.' I learned this technique when working with my colleague, Dr. John Wood during his sessions on the application of mindfulness for leadership. This is particularly useful if you have been triggered by an event and are finding yourself feeling stressed or overwhelmed.

Start by sitting comfortably and close your eyes. Place your attention at your feet. As you inhale slowly through your nose, imagine you are drawing your breath up from your feet towards the top of your head. As you do this, count to four. Pause at the top of your head, holding your breath for a count of two. Exhale slowly through your mouth for a count of five, taking your awareness down your body and back towards your feet. Repeat this '4-2-5' rhythm for a few breaths or until you feel more relaxed and open. Remember, it is a simple equation of '4-2-5' beats.

This is how I optimise it and gain the most value from it

I consciously use slow deep breathing throughout my day. I start my day with five deep breaths and consciously use slower breathing through the day to bring down my reactions and give my body an opportunity for recovery. It is useful when I'm sitting in busy traffic, running late for appointments, being in stressful phone conversations or just feeling overwhelmed with situations. When I notice that I am in the grip of stress and feeling tight, I pause and take a couple of deep breaths to calm and centre.

I use spot techniques, short mindfulness techniques, that can be done 'on the spot' moving through the day. One of my favourites is breathing in through my nose and lifting my shoulders up, holding this for a few seconds, and then breathing out through my mouth, while gently lowering the shoulders. Repeating this a few times brings me back into the present moment and my body feels more at ease.

Where you can discover more

The Chopra Centre describes different breath techniques such as alternate nostril breathing for anxiety, ocean's breath for cooling your mind when you are feeling angry, irritated or frustrated and energising breath when you are feeling sluggish: www.chopra.com.

If you are living in Australia, the Life Flow Meditation Centre in Adelaide offers a range of classes and retreats using mindfulness practice and effective techniques that are designed for taking a well-earned break from stress, letting your body restore itself: www.lifeflow.com.au.

Internationally recognised meditation teacher, author and corporate trainer, Davidji offers guided meditations on his site. After a twenty-year career in business and finance, David made a lifestyle change for living what he calls a 'life of wholeness.' He has a wonderful voice with deep timbre that invites you to let go, come back into the moment and find yourself in the stillness. His book *Secrets of Meditation: A Practical Guide to Inner Peace & Personal Transformation* offers practical ways for stress release and mindfulness: www.davidji.com.

For breath is life, and if you breathe well you will live long on earth.

Sanskrit proverb

2. Re-aligning Your Posture

A strategy for identifying the way the body expresses daily discomfort and stored tension.

Useful for: easing one's stress levels and increasing tolerance.

Future proofing: 'Is this how I wish to show up?'

Shifting your posture can affect your mood and energy. The relationship between our mind and body runs both ways. The mind influences the body's posture and the body activates your mind and emotions. Knowing that this connection exists, you can use it to your own advantage, first by restoring and then sustaining your physical energy.

How this strategy offers you an alternate coping approach

Given the strong connection between posture and mood you can use this deliberately to change your state. If you want to feel happy, start to smile. If you want to feel alert and focused sit up straight. In contrast, look down at a computer screen or iPhone and take your body into a slouched position with your head down which will create the opposite effect. Studies show that when people sit with slumped posture they find it more difficult to experience positive emotions because a downward posture is associated with feeling helpless, hopeless and powerless and it activates the body to release chemical messages that match the posture and associated emotion.

Social psychologist, Amy Cuddy, shares that body language not only affects how others see us, but it may also change how we see ourselves. Rather than worrying about making an impression on others, she advises that we change the impression we are making on ourselves. In a popular TED talk called *Your Body Language Shapes Who You are*, she explains that taking on 'power posing' can liberate us from fears and doubts. To stand in a posture of confidence (like *Wonder Woman*), even when we don't feel confident, helps with generating feelings of personal power. This in turn, can influence positive shifts in self-evaluation, emotions and mood.

This is how you can delight and enjoy its benefits

If you are feeling sad, defeated or overwhelmed, more than likely you will be slouched over with your shoulders curved forward, head down, and eyes looking at the ground. You will probably walk slowly, frown and sigh a lot. On the other hand, if you feel confident, your posture will be upright, chest open and expanded, head up with eyes forward or up. As a result, you appear taller, and feel taller!

You may find that when you work towards a deadline, a difficult conversation or an important event which looms 'larger than life,' you are holding your body tight. Anxiety will trigger the release of stress hormones in the body and one of the effects is your muscles will tighten ready for 'fight or flight.' In these moments, notice the tightening and shift your posture by moving your shoulders down (rather than being up against your ears!). To regain your balance, move your head into a neutral position rather than tilting forward and you will start to feel the tension ease off.

This is how I optimise it and gain the most value from it

As I move through my day, I often do this quick body audit – a personal check to see how I am showing up and what my body is telling me. Regularly, I tweak my own body language to empower myself to feel resilience within my body.

As you are reading this book, do your own quick audit on your own body. What are you noticing about your posture? Are you slouching in a chair, lying down, or sitting up straight? What is the position of your head and shoulders? In this moment how do you feel? What is your mood like? Now adjust your posture and lift your head up, chest out, back straight, and smile. Notice how these slight changes shift your energy?

By paying closer attention to my body posture, I can consciously make the adjustments that will trigger my brain in more positive ways. For example, if I wake up feeling flat, or drop into a low mood during the day, I simply get up and move my body, look up at the sky, wave my arms, smile and say out loud 'Yes!' In moments of vulnerability I cross my arms and put my hands on my shoulders which creates a feeling of reassurance. I hold this pose and gently move side-to-side which evokes a feeling of comfort. This is how I work with my body through the day. I support my posture and in turn my body supports my energy.

Where you can discover more

Amy Cuddy explains in her book *Presence: Bringing Your Boldest Self to Your Biggest Challenges,* the science underlying the connection between body posture and mental state. She shows us how we can become more self-assured and composed in high-pressure moments.

The Body Speaks by Lorna Marshall shows us how we can recognise and then lose unwanted physical inhibitions that we have learned throughout life. She explains how good performers use their bodies to their best effect. Focusing on actors in training as well as those on stage she provides methods to unleash potential and express ourselves more clearly.

> *Emotions and thoughts affect our posture and energy levels; conversely,*
> *posture and energy affect our emotions and thoughts.*

> Erik Peper, Professor of Psychology, San Francisco State University

3. Fragrant Pauses

A strategy designed to sustain your physical energy.

Useful for: Finding your verve and overcoming fatigue.

Future proofing: 'Have I found delight in my daily joy?'

This strategy focuses on using day time rest or pauses as an effortless way to aid physical energy. Pausing involves taking brief and regular micro breaks through your day, which enables you to sustain your physical vitality and your mental concentration. You've heard the saying, 'stop and smell the roses.' Think of this approach as building a rhythmical flow throughout your day – a fragrant pause.

How this strategy offers you an alternate coping approach

You are not a machine. Humans have a pulse, and move from different intensities towards a resting recovery. Ideally, you build in this healthy pause throughout your day and week. If you have been under high periods of intensity and stress in your life, create welcome periods of recovery.

Studies by Nathaniel Kleitman and William Dement found grounded in our body's physiology are 'ultradian rhythms' which are 90-120 minute cycles. During this period our bodies slowly move from a high energy state into a physiological trough. Towards the end of each cycle the body aches for a period of recovery. This craving shows up in the form of physical restlessness, yawning, hunger, thirst and tension. Tony Schwartz, CEO of *The Global Energy Project*, points out many of us ignore the signals and just keep working. The consequence is that our physical energy reservoir can deplete and power down as the day wears on.

Research shows that intermittent breaks for renewal result in higher performance and energy. The length of the renewal seems less important than the quality. *The Quality of Life @ Work Study* found it is possible to get a great deal of recovery in a short time; as little as several minutes in fact. People who take a brief break every ninety minutes reported 28% higher levels of focus than those who take just one break or no breaks at all. They also reported a 40% greater capacity for creative thinking and 30% higher levels of health (published in the White Paper: *The Human Era @ Work*).

Human performance expert Dr. Adam Fraser found that by taking rest time to unwind and access moments of stillness builds recovery for your body and brain. By taking a micro rest, you can easily shift your brain and body chemistry into the relaxation response. In doing so, you will feel calmer and clearer. In his book, *The Third Space*, he explains that by using the moment of transition between the first and second activity, by taking a brief rest, you are better able to physically and mentally show up for whatever comes next. By using micro moments throughout the day, you will replenish your energy and enhance your performance.

This is how you can delight and enjoy its benefits

There are several different ways to build 'pause' and 'pulse' into your daily rhythm. When you are busy, schedule regular breaks. Do this by working intensely for twenty minutes then break for five minutes. If you need a reminder, set a timer, or alarm on your phone. If you wish to stay focused on the activity for a longer duration, go for ninety minutes, then rest for twenty minutes. This is useful if you are using a lot of brain power or physical exertion.

There is also the notion of 'micro recovery' which you can play with between activities. At work, these moments of rest may be as simple as getting up from your desk and going for a brief walk, to have a cuppa or a chat with someone different. When walking between meetings rather than thinking about what was discussed or even your next meeting agenda, de-focus by noticing your walking or by counting your steps. Alternatively, you may choose to sit quietly for a few minutes, to shut your eyes and do some deep breathing or listen to music. If you are near a park or garden, head outside at lunch-time and rest in the sunshine as this is a great energy lifter. Better still, find some grass, take off your shoes and put your feet on the earth, or lie down on the grass as this will give your body even more of a re-charge.

This is how I optimise it and gain the most value from it

I have learned the hard way to build in my recovery time. Throughout my day I now take regular breaks. This involves regularly getting up and making a cup of tea or having a glass of water before standing outside in the sunshine and doing some stretching. A short energy routine or some breathing exercises picks up my energy. If I have been teaching or carrying an intense workload, I schedule two days when I deliberately have a lighter load.

Where you can discover more

In the TED talk, *Three simple steps not to take a bad day home,* Dr. Adam Fraser shares a simple formula about how to use the gap between work and home, as a chance to re-connect to those most important to you and to create more harmony in your relationships. He offers practical strategies for you to effectively use the transition space to re-charge and re-set your energy so you can show up at your best in both spaces. An over-arching strategy for transition involves three clear phases – first: Reflect, 'What went well?' (rather than what didn't go well); second: Rest, garnering a moment of stillness through meditation, mindfulness and to pause; third: Re-set, by asking yourself, 'How do I wish to show up in the next space? How do I want to behave? What type of energy do I want around me?'

> *When demand in our lives intensifies, we tend to hunker down and push harder.*
> *The trouble is that, without any down-time to refresh and re-charge, we're less*
> *efficient, make more mistakes, and get less engaged with what we're doing.*

Tony Schwartz, CEO of the Energy Project

4. Touching Moments

A strategy designed to release the body's natural hormones of pleasure.

Useful for: Uplifting one's spirit, contentment and enjoyment.

Future proofing: 'How do I remain deeply in touch with those around me?'

Physical touch in the form of a hug, pat on the back, and even a hand-shake can have an instant positive impact upon your physical body and mind. It works the same whether you are the person initiating the touch or you are receiving it. These forms of physical contact are processed by the reward centre in the brain which contribute to feelings of happiness.

How this strategy offers you an alternate coping approach

Touching moments are a powerful way to lift your sense of joy and help others to do the same. Research on physical touch by Dr. Dacher Keltner, Professor of Psychology at University of California Berkeley has found that touch is fundamental for all human communication, bonding and health. He emphasises:

> 'The science of touch convincingly suggests that we're wired to — we need to — connect with other people on a basic physical level. To deny that is to deprive ourselves of some of life's greatest joys and deepest comforts.'

Physical touch encourages your body to release the uplifting hormone, oxytocin. Often called the 'feel good hormone,' oxytocin helps you handle life's stressors, encourages social bonding and improves your health. It counters the stress hormones, such as cortisol that are being produced in your body under stress which in turn lowers your blood pressure and heart rate. When oxytocin levels are elevated above normal, most people experience intense feelings of love, joy, wholeness and empathy. This helps you feel connected and more compassionate with yourself and others.

In his book, *Touch: The Science of Hand, Heart and Mind*, neuroscientist David Lindon explains that soothing, warm touch creates a bond of trust and cooperation between people. Physical touch such as a friendly pat on the back or touch on the arm activates the Vagus nerve in your body. This is the major nerve which governs the parasympathetic nervous system which in turn regulates your 'tend-and-befriend' response. When activated, it slows down your heart rate and creates a calming effect in your mind and body. This makes you more open and responsive to connect with others.

This is how you can delight and enjoy its benefits

To obtain the benefits from a natural release of oxytocin in your body, look for diverse ways through your day and week to increase touch. The easiest way is to have warm, loving and close relationships, whatever stage of life you may be in.

If you are not in an intimate relationship, look for other points of connection. Soothing yourself, by stroking down your arms with your hand, or placing your hands on your shoulders and rubbing, or gently caressing your face will create a flowing release of feel good hormones. Stroking your pet for a few minutes is also a quick way to gain an oxytocin release.

A body massage, foot rub, giving or receiving a back rub from someone are effective ways of self-soothing. Many studies have shown massage to be effective in treating anxiety. It increases serotonin, the same neurotransmitter affected by many anti-anxiety medicines. Massage also provides pain relief for pain disorders, low back pain, asthma and other related health problems. It releases endorphins that relieve pain and make you feel capable to address stressful situations in your life.

This is how I optimise it and gain the most value from it

I give and receive a hug whenever I can! When hugging someone close, I try to extend the hug for a minimum of ten seconds and fifty seconds is even better. This way the body is guaranteed a release of oxytocin. I have regular body massage and acupuncture sessions to receive the benefit of hands-on touch.

Another approach I apply is a comforting technique called the 'Triple Warmer / Spleen Hug' developed by *Energy Medicine* authority, Donna Eden. It works by calming the stress response and simultaneously energising the spleen meridian which helps to relax, support and re-charge the body's batteries. Please try it for yourself by applying the following steps:

1. Wrap your left hand around your right arm, just about the elbow.

2. Wrap your right arm around the left side of your body, just underneath your breast.

3. Hold this position for at least three deep breaths.

4. Reverse sides.

Where you can discover more?

In the book *Touch*, Dr. Tiffany Field, Director of the Touch Research Institute, explains that touch has been shown to have positive effects on growth, brain-waves, breathing and heart rate; and decreases stress and anxiety. Since an initial study (with premature babies) she has conducted numerous experiments involving massage therapy and has found that massage enhances attentiveness, lowers stress hormones, improves immune function and reduces pain.

To touch is to give life.

Michelangelo

We need 4 hugs a day for survival. We need 8 hugs a day for maintenance. We need 12 hugs a day for growth.

Virginia Satir, Psychotherapist

5. Sleeping Softly

A strategy designed to re-align the body's natural rhythms.

Useful for: Insomnia and over-coming restlessness.

Future proofing: 'How can I gain the most from my rejuvenation?'

Sleep affects everything we do. It occupies one third of our life. We need our sleep. Without it we become tired and irritable and our brain functions less well. After a good night's sleep, we feel refreshed and restored. Arianna Huffington, CEO of the *Huffington Post*, names sleep as her keystone habit. Her view is a good day begins the night before. After an accident caused by her sleep deprivation, she changed from three hours a night, to now having nine hours a night and says it has changed her life.

How this strategy offers you an alternate coping approach

There are many good reasons to get a good night's sleep. Many of us are not getting sufficient rest because of stress, diet, environment or lack of sunlight and this can feel like we are walking around low on energy and alertness.

Sleep advocate and neuroscientist, Professor Matt Walker, emphasises that, 'sleep is a time of immense benefit for your body.' His sleep research shows that most of us are needing between seven and eight hours sleep a night to maintain our optimal mental and physical functioning. Lack of sufficient sleep can have a significant impact on the body's self-healing ability and repair functions. He says, 'human beings are the only species that deliberately deprive themselves of sleep for no apparent gain.' What this means is that many people walk through their lives in an under-slept state, and do not realist it.

Lack of sufficient sleep can upset your metabolism and its ability to fight disease. If you have only four hours sleep in one night, it impairs your immune system by 70%. What's more, attempting to sleep off a sleep debt doesn't actually work. Sleep doesn't function like a bank where it is possible to carry debt and pay it off later. Once it has gone, it can't be reclaimed. While you may sleep longer the next night, Professor Walker argues that you will never achieve the full eight-hour re-payment. He says, 'the brain has no capacity for getting back that lost sleep that you've been lumbering it with during the week in terms of a debt.'

This is how you can delight and enjoy its benefits

Have you ever worked on your computer until just before you fall asleep, or even worked in bed, eaten dinner late, had a few glasses of wine, and then struggled with sleep, waking up tired in the morning? Then you might consider this 'Five-Step' ritual as an alternative.

1. In the evening, eat a light dinner and take a stroll after you eat and minimise mentally intensive activities such as dramatic movies, gaming or complex work problems.

2. Shut down your work two hours before your bed-time as this gives your brain the opportunity to power down. Then one hour before getting into bed shut down all devices and take yourself mentally 'off line.'

3. If you enjoy a soak in the bath, run a hot bath and add a few drops of lavender oil, as it is a relaxing and soothing essential oil.

4. Select some light-hearted reading or you may choose a gentler reflection of your day, saying your graces by giving gratitude and thanks for your day.

5. As you settle down to sleep, close your eyes and notice your body. Breathe in and around any area that may be feeling tense. You may choose to play a background guided meditation as a comforting sound or soothing voice which turns itself off.

This is how I optimise it and gain the most value from it

I prefer not to work on my computer two hours before sleep. Being a hot sleeper, I've found that having a cool shower and cooling down my feet with soothing foot crème works with bringing down my core temperature. On the bed, my preference is for natural fibres such as bamboo sheets, silk pillow cases and cotton blankets. In the winter it is wool blankets rather than a doona. These steps work to prepare and keep my body comfortable within its resting cycle.

If I am struggling with sleep or wake up in the night, I turn on a dim light and read a book, no screens or phones. The option is to use a mindfulness practice and to say gently, 'settle back down' and count my breath up to ten and back down again …

> *breathe in one, breathe out one, breathe in two, breathe out two.*

Where you can discover more

Sleep apps are becoming a fashionable way to aid better sleep and they each offer different benefits. It depends on what you need to experience in order to obtain better quality sleep. Some apps analyse your sleep-cycle so you can see what is happening in the night; others track your day activities and your sleep duration, cycle and efficiency; while others provide ways to calm and settle your mind using mindfulness and ambient sounds.

Pzizz is a sleep and power nap system app. It plays a sleep optimised mix of music, voice-over and sound effects, quickly quietening the mind, putting you to sleep, keeping you asleep and you will wake up feeling refreshed.

Insight timer is a free app that has guided meditations for deep sleep.

Smiling Mind is another free app with mindfulness meditations called 'Sleep and Gratitude' that help you prepare for a good night's sleep.

> *We are in the midst of a sleep deprivation crisis, and this has profound consequences on our health, our job performance, our relationships and our happiness. What is needed is nothing short of a sleep revolution.*

Arianna Huffington, Co-Founder and Editor-in-Chief of the Huffington Post

6. Sultry Siestas

A strategy designed for optimising recovery cycles.

Useful for: Dealing with high demands or taxing times.

Future proofing: 'How do I manage sustainable performance and not burn out?'

If you are someone who is not getting sufficient sleep at night, or experiencing your energy drop off in the afternoon usually after 3:00pm, the power nap may be a ritual you could use. A power nap is described as a short sleep which ends before you fall into deep sleep. First named by social psychologist James Maas, it was designed to give you sufficient rest to allow recovery, but not so much rest that you would fall into a normal sleep cycle.

How this strategy offers you an alternate coping approach

Napping has been shown to have considerable physical benefits. It helps reverse the effects of stress such as elevated levels of cortisol, increased blood pressure and elevated sugar levels. It activates the body's healing response, which enables time for repair, maintenance and recovery.

While everyone is different, the research shows that the most effective time is between ten and thirty minutes. A thirty-minute nap may also reverse the hormonal impact of a night of poor sleep or reverse the damage of sleep deprivation. Even naps as brief as six and ten minutes have been found to restore wakefulness and promote performance and learning.

Sleep expert, Dr. Sara Mednick found from her research that a short nap is far more beneficial for you than a hit of caffeine from coffee or energy drinks. In her book, *Take a Nap! Change your life*, she recommends a short six-minute rest. This quick interlude not only picks up your performance and creativity temporarily, it will actually sustain your levels through the afternoon and into the evening.

This is how you can delight and enjoy its benefits

Sleep expert and clinical psychologist, Professor Leon Lack, recommends the best way to optimise your 'napping' is to keep it short. His research has found that ten to fifteen minutes of sleep seems the optimal period to improve alertness and performance. Longer than twenty-five to thirty minutes may make you drowsy and less alert. Generally, the best time is six to eight hours after you wake up.

The best time of the day to take a nap will depend on your own rhythm and energy cycle through the day and night. If you are a 'lark' and wake up early with zest in the morning, this window is between 12.00 noon and 1.00 pm. If you are an 'owl' and tend to pick through the afternoon and evening, a power nap between 2.00 pm – 4.00 pm in the afternoon would be better for you. If you do not fall fully asleep that is fine. Resting is almost as beneficial.

Where can you find a place, so you can close your eyes? If you are at home, lie down after lunch for a short siesta. At work, find a quiet place and close your eyes. Some of my clients have a yoga mat in their office and they lie on the floor for ten minutes. Others go outside and find a park, and sit with their eyes closed. Doing a yoga class or a meditation class at lunch-time is another way you can find the stillness. Progressive companies like Google and Nike provide quiet rooms and sleep pods for employees to have power naps. Huffington Post provides unplug sessions which offer employees practices for 'unplugging' from technology and their routine for a while and accessing some silence. These sessions are used for reducing stress and finding a calmer balance by letting go of worry and fatigue. The aim is to give their employees a valued sense of renewal.

This is how I optimise it and gain the most value from it

More and more I trust my body to tell me when it needs a resting moment or two. Rather than pushing through tiredness, I build in recovery space through my day and 'lie down.' If I'm working from home, I will rest in the afternoon for ten minutes. If I find that I don't fall asleep, I rest my mind and I lie down and close my eyes or sit out in the garden and do some mindfulness breathing.

In the words of comedian Ali Wong and Sheryl Sandberg, CEO of Facebook, in her book *Lean In* where she tells women to lean-in … 'I just want to lie down!'

In Australian culture, napping is not something that is a common practice. I remember first going to Spain and Italy and taking pleasure in the daily practice of shops shutting for several hours in the middle of the day for lunch and siesta. Part of my challenge to embrace napping has been to step outside my 'cultural portal' which doesn't value it and go with what my energy needs. From my experience, I feel re-energised and more productive after a nap. No need to feel guilty – it works!

Where you can discover more

In the TED talk, *Give it Up for the Down State*, Sara Mednick Ph.D. talks about the impact of naps on cognitive performance.

The book, *Rest* by Alex Soojung-Kim Pang is full of tips for upping your down-time, from sleep to hobbies and holidays. It gives practical ways to find renewed energy and inspiration, so you can have more of your own verve and sway.

There are apps that can help you fall asleep fast and time your power nap. As previously mentioned *Pzizz* is a popular sleep app for iPhone and Android and has a power nap module. Another app for the iPhone is the sleep cycle power nap.

If you want rest, you have to take it. You must resist the lure of busyness, make time for rest, take it seriously, and protect it from a world intent on stealing it.

Alex Soojung-Kim Pang, Researcher, Institute of the Future

7. Fluid movements

A strategy designed to increase your fitness and agility in smarter ways.

Useful for: Reducing a sedentary or time-crunched lifestyle.

Future proofing: 'What does my body need to remain fluid?'

Rather than spending hours working out in the gym, running for miles and pumping iron, there is a more efficient way to build your cardio fitness and strength. This approach is called *Fast Exercise* or 'HIT' which stands for High-Intensity-Training. With this approach, short bursts of intense exercise are interspersed with longer periods of recovery. Used in combination with movement throughout the day this fitness regime is a way to counteract the impact of a sedentary lifestyle.

How this strategy offers you an alternate coping approach

Expert on body movement and health, former NASA Scientist, Joan Vernikos, Ph.D., reports that on average we sit between five and ten hours per day; that's a lot of hours. Through the so called 'convenience' of modern technology we have lost a substantial amount of perpetual motion in our daily lives. Numerous studies are now finding a direct relationship between hours of sitting and Type 2 Diabetes, obesity, heart conditions and stroke. Clearly, the lack of frequent moving is having a high cost on physical health.

This new fitness formula has been designed by Michael Mosley, medical doctor, British television journalist and author. In his quest to live longer and healthier, he has researched and dispelled many myths about exercise, fitness and diet. He discovered the extraordinary impact of ultra-short bursts of high intensity intermittent training as a way to gain optimal fitness benefits in short periods of time. Some of the proven benefits of his fitness approach are improved aerobic fitness and endurance, reduced body fat, increased upper and lower body strength and improved insulin sensitivity.

A modification of the HIT formula is to use intermittent movement throughout the day. Sitting for lengthy periods has been found to have side effects such as slower metabolism, poor posture, and subsequent back problems. Temporary vigorous movement doesn't compensate. What does work is frequent movement throughout your day because it causes the physical body's metabolism to steadily rise above its resting state.

This is how you can delight and enjoy its benefits

High-Intensity-Training is a short, sharp work-out in which you push yourself as hard as you can for twenty seconds, then take a break for one minute and repeat the cycle three times. A total of four minutes. This can be done in the gym on a standing bike, treadmill, cross trainer or rowing machine. Equally it can be done outside, running in the park, cycling or swimming. Any form of exercise that allows you to use a short sharp intense effort, then a brief measured recovery, works as a HIT formula.

For the best results, HIT is most effective done two or three times a week and coupled with resistance exercise. This involves an additional three-minute routine doing push ups, squats and plank exercises, all designed to build core strength. The other part of the formula is incidental exercise. This requires moving through your day, getting up every thirty minutes and going for a short walk. In addition, with your regular HIT workouts, add in intermittent movement into your daily life. Move and exercise your body frequently whenever you can. A usual ratio to interrupt your sedentary state is thirty-five times a day, and if sitting, get up four times an hour. Perhaps, putting a sticker near your computer could remind you – move four times an hour; then intermittently shift your posture thirty-five times per day = body energy. In this way, you are moving your energy constantly and shifting your body.

This is how I optimise it and gain the most value from it

I use the process of HIT three times a week in the gym preferably on the standing bike. I am very conscious of incidental exercise and the need to move throughout the day. Some of the ways I do it is by parking my car some distance away, so I can walk for at least ten minutes to my meetings. I climb the stairs rather than use a lift if it's below level 3 and choose to walk up and down moving escalators. In between working at my desk, I pause and do a physical energy routine, or go for a short walk or bounce on my mini trampoline. I have a daily mantra – *Move, Move, Move.*

Where you can discover more

In the book, *Fast Exercise,* Dr. Michael Mosely and Peta Bee investigate the science of high intensity training for getting fitter, stronger and better toned in just a few minutes a day. Their focus is dispelling fitness myths and showing ways you can get the most out of exercise, whatever your age or level of fitness. They offer practical, science-based advice and a range of different work-outs that can be done anywhere, anytime.

In her book, *Sitting Kills, Moving Heals,* Dr. Joan Vernikos shows that the key in reversing the damage of sedentary living is to put gravity back into your life. This can be done through frequent, non-strenuous actions that resist the force of gravity through the day, every day!

A few weekly doses of intense exercise may deliver many of the health
and fitness benefits of hours of conventional exercise.

Michael Mosley, M.D. TV Journalist and Author

8. Chi of Life

A strategy designed for internal balance and vibrancy through food.

Useful for: When feeling sluggish and depleted.

Future proofing: 'Where will my nourishment come from?'

'Food is Medicine' is a term which was originally coined by Hippocrates, the father of Western medicine. It was his belief that eating wholesome food is the basis for all good health. Hippocrates said almost 2,500 years ago:

> 'Leave your drugs in the chemist's pot if you can heal the patient with food.'

Approaching food as medicine is a novel way of thinking about eating and nutrition. For many years, a major focus on food has been weight-loss or weight management. Increasingly, the focus is now shifting towards eating food for vitality and thriving.

Evidence is now more supportive of intuitive eating. This is where you listen to what your body tells you it needs to sustain itself. Often it can simply be a trace mineral or element found in certain foods that is lacking in your body; a depletion. What if you were to take it further from seeing food as fuel toward it being a natural medicine – one that helps your body to heal and thrive?

How this strategy offers you an alternate coping approach

The Medical Medium, Anthony William, reminds us that 'food is the new frontier' to counteract the negative health issues from our modern lifestyles. In the book, *Life Changing Foods,* he delves deep into the healing powers of what he calls 'the Holy Four' - fruits, vegetables, herbs and spices and wild foods. He explains that the *Holy Four* groups are filled with endless life-healing and life repairing nutrients that protect us from health threats, particularly stress and pollution.

> 'The Holy Four foods, which come from the earth – have a whole host of benefits that go beyond physical nutrition. They can offer you a feeling of in-the-moment comfort and grounding, and they also offer longer-term resolution you never knew possible.' (p. 29)

This is how you can delight and enjoy its benefits

Self-care revolutionary, Don Toleman, urges that in today's world of pharmaceuticals it is imperative that you gain knowledge and confidence in 'being your own doctor' and re-learn a trust with your body's own ability to first heal and then to sustain itself. His approach for overcoming nutritional deficiencies lies with consuming 'living plant whole-foods and getting enough sunlight each day.'

Plant wholefoods are unprocessed or unrefined or minimally processed before being consumed. They are loaded with anti-oxidants, vitamins and minerals which are essential for removing toxins and balancing the body's pH levels to reduce inflammation and keep the immune system strong. These wholefoods include raw fruits and vegetables, nuts, seeds, pulses, hemp oil, coconut oil and high-fibre foods such as organic oats, brown rice and millet. How could you add more of these foods into your own daily smorgasbord?

This is how I optimise it and gain the most value from it

An essential part of my self-care approach is being what Don Toleman calls a 'wholefood farmacist' by finding solutions from nature. High on my list of foods are a group of superfoods which are pumped full of nutritious, healing properties. They are thriving plants that are packed with antioxidants, micro-nutrients and other powerful goodies that the body needs to heal and thrive. These super healing foods include easily accessible plant foods such as celery, coriander (cilantro), blueberries, papaya, spirulina, sprouts, garlic, ginger, coconut water and lots of leafy greens.

Anthony William emphasises:

> 'Food is meant to be a joyful part of your life. Healthful eating isn't meant to be an exercise in deprivation. We're so used to reading articles on nutrition that solely talk about fibre and blood pressure and sodium levels that it can be easy not to realise: when you know the right foods to eat, and how to tap into their benefits, food can feed you on every level.' (*Life-Changing Foods*)

I have intuitive knowing that by eating a plant-based diet, doing plenty of exercise, getting sunlight and staying hydrated, my body will sort out its balance and release acids that accumulate. If there is a signal that my body might be on the acidic side, simply adding a half a teaspoon of bicarbonate of soda or apple cider vinegar in some water assists it to get back into a natural balance.

Where you can discover more

If you want to learn more about self-care, the *Farmacist Desk Reference (FDR)* by Don Toleman provides a wealth of information based on the wisdom of ancient, disease-free cultures and how they lived long without reliance on pharmaceutical drugs and medical treatments.

Life-Changing Foods by Anthony William investigates the healing powers of over 50 foods – fruits, vegetables, herbs and spices, and wild foods – explaining each food's properties, the symptoms and conditions it can help relieve or heal. He describes in detail the quality of each superfood.

Health expert Sue Rudd, believes good nutrition and good health start in your kitchen! In her beautiful cook-book, *Food as Medicine*, she offers 150 delicious plant-based recipes developed by a nutritionist and cook.

We now know that food is medicine, perhaps the most powerful drug
on the planet with the power to cause or cure most disease.

Dr. Mark Hyman, Physician

9. To Stomach Everything

A strategy designed for your immune system and to build inner resilience.

Useful for: Aiding digestion and easing physical discomfort.

Future proofing: 'How can I eat and replenish with choice?'

This strategy is about how you can strengthen your gut health. There are as many micro-organisms as there are cells in your body and most of them live in your gut. You may not have thought about yourself being a walking incubator for a vast population of bacterial organisms, however, that's what you are. What is more interesting is the bacteria community in your body has a distinct composition. It is called your 'microbiome' and it is as unique to you as the iris of your eye and your thumb print. That means everyone is different.

How this strategy offers you an alternate coping approach

What ancient cultures have known for centuries western science is now revealing – that gut bacteria, which number more than one hundred trillion cells, have a significant effect on the health of our brain and body. Not all gut bacteria are created equal. The 'good' gut bacteria are called probiotics and are responsible for strengthening your immune system, balancing blood sugar levels and manufacturing the vitamins your body needs. The 'bad' bacteria can cause digestive distress, skin conditions and discomfort.

A healthy gut is created by having balance, limiting the 'bad guys' and boosting the 'good guys' so they can grow and flourish. Imbalances in your gut flora caused by antibiotics, processed and refined foods, high sugar diet, and stressful lifestyles can all contribute to dramatically reducing the number of beneficial bacteria. When this occurs, the natural balance between good and bad bacteria is thrown off and this results in an over-growth of 'bad' gut bacteria which has been found to create inflammation, food allergies and intolerances, weakened immune system and mental health problems.

The gut produces over 80% of the body's serotonin, a neurotransmitter which controls how your body reacts with food and to stress. Research is showing that serotonin is a key brain chemical involved in mood control, depression and aggression. It is now understood that a reduction in healthy gut flora is related to lower serotonin levels, which in turn increases depression and anxiety. Furthermore, 80% of the immune system is in the gut, so it is key in optimising gut flora. A happy gut, makes for a calm and happy brain and a healthy body.

This is how you can delight and enjoy its benefits

Making a few key lifestyle changes can have a very positive impact on your gut balance. When you eat more fibre in your diet you encourage the growth of good bacteria. Where possible avoid processed and refined foods, sugary carbonated drinks and alcohol as they have been found to be one of the causes of harmful bacteria proliferating and becoming overgrown.

You may include fermented foods in your diet as they contain higher levels of beneficial bacteria (probiotics) and create anti-inflammatory compounds. This includes fermented vegetables (i.e.

sauerkraut, kim-chi), fermented milk (kefir) and fermented soy (natto and tempeh). If you are unable to access these types of products, take a high-quality probiotic which adds live culture into your gut. Integrative medical doctors are becoming savvy about the detrimental impact antibiotics have on gut flora. There are now specific probiotic powders designed specifically to counteract the overgrowth of bacteria created by certain antibiotics.

This is how I optimise it and gain the most value from it

I always travel with a high-quality probiotic and I mix them around to ensure I am getting different strains of culture. When possible, I make my own fermented coconut yogurt, kefir and I buy fermented veggies at local markets.

A recent addition to my gut health program has come from Anthony William, the medical medium. He recommends a glass of fresh celery juice on an empty stomach, either first thing in the morning, or two hours after eating. It is strongly alkaline which helps prevent and counteract acid reflux, headaches, fatigue, constipation and bloating.

Where you can discover more

In the first episode of *Trust Me, I'm a Doctor* Season 6, Dr. Michael Mosley and Dr. Saleyha Ahsan examine whether taking a supplement, consuming a fermented dairy drink or eating foods high in inulin are better at encouraging a healthier gut flora, and whether commercially produced or alternative probiotics are better. The experiments found that home-made varieties were found to contain higher levels than commercial varieties.

In your local area, find a raw and fermented food instructor who offers classes in how you can make fermented veggies, coconut kefir and yogurt. These staples of good gut health are easily made at home. In Australia we are so fortunate to have the remarkable Remedy Bliss, a pioneer in fermented and raw foods. Internationally, Donna Gates is a leader in the emerging field of body ecology, diet and healing.

Microba Australia has developed a test that maps your complete microbiome. Using advanced technology, it can sequence all the genes of the micro-organisms in your gut. The report can help you understand your unique make-up and offers lifestyle changes which can improve your gut health.

Let's face it a happy tummy, is a happy YOU. Good digestion is everything. Much of your immune system and serotonin production is housed in your gut. Re-establishing the microflora ecosystem will help you feel healthier, happier, more balanced.

Remedy Bliss, Food Instructor

10. Refreshing Raw

A strategy designed for ensuring a balance of healthy enzymes.

Useful for: Getting your body to absorb the most amount of nutrients.

Future proofing: 'Where is my fuel to increase tomorrow's vitality?'

Live foods are raw, uncooked foods such as fruit, vegetables, sprouted grains, nuts and seeds, and fermented foods. In raw form, uncooked foods are rich with all the vitamins, minerals, enzymes and phyto-nutrients that our body needs. The closer they are to a natural and fresh state, the more 'life force' your food contains.

How this strategy offers you an alternate coping approach

'Locavore,' is a powerful concept that means sourcing your nutrition from your environment and keeping you in balance with your local chi or energy from your surrounds. It also offers your body a much-needed variety to accommodate the changing seasons. Supermarkets offer different foods all year round, but do these really sit within the climate of where you live? For centuries, Asian cultures have taken a biodynamic approach to food and health. These traditional Asian cultures have a term called heating and cooling foods, each balances the body's need to combat extremes in weather, or over-indulgence.

Have you walked around a local market recently or visited a place where you are able to eat fruit fresh off the vine or from the garden? What does it do for your senses as you wander the rows of brightly coloured, fresh veggies and fruit? Does your mouth water? Do you feel hungry? How does it taste when you take that first bite? Delicious, refreshing, mouth-watering? Locally grown produce is more likely fresher than produce that has been transported and sat on shelves in a supermarket.

It makes common sense that food that is fresh will have more vitality and 'aliveness.' Food chemistry shows that raw foods are rich in enzymes, called the 'spark of life.' Enzymes have a multitude of uses from helping your digestion to work better to optimising the uptake of nutrients from your food. The quickest way to make sure you are getting heaps of enzymes is to eat plenty of fresh and raw foods. You can top that up by taking some chlorella or spirulina each day as they are some of the most nutrient dense foods on the planet.

This is how you can delight and enjoy its benefits

There are simpler ways for boosting the raw, 'live' parts of your diet. Juicing, making smoothies, eating salads, or steaming veggies are options. Another way is drinking water and adding a squeeze of lemon and mint in the summer for cooling, or in the winter adding some fresh ginger for internal warmth. Buy from local farmers markets and supermarkets that stock mainly locally-produced fruit and vegetables. Go for what is in season as it's aligned with nature's four seasons, giving your body what it needs to stay healthy during this passage of time.

Being intrinsically connected with nature, our bodies adjust and change with the season, and so do our nutritional requirements. Let nature guide your choices. For example, in summer there are lighter fruits such as pineapple, papaya, peaches, apricots, tomatoes and berries which have anti-inflammatory properties and are good for helping the body to cleanse, repair and rebuild. In autumn and winter, citrus fruits become available, which are high in Vitamin C and other minerals for keeping our immune system strong.

The deeper the colours of fruit and vegetables and the more variety, the better. Brightly coloured fruits and vegetables provide the highest 'phytochemical' content. These are non-nutrient plant chemicals which have protective qualities against most disease. Plants use phytochemicals as defence against potential threats which may be bacteria, viruses, moulds and fungi. When we consume these plants, the inherent defences are passed onto us to fight off potential threats to our health. The current research is exploring the role of phytochemicals in interfering with processes that cause chronic disease. One example is that phytochemicals may prevent carcinogens (which are cancer-causing agents) from forming.

This is how I optimise it and gain the most value from it

As much as possible, I consume whole-foods that are seasonal, local and rich in different colours. Each meal, smoothie or snack is an invitation to create a fruit and vegetable rainbow. There are five main colour groups and each has a unique set of phytochemicals and health-creating properties – red, purple/blue, orange, green and white/brown. Without knowing the specific qualities of each colour, I know that by including the different colours, I am giving my body what it needs in order to be at its best.

In creating the colour palette, I am also guided by the body's innate intelligence to understand what it needs at a particular time. This requires listening and remaining 'tuned in.' For example, I may be 'pulled' towards eating more white vegetables such as garlic which is high in a phytochemical called allicin and known for its anti-viral and antibacterial properties. While I may not be aware of it, my body is probably fighting an infection and needs an extra boost which the garlic provides.

Where you can discover more

The documentary *Food Matters* features interviews with leading health experts who reveal the best natural healing choices you can make for you and your family's health. In the film, you will discover what works, what doesn't and what is potentially harming you when it comes to your health.

> *When you gain the knowledge and confidence to embrace the principles of health, you no longer live in fear and uncertainty because you realise that no 'credentialed expert' could possibly know more about your body than you.*

Don Toleman, 'Indiana Jones of wholefood medicine'

11. Sweet and Sour

A strategy designed to optimise energy levels.

Useful for: Balanced and long-term sustainable energy.

Future proofing: 'How do I want my body to remain healthy for longer as I grow older?'

This strategy is about how you keep your blood sugars balanced so they can sustain your physical energy and vitality. In terms of your body's physiology, the most effective way for doing this is through managing your diet and reducing stress levels. This has been found effective with blood sugar management and to prevent diabetes. There are many diets on the market, and each of us is different. That means there is no one size that fits all. It is about you knowing your body and what works best for it.

How this strategy offers you an alternate coping approach

A diet that has been proven effective for keeping blood sugar levels stable and reducing inflammation is a low carbohydrate Mediterranean-style diet. It emphasises eating lots of green leafy vegetables and plant-based foods, small serves of protein, complex carbohydrates such as wholegrains and legumes, moderate amounts of healthy fats such as olive oil, nuts and yogurt. This combination enables the body to sustain a normal blood sugar. At the *2017 Healthy Ageing Conference* in Adelaide, leading neuroscientist Dr. Fiona Kerr, emphasised that the Mediterranean Diet remains the most effective diet to sustain a healthy brain and body as we age.

In examining the role of diet, nutritional expert, Dr. Axe, emphasises that it is not that you must avoid consuming any carbohydrates when trying to maintain normal blood sugar; rather you just balance them out with protein and fats and focus on getting them from real, whole foods. Eating a source of protein, fibre and healthy fat with meals can help stabilise blood sugar because it slows down the absorption of sugar into the blood stream, which manages your appetite and is important for metabolism. The easiest source is to consume nuts, seeds, fruits and vegetables.

This is how you can delight and enjoy its benefits

Consider how you can incorporate high quality protein and fats into your daily diet. The best proteins for managing your blood sugar levels include plant-based options such as hemp powder, chickpeas, lentils, quinoa, buckwheat, amaranth, nuts and seeds, particularly chia seeds. If you prefer animal protein sources, include fish such as salmon, free range eggs, grass fed beef or lamb and raw dairy products such as kefir, sheep or goat yogurt and free-range poultry.

If you want to improve your fat intake, consider high quality fats such as virgin olive oil, coconut and hemp oil, nuts and seeds such as chia, hemp and flax. In each meal include high-fibre foods such as vegetables and whole fruits as the fibre means they take longer to digest and this helps keep blood sugar at normal levels.

The jury is out on processed tofu as it contains higher levels of phyto-estrogens, a plant-based oestrogen called isoflavones that may mimic the activity of the hormone estrogen in your body. The effects of isoflavones on human estrogen levels are complex and is different for each person. While it is a dietary staple in many Asian cultures, it may not be so relevant in western culture. If you like soy products, choose GMO-free sources, and consume in moderation. An alternative is to have it as fermented products such as natto (Japanese) and tempeh (Indonesian).

To assist with sugar balancing, avoid foods that spike your insulin levels and increase inflammation in the body. Studies show that the main two culprits are refined sugar and processed carbohydrates. Refined sugar is now added into many every-day items such as yogurt, fruit juice, pre-packaged foods and meals (even the one's sold as 'healthy'). Processed carbohydrates include bread, pasta, biscuits and crackers. Wherever you can, consider the option of whole, fresh foods instead of packaged foods.

This is how I optimise it and gain the most value from it

I am observant of my sugar levels and pay attention to keep them stable. In times of stress I find it is even more important to maintain my sugar levels within a normal range. Stress produces elevated levels of the hormone cortisol which elevates blood sugar levels (helps the body face the 'fight or flight' response). Sustained cortisol leads towards inflammation and poorer absorption. That means I watch both – what is going into my mouth; and how much angst I have in my body. To re-set the balance, the first place I start is to lower my stress before I eat. Sometimes however, a simple piece of fruit will do the trick.

Where you can discover more

The 8-week Blood Sugar Diet by Dr. Michael Mosley has been recognised as an excellent way to lose weight and to re-program your body's health and energy. It is based on the Mediterranean diet with a twist – it is a low carb version and may include intermittent fasting.

This diet has the 5:2 ratio which is five days of low carb Mediterranean-style eating, two days of 800 calories each (fasting). As a way of life, this lifestyle diet has substantial results such as weight loss, improved blood sugar, hunger settles, you will feel fitter and better, and health risks of diabetes are reduced and reversed.

Dr. Mercola, has a portal on alternative health and he writes about how you deal with a sugar addiction. You can find a wide array of research and information at www.mercola.com:

When blood sugar levels are up, you feel energised. When they drop, energy levels plummet. So, if you eat frequently to keep your blood sugar levels steady, you'll feel more energised all-day long.

Susan Kleiner, Scientist and Nutritionist

12. Perfumed Pleasures

A strategy designed for shifting one's state of mind or altering one's mood.

Useful for: Overcoming the staleness of one's thoughts and to improve memory recall.

Future proofing: 'What do I wish from a lingering fragrance?'

Essential oils are concentrated extracts taken from the roots, leaves, seeds or blossoms of plants. They can be inhaled, diffused or applied on the skin in a crème or oil base. Today, the health benefits of essential oils are gaining new attention as an alternative treatment for stress, emotional balance and digestive problems. This strategy provides methods to increase these perfumed pleasures in your life.

How this strategy offers you an alternate coping approach

The use of essential oils has been around for over 6,000 years. The ancient Chinese, Indians, Egyptians, Greeks and Romans used them in cosmetics, perfumes and health remedies. Recently, the use of therapeutic oils has become more popular in our modern-day lives as a substitute for toxic cleaning chemicals in the home and thus to promote and provide physical health and mood benefits.

Smell stimulates olfactory receptors in the nose that send signals through the nerves to the limbic system (which effects one's mood and emotions). What we smell can have a profound effect on our body and emotional state, it can lift and open our response, or activate a stress reaction. Have you ever walked into a café or someone's home and the smell of cooking takes you instantly back into your grandma's kitchen and you feel nostalgic? Many travellers talk about coming home when noticing familiar smells. One of the things that Australians living overseas miss is the aroma of eucalypt that fills the air.

Medical aromatherapy in Europe is used as a clinical therapy. Studies have found that lavender is useful for mild sleep disturbances. Oils such as thyme, rosemary and sage have the highest anti-oxidant properties which help the body remove free radicals. Peppermint is often found useful for aiding digestion. Frankincense has over seventeen active agents and has a variety of health benefits, including helping relieve chronic stress and anxiety, reducing pain and inflammation and boosts immunity. Tea tree oil is well known for its antiseptic properties and ability for the treatment of wounds. It has been found in medical studies to kill certain strains of bacteria.

This is how you can delight and enjoy its benefits

Adding some essential oils into your energy tool-kit can be a useful way to pick up or calm down energy. The compounds in the various oils can add flavour and fragrance into your home environment or your food and cooking. Some make a wonderful substitute for commercial perfume. They can be used to help your body fight colds, handle pain and digestive discomfort.

There are so many oils on the market. Depending on your needs, buy a few and try them out. There are a variety of oils that you can add into your cooking to give a boost such as orange, lemon, clove, ginger and cinnamon. If you are studying or want to concentrate, use rosemary as it releases a neurotransmitter that helps with memory performance and alertness. To keep your home fresh and clean, you can mix up a spray bottle of water with tea tree oil. It has anti-bacterial and anti-microbial properties. It is also useful to assist the body to clear coughs and colds. Rubbing it on the chest (mixed with some oil), using a diffuser or putting a drop on your pillow at night will help with breathing.

This is how I optimise it and gain the most value from it

I love essential oils and use them in a variety of ways. My favourite is rose oil. She is the queen of the oils and the most expensive. It takes thousands of rose petals to make a small bottle of essential oil. I use it as my perfume. I always have peppermint oil in my handbag and take a drop in some water after a meal to help digestion. At night before sleep, I diffuse lavender oil in my room. Apart from smelling wonderful, it is beneficial to relax and calm the nervous system.

Have you ever walked into a room and been overwhelmed with the smell of perfume and aftershave? For over ten years I have ceased wearing commercial perfumes and replaced them with a spritzer bottle and a blend of essential oils. One of my favourites is the relaxing and uplifting combination of bergamot, ylang ylang, geranium, jasmine and rose. You may want to try to make your own. Choose the oils you love, add ten drops of each into a spray bottle filled with pure water, shake and spray.

Where you can discover more

Always buy pure grade, organic oils and know the source. There are many oils on the market that are not pure. If you are putting oils on your body and breathing them in you want them to be of a high quality. Remember some oils are photo-sensitive, which means that if you put them on your skin and go out in the sun, you may burn more easily or have a skin reaction e.g. orange oil. Young Living Oils and Doterra both produce a range of high-quality essential oils.

To explore how you can use essential oils, *The Complete Book of Essential Oils and Aromatherapy*, by Valerie Ann Worwood, is a useful resource guide. It offers over 800 natural, non-toxic, and fragrant recipes to create health, beauty and safe home and work environments.

If you want to examine the connection between oils and emotions, *Aromatherapy and the Mind*, by Julia Lawless analyses the development and role of fragrance and its healing effect on the human psyche.

The splendour of the rose and the whiteness of the lily do not rob the little violet of its scent nor the daisy of its simple charm. If every tiny flower wanted to be a rose, spring would lose its loveliness.

Saint Therese Lisieux, Carmelite nun

13. Verdant Green

A strategy designed to refresh and stimulate dynamic energy.

Useful for: Clearing the mind and enlivening one's energy.

Future proofing: 'Am I still in touch with my surroundings?'

To step into nature, whether it be a local park, garden or national reserve, is a sure way to change your mood and shift your energy. Put your hands in the soil in your vegetable garden, get out and spend time doing the gardening or simply looking at a beautiful nature scene, essentially has the same impact. Nature and its quintessential beauty can affect our brains and energy fields in positive ways. Grounding oneself within nature is a powerful way to reality test your moment, as it provides a sense of feeling solid within your reality.

How this strategy offers you an alternate coping approach

For centuries healers have recommended connecting with trees, sitting near them, leaning into them or walking near them for healing and balance. Instinctively as children we climb trees to sit and play in them.

Connecting with nature allows you to recuperate and recover quickly after stressful experiences. Studies show that within three to four minutes of being in nature, or simply looking at images of nature, you can significantly reduce your blood pressure, heart rate, muscle tension and stress hormones. When this happens, your mood becomes calm and contented. Being in nature has been found to reduce rumination or nagging niggles from consuming your mind with worry. Walking, or even better, trekking for ninety minutes in nature, significantly lowers excessive negative thoughts and reduces neural activity in the part of the brain that impacts on mood. The result being you feel calmer.

In Japan, 'Forest Bathing' (*Shinrin-yoku*) is the practice of taking a short, leisurely visit within a forest and has surprising health benefits. *Shinrin-yoku* is a term that means 'taking in the forest atmosphere' or 'forest bathing.' It was developed in Japan during the 1980s and has become a cornerstone of preventive health care and healing in Japanese medicine. It has been proven to lower heart rate and blood pressure, reduce stress hormone production, boost the immune system, soothe the spirit and improve overall feelings of ease with life. The practice has now spread to California and Victoria, Australia.

This is how you can delight and enjoy its benefits

Spend time walking and being in nature whenever you can. If you are feeling drained of energy leaving you flat and without your usual spark, take yourself into a park and wander within its splendour. Just be with trees. Studies have shown that the vibration of trees has the same positive benefits as walking in nature. If you love trees, give one a hug for a couple of minutes, soak up its towering strength and years of standing tall and proud.

Alternatively, you can apply what is referred as 'Dendrotherapy' which is healing by trees or with the help of trees. Russian scientist, Mikhail Vinogradov, has devoted his life to the research of trees, as donors and recipients of energy. He says, 'Trees really can cure, heal, make wholesome, feed energy. The best in this respect are oak, birch and pine, but almost equally valuable are cedar, locust, maple, rowan, apple, plum and others.'

He invites you to try the practice of Dendrotherapy by using a few simple steps. Start by standing forty to sixty centimetres away from a tree. Set your intention to focus on receiving the tree's energy. Visualise this flow as a warm wave of energy slowly rising through your body from the feet upwards. After you feel relaxed, start doing the following breathing exercise as this will help you distribute the received energy throughout the body. Inhale and hold the air in the lungs for a count of four seconds, then exhale, hold for a count of four when the lungs are empty until the next breath. While you are holding the breath, visualise the energy of the tree 'spill' and be converted into your bioenergy field. A healing exchange takes place.

This is how I optimise it and gain the most value from it

I find beautiful parks and gardens wherever I am and spend time walking through them, pausing and absorbing nature's resonance. On a regular basis I travel to an energetic sanctuary in Tasmania nestled beside the Tamar River and then just sit within a stunning garden of trees and roses. I have my favourite elm tree and lean into her for a nourishing exchange with deep appreciation of her presence and energy. Other ways including taking my shoes off and walking barefoot on the grass or on the beach, which allows me to feel grounded or what my body calls being in touch with my surrounds.

Where you can discover more

A Little Handbook of Shinrin-Yoku by Amos Clifford explains the gentle, healing practice of 'Forest Bathing' and other nature-based healing practices that are making their way into the rest of the world. As an experienced wilderness guide, he suggests leadership strategies to take people on *Shinrin-Yoku* walks.

Blinded by Science, author Mathew Silverstone, proves scientifically that trees do in fact improve many health issues such as concentration levels, reaction times, depression, stress and other various forms of mental illness. He even points to research indicating a tree's ability to alleviate headaches in humans seeking relief by communing with trees.

Keep close to Nature's heart ... and break clear away, once in a while, or climb a mountain or spend a week in the woods. Wash your spirit clean.

John Muir, Naturalist and Conservationist

14. Essences of You

A strategy designed to increase your body's vibrancy and vitality.

Useful for: Combating emotional stress and physical fatigue.

Future proofing: 'How do I age gracefully and feel full of life?'

Minerals and antioxidants in our diet are essential for a wide range of body functions. They are important for building strong bones, teeth, blood, skin, hair, nerve function, muscles and a full range of metabolic processes. There are two different types of minerals – macro minerals and trace minerals. While your body needs larger amounts of macro minerals than trace minerals, both are essential for sustaining health. This strategy explores how you can maintain sufficient minerals so-as to function on 'all cylinders.' Without these essential essences you can feel depleted and left with no fuel to sustain a vibrant lifestyle.

How this strategy offers you an alternate coping approach

Minerals and antioxidants are important for the optimal functioning of the body. Electrical and chemical reactions are happening all the time and minerals play a critical part in these reactions. That means it is necessary to constantly replenish minerals in our bodies on a daily basis. They are not something the body produces, it needs to extract them from the food we consume. In today's fast-paced world, we must heed the body's intrinsic need to stay productive. Mineral essences are often the invisible and missing ingredient that keep everything flowing for wellness.

The main macro minerals are magnesium, calcium, sodium, potassium, phosphorus, chloride and sulphur. They play major roles in key functions such as building bones, maintain body fluids, keep proper pH in the body tissues, transmit nerve impulses, maintain cell membranes and facilitate enzyme action. Without them, the infrastructure of our body suffers. The best way to ensure you obtain enough of these super essences is to start with your diet. If possible, eat organically grown fruits, vegetables, wholefoods and superfoods such as spirulina and chlorella.

The focus on the importance of trace minerals has recently become stronger. Some modern farming techniques are causing mineral depletion from the soils. Coupled with people living more stressful lives and eating more nutrient deficient foods, this is leading to widespread mineral deficiencies. Trace minerals are needed in micro concentrations and exist in relationship with one another. Too much of one trace element can lead towards imbalance in others and, therefore, they must be taken in combination to enhance their effectiveness.

Certain minerals such as zinc, copper and selenium are antioxidants and help to remove free radicals from the body. Fulvic acid which is found in rich dark soil untouched by farming and full of micro-organisms is one of the most powerful free radical scavengers. Science now confirms what ancient Indian medicine (Ayurveda) has affirmed; that using 'fluvic acid minerals' helps to nourish the thyroid and adrenals, aids in detoxification, reduces signs of aging, and supports the immune system. Trace elements can be taken in liquid form daily. Fluvic acid is also available in a bio-available liquid form.

This is how you delight and enjoy it

Magnesium is one of the macro minerals which has become extremely important in our modern lifestyle. It is called the 'master mineral' because it has the most functions in the body. It is key to over 300 biochemical reactions within the body. It helps increase energy, calm nerves and anxiety, helps with digestion, relieves muscle aches, supports a healthy immune system, keeps the heart-beat steady and regulates blood sugar levels. Carolyn Dean, medical doctor, naturopath and author of *The Magnesium Miracle* emphasises that magnesium is an essential nutrient, indispensable to your health and well-being. She reminds us that it is often overlooked and plays an essential role in guarding against and alleviating conditions such as heart disease, osteoporosis, diabetes, arthritis and asthma.

A simple and effective way to give your magnesium levels a boost is a combination of magnesium supplement plus applying transdermal magnesium that is absorbed via the skin. While there are many types of magnesium supplements on the market, naturopaths recommend products with magnesium citrate. With transdermal magnesium, the most effective crèmes are based on magnesium chloride which is the most bio-available form of magnesium for skin absorption. You can apply it in the form of a crème that is infused with magnesium chloride, have a bath or foot bath using magnesium flakes or a magnesium spritz oil containing a high concentration of magnesium in a water-based solution.

This is how I optimise it and gain the most value from it

I use a magnesium crème each day and put it over my whole body – once in the morning after a shower and then again at night before sleeping. If I have muscle tension from working at the computer or after doing a work out, I apply some more. I travel with a small tube in my bag in case of restless legs or muscle tightness. With my diet, I aim to include magnesium rich foods, particularly dark leafy greens, avocado, almonds and pumpkin seeds. I take mineral supplements – magnesium citrate powder supplement, trace mineral liquid and fluvic acid liquid daily.

Where you can discover more

Elekra Magnesium produces a range of cremes and food-grade products that contain magnesium chloride; Australian based, natural products.

Grain Fields Australia (called agmfoods) have an ionic mineral liquid that contains seventy-two minerals in a form that is easy for the body to absorb.

Morningstar Minerals has a blend of fluvic and humic minerals in an all-natural, completely organic supplement. Derived from plant matter rich in minerals, vitamins, trace elements and amino acids. They can be purchased online via www.iherb.com.

> *Kale is a leafy vegetable that is bold and bitter, but it's packed with vitamins and minerals. You can juice it like you would carrots, putting whole stalks into a vegetable drink. It'll boost your greens and your energy levels.*

Chi Lang

15. Grounding Delights

A strategy designed for being physically grounded.

Useful for: Finding one's balance and being in the moment.

Future proofing: 'How do I get the most from now?'

Grounding is essential for our health and vitality. The technique is as simple as kicking off your shoes and walking barefoot outside on earth be that grass, dirt, sand on the beach, wherever you can connect directly. The benefits of earthing include better sleep, reduced pain and inflammation by activating an improved circulation. This strategy examines ways that you can incorporate natural earthing methods and technologies that both soothe and strengthen your body's bioelectrical system.

How this strategy offers you an alternate coping approach

Earthing involves coupling your body with the Earth's surface energies. It means walking barefoot on the earth, or sitting, working or sleeping while connected to a conductive device that delivers the natural healing energy of the Earth into your own body. Modern day pioneer in the field of Earthing, Clinton Ober, says:

> 'We have essentially lost our electrical roots. Our bare feet with their rich network of nerve endings rarely touch the ground. We wear insulated synthetic-soled shoes. We sleep on elevated beds made from insulating material. Most of us in the modern, industrialised world live disconnected from the earth's surface.' (*Earthing: The Most Important Health Discovery Ever?* p. 4)

The research shows that immediate positive physiological changes happen when you start earthing. Our bodies have an electrical energy; it is made up of water and minerals and both are efficient conductors of electrons. In our modern lifestyle, we can take on too many positive electrons in the form of free radicals. The high prevalence of electromagnetic waves, Wi-Fi and mobile phone waves causes a build-up of positive electrons in our bodies and cells. This imbalance has been shown to lead to increases in conditions such as inflammation, pain, disrupted sleep and muscle tension.

The good news is that the Earth has an infinite reservoir of negative ions which neutralise the positive electrons (free radicals) making them harmless. Research indicates that these negative ions have antioxidant effects that can protect your body from inflammation and its many well-documented health consequences. The negative electrons are pulsating perpetually on the surface of the Earth, fed by natural occurrences such as solar radiation, lightning strikes and energy generated from the core. These are easily transferred throughout the body as long as there is direct contact. The solution is to get grounded. Ober explains:

> 'Exposure to sunlight produces Vitamin D in the body. It's needed for health. Exposure to the ground provides an electrical "nutrient" in the form of electrons. Think of these as Vitamin G – G for ground. Just like Vitamin D, you need Vitamin G for your health as well.' (*Earthing: The Most Important Health Discovery Ever?* p.9)

This is how you can delight and enjoy its benefits

One of the most simple and pleasant ways to absorb the earth's healing energy is to walk barefoot on the ground. If you have pain, jet-lag or are feeling worn out, go outside (weather permitting) and put your bare feet directly on the earth. You may start feeling a subtle tingling rising upwards from your feet; this is the Earth re-energising your body through your feet's meridians.

Other ways to generate earthing effects are to wander out into your garden and touch your plants, smell the roses or simply put your hands into the soil in your veggie garden. If you don't have a garden, put some herb or flower pots on the balcony or veranda so you can make contact when you need a grounding for yourself.

If you wish to explore earthing devices you can use indoors, there are earthing floor pads that you can use while sitting at your computer or watching TV and special conductive sheets you can use on your bed for earthing during your sleep.

My recommendation would be to try the natural earthing process first, a little every day and see what shifts for you.

This is how I optimise it and gain the most value from it

In the summer months, I go outside and lie on the lawn in the backyard or stand barefoot on the grass and do some energy exercises. The beach is always a wonderful place for strolling and to receive an 'earth hit.' During the winter months I use an indoor earthing mat when I'm sitting at my computer. On sunny days, I'll go and sit in a park and slip my shoes off.

Where you can discover more

An independent documentary *The Grounded,* is about an Alaskan farmer who experiences pain relief through grounding, and inspires his community to try it with wonderful results. The link is www.mygroundedmovie.com.

Earthing: The Most Important Discovery Yet? by Clinton Ober, Stephen Sinatra and Martin Zucker, describes how by re-connecting with the Earth, symptoms such as inflammation, pain, fatigue, stress and poor sleep can be eliminated.

If you are interested in exploring the use of earthing products within your home or workplace, Barefoot Healing and Ergon Effects Australia are two Australian companies that offer a wide range of different earthing devices.

> *The goal of life is to make your heartbeat match the beat of the universe, to match your nature with Nature.*

> Joseph Campbell, Author

16. Refreshing Your Space

A strategy designed for clearing one's space refreshed.

Useful for: Reducing a mustiness and clutter of lingering moods and energy.

Future proofing: 'How do I remain contemporary and fresh?'

Space clearing is a powerful way for clearing, balancing and shifting your energy. The practice focuses on the actions you can take for creating a more peaceful environment in a subtle, energetic way. This strategy offers ways you can incorporate freshness into your living and work spaces, to create more flow and ease. It is based on ancient practices of Chinese Feng Shui and Native American herbal cleansing rituals designed to revitalise the energies found within buildings.

How this strategy offers you an alternate coping approach

Physical places can get dense with stagnant energy either because there are too many people moving through it, there is not enough light or air movement, or the people in the space have dense energy created by stress and emotion. They need energetic maintenance to be unencumbered and revitalised.

Have you ever walked into a space and felt that the energy was stagnant and heavy and after being there for a while you start to feel the same way? Or you may have entered a room after an argument and can literally feel it hanging in the air. Denise Linn, space clearing expert, says, 'Clutter can clog our lives,' and it is important that you know how you can shift this life debris. This primarily involves removing physical objects from a space. There are also the less tangible types – emotional and mental clutter, which need a regular clean out.

Spaces have a vibration and keeping the energy free and open helps everyone, including you and the people you live and work with. Feng Shui expert, Karen Kingston, suggests it is best to start with clearing clutter and to follow this with space clearing. She explains, 'Space clearing is the most effective way I know of loosening the stuck energy that accumulates around clutter … it works best if you've done a clutter clearing first.'

This is how you can delight and enjoy its benefits

An appropriate time to enliven and freshen up the energy in your home is spring. It makes common sense to open windows, and to let the light in, remove clutter and to shake things out that may have built up over the winter months. Other appropriate times for a space cleanse are after an argument or break-up, after an illness or trauma, or when you are feeling flat. It is also useful for new beginnings, when you move into a new space (home or work) or you finish a project and want fresh energy for a new project or a fresh start.

Space clearing, is an easy and effective thing you can do to seek a fresher state. The traditional way to purify and clear space is to use herbs such as sage leaves, cedarwood oil and sandalwood incense. Begin by creating a strong intention in your mind before space clearing and to bring in a natural vibrant energy. Remove any excess clutter from the space. Next, use a bell or drum and move or walk around the room or building, let the sound reverberate into all the corners. Kingston recommends the vibration from a Balinese bell as being one of the most effective ways to shatter energetic imprints left in buildings. Next, light sandalwood incense or diffuse cedarwood in the space. This purifies the space of unwanted energy.

The second part of the ritual is to burn sage which is called 'smudging.' Smudge sticks are available on-line or from health shops and 'mind-body-spirit' fairs. Move around rooms with a smoking smudge stick, go into each corner and ask the space to be cleared from any lingering energies that may be trapped and then for them to be blessed. Remember to 'smudge yourself' by moving the sage smoke in the space around you. Ideally, if you are doing this with someone else, smudge each other as it is easier this way. After the clearing is complete, open the doors and windows and let in the fresh air. You may want to light a candle, burn calming incense and put on some uplifting music.

This is how I optimise it and gain the most value from it

When I enter a new hotel or work-space on my travels, I use the 'Space Clearing Essence' created from Australian Bush Flower Essences. I set my intention to clear any unwanted energies in the room from previous guests or residual energies lingering from prior meetings, and to create a vibrant and clear space for me to sleep and work in. For longer stays, I take an oil diffuser and space clearing oils.

Where you can discover more

In her book, *Space Clearing: How to purify and create harmony in your home*, Denise Linn explains the four key steps for space clearing and the different methods involved – from using bells, drums, rattles, feathers, smoke and sacred dances. There are simple guidelines to preserve the atmosphere after a clearing, including special blessings and prayers.

Creating Sacred Space with Feng Shui, by Karen Kingston provides a guide for using Feng Shui and other clearing rituals for space clearing your own home and creating sacredness in your life.

If you are interested in buying essential oils for space clearing, natural skin care company, Janesce has organic, pure quality oils that are produced in a beautiful natural and biodynamic environment in the Adelaide Hills: www.janesce.com.au.

Space Clearing is a simple method for harmonising energy in a home or business ... in other words it helps make a room or a space feel good. The practice of Space Clearing has been practiced in ancient India, Egypt, China, Japan and in every native culture around the world since the beginning of time.

Denise Linn

17. Detoxing Your World

A strategy designed to create a safe living environment.

Useful for: Cleansing and refreshing the body of toxins.

Future proofing: 'What am I breathing in and absorbing from life?'

Cleaning up your space and detoxing your world can contribute significantly to your comfort and physical health. Reducing the amount of chemicals in your immediate world can help lift some of the load off of your body and the environment. Knowing that these chemicals exist in your everyday environment gives you the information to make different choices. It is encouraging knowing that we do have other options. The reality is, however, that it does take effort and commitment to create toxin-free spaces. However, there are some small steps you can take which will begin to make an immediate difference.

How this strategy offers you an alternate coping approach

There are chemicals lurking in your personal care products, cleaning products, food packaging, furniture and carpeting that have been found to be a health risk, particularly for women's health.

Studies show that synthetic chemicals cause havoc with both the immune and endocrine systems. Fragranced products typically are high in synthetic chemicals such as parabens, phthalates and synthetic musk. These have been found to interfere with hormone production and release and create adverse reproductive effects such as low sperm count and birth defects and liver and kidney damage.

Bisphenol-A (BPA) is a chemical used to make many plastic products such as water bottles and baby bottles and is found in the plastic lining in canned foods. BPA is an endocrine disrupter – a substance which interferes with natural hormones. It has been linked with reproductive disorders, breast cancer and heart disease.

This is how you can delight and enjoy its benefits

Make your home a haven, a safe environment for your body. A good starting place for limiting chemical exposure is the kitchen and bathroom. Do a 'chemical inventory' of what substances are used to clean your house, identify the chemicals in household cleaning products. There are many hidden toxins, but there are three big ones to watch out for in your kitchen and bathroom. The first is phthalate found in fragrant products such as air fresheners and dish soap. This is an endocrine (hormone) disruptor. The second, is 2 butoxyethanol used in window and multipurpose cleaners, a powerful solvent not to be messed around with! The third, is chlorine found in toilet cleaners and laundry whiteners which is a respiratory irritant and thyroid disruptor.

Do your research about the effects of these toxins and then source a natural, less harmful product, to reduce your chemical load and its subtle influence upon your immune system. Be aware that if a cleaning product claims itself to be 'green,' 'natural' or 'biodegradable,' that doesn't mean it is non-toxic.

A few small shifts in the kitchen can make a difference. Start by reducing plastic and use glass. You can do this by not using plastic wrap or plastic storage containers and instead, shift towards storing food in glass-ware and where practical, buy products in glass. For cleaning, select products that are biodegradable and gentler on the environment and on you.

For your personal products look for products that are natural and both palm-oil and fragrance free. A solution is to switch towards products that have blends of natural oils and botanical extracts that cleanse, revitalise and nourish your body and face. With cleaning products, research shows that eucalyptus oil is a natural disinfectant It is also anti-bacterial and anti-insecticidal which makes it effective in reducing bed and dust mites. Want to prevent mildew and mould in your bathroom? A spray with two cups of water and a few drops of tea tree oil and lavender works. There are many more natural ways to clean your home both safely and cheaply.

Indoor plants are an effective way to reduce chemicals such as ammonia, benzene, formaldehyde and xylene from indoor air. They purify the air from these toxic chemicals and convert Carbon Dioxide (CO_2) into Oxygen. Some of the best space cleaners are Peace Lily, Spider Plant, Aloe Vera and Snake Plant (which is good in the bedroom at night because it releases oxygen and helps you have a better sleep).

This is how I optimise it and gain the most value from it

For sleeping, my sheets are pure cotton or silk and my blankets are wool or cotton. In the winter months, my doona is made from silk which is just delicious to lie under. I wash these using natural products such as eucalyptus oil, as I do breathe within their comfy folds for up to eight hours. With personal products such as hair, face, deodorants and body products, I deliberately choose those made from botanical oils and natural extracts. For mouth hygiene, toothpaste and mouth-wash, I opt for sugar-free, fluoride free and non-toxic products. The candles I burn are 100% soy or bees-wax or a combination that doesn't contain paraffin and are either unscented or scented with essential oils.

Where you can discover more

There are an increasing number of online guides that offer links to find safe, non-toxic beauty and home-care products. Safe Cosmetics Australia offers a 'toxic-free' list.

Super Natural Home by Beth Greer offers choices and recipes to 'live clean' in a toxic world.

> *If you don't take care of this the most magnificent machine that you*
> *will ever be given ... where are you going to live?*

Karyn Calabrese

18. Keeping Your Vibration High

A strategy designed to lengthen and strengthen your energy.

Useful for: When feeling sluggish or tired.

Future proofing: 'How can I extend my dynamic self?'

This strategy is designed so you can engage easily with your own natural frequency. Maintaining this vibration is a key to being fully alive. In today's world, it is easy to deplete your frequency or find that it fades into the background with so many competing energies coming in on you. This strategy shows you ways you can pick your energy up when you find yourself feeling sluggish or tired. In doing so, you can then bring yourself and your frequency to the forefront, and in doing so, be your own uniqueness with a larger movement of energies.

How this strategy offers you an alternate coping approach

Your vibration describes your overall state of being. Everything in the universe is made up of energy vibrating at different frequencies. Famous physicist Nikola Tesla said:

> 'If you want to find the secrets of the universe, think in terms of energy, frequency and vibration.'

Even things that look solid are made up of vibrational energy fields at the quantum level – this includes you! In the emerging field of energy medicine, there is a growing appreciation of the clinical importance of human energy fields. These fields, which are now called 'biofields' are measurable physical phenomena. Studies into the significance of bio-magnetic fields produced by the human body are now being done in major medical centres around the world. What is being discovered by science is something that the ancients have always known – there is an interdependent relationship between the health of the human body and the health of the energy field.

Research indicates that every living thing has a frequency (measured in megahertz, Mhz) and moreover, we are all affected by the frequencies around us. Specialising in methods and products for sustainable agriculture, Dr. Bruce Tainio of Tainio Technology invented several instruments to minimise environmental stress from environmental frequencies. In examining the relationship between frequency and disease he found that the human body has a frequency that sits in a range between 62-68 Mhz and that sickness and disease can begin to take effect at 58 Mhz. That means by keeping your frequency in its natural groove above 62 MHz, you are more likely to stay within a healthy range for your vitality.

This is how you can delight and enjoy its benefits

There are many simple ways you can lift your own vibration. Become aware of your own inner dialogue. Positive and negative thoughts have been found to impact your frequency. Research has found that negative thoughts lower the human frequency by about 12 Mhz while positive thoughts raise the frequency by 10Mhz.

Find a sacred space to reconnect with your serenity. Prayer and meditation have been found to raise the frequency by 15 Mhz.

Be conscious of the food you eat. A diet high in fruit, vegetables and natural, unprocessed foods are high in vitality and nourishment. According to research by scientist Dr. Royal Raymond Rife everything has an 'electromagnetic signature or pattern of oscillation (frequency).' Fresh produce has a frequency up to 15 Mhz, dried herbs from 12-22 Mhz and fresh herbs from 20-27 Mhz. In comparison, processed and canned food were found to have a frequency of zero.

Choose friends that are kind and generous of spirit, give to givers who in turn will give onwards, rather than to takers who will only come back, to seek more from you. That also means removing from your life toxic relationships, steeped in drama that drain your energy and lower your vibration.

Avoid sitting too long inside under fluorescent lights or looking at a computer screen. When you start feeling tired from being inside, go outside into the sunlight. Rather than lying down or sleeping in air conditioning, use a fan, instead to move the air.

This is how I optimise it and gain the most value from it

I am very aware of my own natural frequency. When I'm in the groove I feel light, in ease and joyous, there is a love of life and connection with people. I want more of this feeling in my life. That means I do many smaller things each day that can strengthen and sustain my frequency's resonance. Earthing, standing in the sun, looking-up, tapping, moving, loving and connecting.

The most important thing is noticing when my frequency is off and asking the question, what do I need? Sometimes it's as simple as going for a walk in a park, having a rest, having a quick chat with a close friend, or sitting quietly and meditating. Other times, it is releasing the build-up of emotions that are heavy and flattening.

Where you can discover more

Vibrational Medicine: The #1 handbook of subtle-energy therapies by Richard Gerber, M.D., is a combination of ancient wisdom and the new science of energy medicine. Trained in a variety of alternative therapies as well as conventional Western Medicine, Dr. Gerber explains current theories about how various energy therapies work and offers new insights into the physical and spiritual perspectives of health and disease.

The Encyclopedia of Energy Medicine by Linnie Thomas and Carrie Obry presents the emerging disciplines of tomorrow's healing techniques. Many methods in the book rely on a growing appreciation of the clinical importance of energy fields.

> *The law of vibration ... nothing rests; everything moves; everything*
> *vibrates ... We are the same as plants, as trees, as other people, as the rain that*
> *falls. We consist of that which is around us, we are the same as everything.*

Gautama Buddha

Your Cognitive Energy

CHAPTER THREE

Cognitive Awakeners

What we believe to be true in life may be more powerful than what others accept as truth.

Gregg Braden, Author

Cognitive You is about making sense of the world around you. It is how you connect with the world through your senses and then create an internal representation of what you want from life and dream for the future. This becomes the basis of your mind-set and living your lifestyle. Your beliefs form your preferences and prejudices which become your unique reality to seek out and then interact with certain aspects of life. This interplay involves your thinking, perceptions and responses with information as it comes to you. Your own brain power, plus exposure from other's wisdom passed down through cultural stories, beliefs, assumptions and attitudes for living a worthy life, will shape how you will engage with the larger world and then adapt to its changing pace.

Mental health or well-being can easily be viewed by others as the ability to have an agile conversation, thereby offering an openness of opinion and desire to discover different points of view. These individuals actively engage without any thought blocking or confusion. They display a genuine curiosity to find answers by asking questions rather than ruminating about self or issues faced. They are invariably responsive with either a quick repartee or wit, lightening or adding more substance to the interaction. Articulating a deeper meaning and comprehension, a shared pleasurable exchange.

Engagement and disengagement are two of the most critical factors for your cognitive balance and flow. Engagement is about the 'how' of connection, attachment and involvement. Disengagement is the capacity to disconnect, release and separate. These processes determine the extent with which you move towards or away from situations, people and information. It also shapes your ability to create space between the information coming into your senses and your reactions towards it. It sets up the choices you make.

Ultimately with the mind, it is about discovery, exploration, creativity and learning because we are 'learning beings.' While there are the lower parts of the brain that are about survival and keeping you safe, the higher parts of the brain are about the intrigue of novelty and learning.

One of the key chemical messengers (neurotransmitter) in the brain is dopamine and it is released when we are learning something new or have curiosity. One of the functions of dopamine is to maintain alertness and this is what we need to learn new things and to expand the basis of our knowledge. When dopamine ramps up the brain, it becomes more like a sponge ready to soak up what is happening. Research has found that curiosity triggers the activity of dopamine and aids in our ability to learn more rapidly. In our higher brain functions we are wired to seek out wonder, marvel, and to take a broader interest in our world. The challenge is how to sustain our cognitive energy so we can learn, grow and expand our mind-set.

Cognitive energy issues of imbalance. There are five common effects found lacking in an agile mind-set. They are typically associated with our mental resources being either over stretched, under stimulated or dominated by a stress reaction when facing challenges and adversity:

1. Boredom, monotony, and dullness

2. Being stuck and in a muddle

3. Anxiety, fear, doubts and worries

4. Distractions, deflections and pastimes

5. Beliefs structures, fixed thought patterns.

These common effects can act a as a signal that something is lacking for our mental energy and sharpness. Boredom and frustration can let you know that the choices you are making are not working for you anymore and it may be time to try something different. Anxiety and fear may let you know that you are stepping outside your area of comfort and while it can feel uncomfortable to keep pushing your growth edge.

Curiosity and meaning will drive us outwards in search of knowing more. Sadly, at times, we can become preoccupied with self and focus more on getting it right in order to achieve perfection. There are no right or wrong answers to live your life regardless of the experts, and the mind or cognitive realm has many plying their trade with what you should or shouldn't do, in any given situation. Keep it simple by being active and direct your own mind to a discovery of something it enjoys learning.

According to neuroscientist Dr. Joe Dispenza we can use our curiosity to change our thoughts and this can change our destiny. He proposes that total transformation is possible and it all starts with the mind and is as simple as asking 'What if?' He puts the proposition:

'If you were to sincerely think about a greater ideal of yourself before you started your day, you would begin to make your brain fire in new sequences, patterns, and combinations. And whenever you make your brain work differently, you just changed your mind.' (*Evolve Your Brain: The Science of Changing Your Mind*)

Building mental agility requires us to stretch beyond what we know and build new connections in our brain.

The Cognitive Realm seeks a daily awakening of the following:

Mindfulness	Being non-judgemental, present and open. Free from hooks and conditioned responses.
Creativity and Ingenuity	Having originality and using imagination to create new and different thoughts, ideas and solutions.
Problem Solving	Finding resolutions, answers and clarification to immediate issues and future challenges.
Insight and Learning	Discovering and expanding understanding, knowledge and wisdom.
Research and Discovery	Using investigation, study and exploration to find new ideas and patterns of new thinking and perspective.
Critical Discernments	Making important judgements with sensitivity, astuteness and awareness.
Taking Calculated Risks	Taking a chance after careful and deliberate estimation of the probable ability.
Sharpness of Recall	Recalling memories with a quickness, astuteness and intelligence relevant in any given moment.
Abstracting	Having the mental capacity to think about something conceptually or theoretically, a layering of complexity.

Dr. Bruce Lipton, author of *The Biology of Belief*, states that we have around sixty thousand thoughts per day and 80% of these thoughts we had yesterday. The conscious brain is the creative, learning program that thrives on novelty and development. In contrast, the subconscious brain is more like a machine that stores everything in the form of programs. It records, pushes a button and plays back. Science is recognising that these programs begin in uterine, and continue onwards by being embedded throughout family systems, culture and societal norms, with the majority laid down by the age of seven. Without cognitive awareness, we are running on auto-pilot. Which is why the unconscious mind acts as a powerful filter to the world around us.

There is a common principle in neuroscience that says, 'Nerve cells that fire together, wire together.' The phrase was first used in 1949 by Donald Hebb, a Canadian neuropsychologist known for his research in the field of learning. Since then it has become a learning rule in the field of cognitive development. This means if you are repeatedly thinking and acting in an identical way on a daily basis, your brain will become moulded into a specific pattern. Dr. Joe Dispenza says:

'It's ironic. Most people routinely think the same thoughts, perform the same actions, and secretly expect something different to show up in their lives.'

Thought leader in emotional health, Dr. Susan David, identifies that we can all become hooked by rigid, negative patterns of thinking and behaving. The result being we find ourselves coping by either bottling up or suppressing difficult emotions, or we are brooding and ruminating on them. How do we un-hook ourselves from this? In her book, *Emotional Agility* she explains the solution is not about ignoring difficult thoughts rather it is about holding them loosely. During the day, we speak sixteen thousand words, but our internal dialogue is thousands more. That means we are being strongly influenced by what is going on inside our head. If we are not aware of the conversation, our responses tend towards being reflexive and we run off auto-pilot. Consequently, our decisions are not the result of our decision-making, but our habits.

The good news is that we can change them by finding clues and rewards that fuel the habits and deliberately replace them. The challenge to being cognitively awake is to first spot the clues, then face them courageously before walking past them with different or alternate choices. The task is to free ourselves from emotional rigidity and thoughts that limit us and can lead to a range of mental health conditions. The solution lies with what Susan David calls being emotionally agile:

'Being flexible with your thoughts and feelings so that you can respond optimally to everyday situations – is key to well-being and success.'

The eighteen cognitive awakeners help you to enhance your mental energy. They will provide you with resources and strategies to assist in answering the following questions:

How do you find and then communicate clarity of your thoughts?

How do you keep your mind engaged and vibrant?

How do you broaden your preferences and pre-judgements?

How do you live your beliefs and values?

How do you reduce your stressors, anxieties, doubts and worries?

The classical fields of understanding in regard to psychology and neuroscience have made great advances with regard to the well-being of the mind and aging. Plasticity is a progressive concept drawn from years of research and sound client practice. It refers to the brain's amazing ability to change through life, to reorganise itself and make new connections. We now know more and realise the mind's capacity to heal itself. With aging there has been a natural increase and focus on dementia, its wear and tear. Agility and reasoning have become more important to keep our faculties healthy. *Lumosity* is a company that offers a series of mindful tasks and games geared to enhance fluidity.

The emergent fields of Energy Psychology, Epi-genetics and Mindfulness, are discovering new and faster ways to download information at the subconscious level in order to re-write out-dated beliefs, habits and to build new neural pathways to create an exceptional self.

A healthy mind moves swiftly through what is known to pursue what it has yet to learn. It seeks new or different information as to how we can make sense of our surrounds and then works out better ways to live. It craves daily stimulation, together with its inverse, contemplation and provides a mindful work-out that keeps mental agility both poised and sharp.

Cognitive Awakener Strategies

Cognitive Awakeners provide a series of strategies and techniques to mindfully make sense and to find meaning from a myriad of information and distractions. They awaken your natural verve and sway.

Cognitive Verve: is a focused process to seek your truth or answers, a cause and effect, a resolute problem-solving, analysis and finer discernments.

Cognitive Sway: is more an abstract process to expand the mind's capacity, a curiosity, a free-association, a humour, a creativity and day-dreaming.

These awakeners are the substance of what successful individuals use when they need to optimise their mental strength and agility to process information, create meaning and make sense of complexity. They relish having sharp thinking and being resilient to resolve issues and challenges.

Awakener	Description
1. Be Alert	Being more aware of your surrounds and then able to direct your attention and focus towards when and where you need it most.
2. Spacious Clarity	Obtain space from all your thoughts and reactive patterns; create the room to observe and participate, rather than just reacting.
3. Say Enough!	Limit your negative self-talk by noticing and naming it, then not to choose to be in alignment with it. Getting your negative self-talk to 'back off.'
4. Living You	Focus on what your mental energy wants to thrive, rather than what you don't want; set your direction toward a positive outcome.
5. Relieve & Restore	Be in the moment using meditation to activate slow brain patterns that evoke deep physical and mental relaxation and healing.
6. See Your Truth	Get into the core of what matters by asking better questions of self that gain a richer perspective and understanding of what is truly important.

7. Your Best Friend	Be a friend to yourself, 'a best friend' by making sure that you are thinking positive thoughts about what you want in the world.
8. Lean into Strength	Use your learned and innate strengths along with your natural talents, adding an intrinsic motivation to ensure an enriched life.
9. Change Your Mind	Reflect openness in how you engage the world, find yourself becoming more accepting, re-framing criticism and deal with regrets.
10. Resonate Positively	Be fully aware and considerate with the messages you are transmitting to yourself and others through a kinder and thoughtful thinking process.
11. Press Pause	Build healthier habits that easily recover a mental energy, such as pausing, reducing multi-tasking, doing cognitively challenging activities first.
12. Down Time	Allow yourself some 'mind wandering' time when you are 'un-goal' focused and not intensely concentrating, but rather revelling in a state of day-dreaming.
13. De-program Self	Move beyond your preference and prejudices, affording you an insight into how and when you are triggered, so you can move away from your old self.
14. Stand up for Self	Manage your own work and life boundaries by setting limits, push back and mark out what is 'enough' for someone else and yourself.
15. Speak to Yourself	Listen to how you speak with yourself and when self-sentencing is detrimental to you shift towards positive affirming words that are more supportive.
16. Nurture Tomorrow	Observe how you receive and give a compliment, tease, challenge, push back and give feedback to others and yourself with grace..
17. Make a Date with Yourself	Build future memories by placing sign-posts six months into the future. Anticipate and set what you want in the future and delete what no longer serves you.
18. Playfully Healthy	Use the power of your mind through mental imagery to activate a healing process, and stimulate the body's natural responses.

Until you are willing to be confused about what you already know, what you know will never grow bigger, better, or more useful.

Milton Erickson

1. Being Alert

A strategy designed for sustaining mental agility.

Useful for: Enhancing one's focus and powers of concentration.

Future proofing: 'What requires my clarity?'

This strategy is about coming fully into the present by managing what you pay attention to, and what stops or detracts you from your immediate focus. It assists concentration, lowers distraction and increases your mental capacity to choose where your thoughts are going. It is one of the foundation skills for becoming mindful.

How this strategy offers you an alternate coping approach

In today's environment we have access to a huge amount of information and technologies which means we constantly find ourselves in the 'on' position. We are being subjected to vast amounts of current news continually coming at us, with an expectation that we will respond instantly. This incessant environment has created what is referred as an 'epidemic of being overwhelmed.'

Attention is a limited resource, and distractions take their toll. Research by the Franklin Covey Institute examined the workplaces of over 350,000 people from all over the world. The study found that most people spend an average of 40% on low-priority or irrelevant activities as opposed to priorities that are important. It is not surprising that with the mind under siege, it is difficult to stay attentive about what truly matters. Mindfulness expert Ramus Hougaard says:

> 'Action addiction is one of the biggest threats to our mental effectiveness and productivity ... it takes away your ability to maintain clear priorities ... When the mind's under pressure – when it never gets a break from being bombarded with information and distractions – it can be difficult to maintain focus, let along prioritise tasks.' (*One Second Ahead*)

A compelling finding from numerous studies is that our brains actually perform better when we are focused and not doing multiple things all at the same time. While multi-tasking may feel empowering, it is a slower way to operate. The switching time required to move between tasks actually reduces efficiency and drains energy. It is no wonder that people experience mental fatigue and exhaustion.

This is how you can delight and enjoy it

Developing your focus is simple, but not easy to execute. You must first manage your brain's natural inclination to react to what it feels is 'urgent' or novel as both give you a dopamine high. Getting a hit from this powerful brain chemical is very seductive. In the moment you will feel busy and productive, but by the end of the day, you will feel cognitively weary and realise you haven't achieved anything that is important.

According to neuroscience research, timing is of the essence. Inhibiting distraction is a core skill to stay focused. That means noticing the distractions before they take you off on a different thought pathway. Once they take hold, your neural circuitry will kick in and you will become distracted.

Thought leader in neuroscience and leadership Dr. David Rock, believes an effective starting point to become more alert is to manage what you focus on. He recommends:

> 'Pay attention to your attention and stop yourself from getting on the wrong train of thought or getting off it before it takes hold and is solidified. This is the opposite of being mindless: it's being mindful.' (*Your Brain at Work*)

Using inhibition is to notice the urges, thoughts and behaviours that are happening early on, and to choose not to follow them. He proposes the technique of 'Pause-Clarify-Decide' which can help you re-wire your brain from reaction to attentiveness. Notice and then practice not shifting with the pulls on your attention … 'Pause' and ask yourself a clarifying question, 'Is this where I want my focus now?' Then, decide 'yes' or 'no,' before refocusing on what matters.

Conversations are a place where your attention and focus can be tested. During conversations practice being aware of your thoughts. How are you listening? Are you wandering off in your own head, thinking about what to say next? What is happening to your energy and attention? Is your state of mind impatient and thus urging you to jump in and interrupt, to add your opinion? Or, are you present with what the other person is saying, listening deeply and allowing the conversation to unfold?

This is how I optimise it and gain the most value from it

When I seek to do some deep thinking or creative writing, I start in the morning when my space is generally quiet and my brain is refreshed and focused. During this time, I have the most mental energy to control my attention span and it is easier to manage distractions. I switch off email and put my iPhone on silent. The space is set up to reduce distraction and any pulls upon my mental energy. This is my rhythm and I realise that it may not be yours. What's important is to know your own cycle of mental alertness and ways to manage your thinking.

Where you can discover more

One Second Ahead: Enhance your performance at work with mindfulness by Ramus Hougaard, Jacqueline Carter and Gillian Coutts, demonstrates that it is possible to train the brain differently in today's constant pressure and distraction world. It offers practical tools and techniques as to how you can process differently so you can be more focused, calm and have less clutter in your mind, and a better management of time and attention.

> *The ability to voluntarily bring back a wandering attention over and*
> *over again is the very root of judgment, character, and will.*

> William James, Psychologist

2. Spacious Clarity

A strategy designed to review your thought processes.

Useful for: Dealing with complexity and confusion.

Future proofing: 'What really matters here?'

This strategy is about getting more space between you and your thoughts. In a single day we might speak about sixteen thousand words. However, on the inside our internal dialogue has thousands more thoughts and words. It is easy when it is noisy inside to believe that our thoughts are real. This technique is about releasing your thoughts from fusing with you and letting go of the belief that just because you are having a thought, it is valid or useful.

How this strategy offers you an alternate coping approach

We can become entangled in our incessant chatter and unhelpful thoughts without even realising it. This happens when we are caught up and dwelling in worries, fears, doubts and regrets about issues and problems. Being 'hooked by your mind' means you are captured by your thoughts and they exert an influence over your actions. When you are hooked, you allow thoughts to push you around, to bring you down or hold you back. Medical doctor and psychotherapist, Dr. Russ Harris explains that repetitive thoughts are one way that your mind copes with uncertainty and in not wanting to deal with tricky situations.

The way out of this quagmire is to use healthier techniques that can break recursive cycles of 'cognitive fusion' caused by believing your thoughts are true. Find simpler ways to detach from unhelpful thoughts and thus create a space which is beneficial to your mental health. From this state you can gain greater awareness and choice about your thoughts and the influence they are having on your mental state and behaviour.

This is how you can delight and enjoy its benefits

Every now and then over the next few days, try to drop in and tune into what your inner chatter is 'banging on' about. What are you detecting? Is a positive conversation going on? To what extent is your inner chatter full of critical appraisals of you? Do you believe them?

You might be surprised at the number of different voices and stories and that the majority are unsupportive. You are not going crazy; this is actually a normal process for the brain when left unchecked. It will naturally focus on and react to perceived threats or find ways to deal with uncomfortable and difficult experiences. Psychologist Dr. Susan David says, 'While we often accept the statements bubbling up from within this river of incessant chatter as being factual, most are actually a complex mixture of evaluations and judgements, intensified by our emotions.'

A way to unhook yourself is to pay attention to your thoughts. In doing so, you will quickly notice the presence of repetitive thoughts and patterns that waste your energy and take away the chance to learn something new and exciting. Shift this dynamic so you can give yourself some mental space by taking charge of your thoughts.

The brain likes its established paths of least resistance and thinking loops provide this path. That is why thinking can be taxing at times because you are asking your brain to change a habitual pattern. You are re-wiring the neural pathways to form new habits of a lifetime.

This is how I optimise it and gain the most value from it

I use a technique called 'diffusion' which comes from a method called 'Acceptance Commitment Therapy' (ACT is a form of cognitive and behavioural therapy that has been developed from the work of clinical psychologist Professor Steven C. Hayes). It is a useful method to create a space from my recurring thoughts. It involves distancing, disconnecting or seeing my thoughts for what they are (streams of words) not what they say they are (truths, dangers and facts). The process involves observing what is happening in my thoughts; how I am interpreting them and how that is affecting me. In that moment, I stop and label the unhelpful thought or story. This instantly creates a mental space between the thought and me.

One of my familiar stories has been the 'I'm not good enough' story. This one usually comes when I want to try something different or unusual which takes me outside my comfort zone. It happened writing this book when voices like 'Who do you think you are? Other writers are so much better and more inspiring!' showed up. Using diffusion, I recognised the story, chose not to believe it was true, and kept writing despite feeling uncomfortable.

What are your stories? Do you have some familiar ones? What about giving them a name and then stopping when they show up and choose not to agree with them. Three other ways you can use diffusion is to acknowledge unhelpful thoughts and say … 'Thank you mind for that one, I've got it from here' or, simply say 'Thinking' or, 'I'm noticing that I'm having the thought that ….' which immediately places you in the role of observer of your thoughts, rather than being caught up in them.

Where you can discover more

If you are interested in learning more of these psychological skills, Dr. Russ Harris teaches a program called *ACT Mindfully,* an introduction to cognitive and mindfulness skills. This approach is about developing mindfulness in daily life without the need for formal meditation.

> *We can use mindfulness to 'wake up,' connect with ourselves and*
> *appreciate the fullness of each moment of life.*

Russ Harris, M.D., Psychotherapist

3. Say Enough!

A strategy designed to reduce one's negative self-critique.

Useful for: Not repeating and reinforcing negative thoughts and self-beliefs.

Future proofing: 'Do I really want to hold myself back?'

This strategy is about limiting negative self-talk. It involves tracking how you speak to yourself and how to change your inner dialogue if it is repetitive and negative. Having a thought, whether it is limiting, 'No one cares,' or enhancing, 'I am loved,' both change your biochemistry in an instant. Once the mind has a thought, the rest is history. There will be a cascading flow of chemicals, either stress hormones in the case of a negative thought or feel good hormones such as oxytocin with positive, loving thoughts. The mind-body connection is a powerful dynamic one which shapes who we are and who we become.

How this strategy offers you an alternate coping approach

The interesting challenge is that we can take charge of our own thoughts. If we do this, it requires that we must go against our own biology. Research shows we have a 'negativity bias' in our internal chatter. This means that most of the time when we are chatting away, it is not making us feel any better or strengthening our self-worth. It is, in the truest sense doing the opposite, eroding our sense of confidence and connection. So deeply ingrained is the habit of replacing positive thoughts with negative thoughts, we do not even realise it. It is the brain's inherent way of keeping us safe from perceived threat.

Most of our thoughts can happen outside our conscious awareness. Often our reactions can come from our unconscious habitual thinking and we are not even aware of them. The solution rests with releasing ourselves from this grip by becoming more aware of our thinking. For David Rock, author of *Your Brain at Work*, this requires us being the 'director' of our own minds – to notice your thoughts and make a conscious decision about who and what is on your internal stage. In other words, we take charge of our inner conversations and dynamics rather than the other way around.

This is how you can delight and enjoy its benefits

It is highly unlikely to not have some negative thoughts, as your brain is wired for it; a natural critique. The key is to reduce spending too much of your time there because these negative thought patterns probably are not serving your best interests. When you realise that your thinking is detrimental, it is important to not give yourself a tough time. This will only fuel the inner critic who needs little encouragement to voice a less than productive use of energy. Know when it is time to say 'enough!'

Another way is being 'okay' with negativity. Notice that you are being negative in your thinking and choose not to dwell there by setting time limits and asking what use this is in creating a healthy dynamic. Comprehend what is relevant and what makes you stuck. Move to focus on what you can shift or do differently within the dynamic, so you can free yourself up. Be negative for say three minutes, get it off your chest, then just move on and leave behind what doesn't work. As a result, you will have less baggage.

This is how I optimise it and gain the most value from it

My way of saying 'enough' is to regularly observe my inner chatter and its sometimes hilarious or torturous discourse. What is the chatter like? What words are being used? Is a positive or negative conversation going on? What vocabulary and labels am I using to describe my experience? Using this approach, I find there is a tendency to use words that exaggerate and over dramatise. For example, I was habitually using the phrase, 'I've been so busy, rushed off my feet,' whenever people asked how I was going. This unconscious response was like a badge of honour and was activating a stress response in my body. To change this effect, the word 'busy' was deleted from my internal and external vocabulary. Now, I choose different options such as, 'I have many other things that I can be doing,' or 'I'm a little stretched at the moment.'

Another habit was to over emphasise my feelings and reactions. Previously when I disliked something, I found myself habitually saying, 'I hate that!' This is an extreme emotion for something that I simply do not like, so I have changed some of my words to, 'I dislike that ...' or 'I have a distaste for that ...' reducing the intensity of my emotional words has helped reduce my reactivity and creates a more open mental space.

Where you can discover more

The Chatter That Matters - Your Words Are Your Power by Dr. Margaret Martin, offers tools so you can pick and choose your train of thought in a constructive way. It is written as an easy-to-use guide to assist you to 'reclaim control of your thoughts, by getting rid of the negative mind chatter,' 'improve the chatter you share with others,' and 'structure the all-important protective chatter.' These are all components that make up 'the chatter that really matters.'

Playing Big – A Practical Guide for Brilliant Women Like You by Tara Mohr is a program so you can play big from the inside out. It is a practical guide to move past self-doubt and to create what you want to create – whether in your career, your community or in a passion you pursue outside of work. It is about living with a greater sense of freedom to express your voice and pursue your aspirations.

Get to know the voices in your head, and which ones to follow.

Tony Robbins, Author and Life Coach.

4. Living You

A strategy designed to explore and achieve what is important to you.

Useful for: Sustaining a direction, overcoming challenges and obstacles.

Future proofing: 'What is my purpose and how do I stay true?'

This strategy can assist to align your purpose, bringing a positive direction which can influence your future thinking. At times when life gets challenging and feels stressful, it can lead towards becoming consumed by self-absorption. Reconnecting with your purpose will immediately take you beyond yourself and how you will show up as a difference in the world. Returning with what is meaningful will shift your focus towards what you want, rather than what you don't want. Leaning into what you want, even when a situation is confronting, helps you stay true with what matters and to be authentic in your world.

How this strategy offers you an alternate coping approach

To know your purpose can help to give your life structure and meaning. Finding your innate calling is not always easy and can be a life-time journey. Margie Warrell in her book, *Make your Mark*, defines purpose as 'a stable and generalised intention to accomplish something that is at the same time meaningful for you and consequentially the world beyond you.' It can be your beacon, a guiding light when you are making choices and decisions about what direction you might take.

How can you define your purpose? The science of a meaningful life shows that it comes from a combination of four intersecting factors: First, your skills, gifts and strengths; Second, what you love doing; Third, what you care about; and lastly, what our planet needs, and how you can contribute. The intersection of these four factors is your larger intention for living life – your life purpose.

Ikigai is a Japanese word whose meaning translates roughly as a 'reason for being,' encompassing joy, a sense of purpose, meaning and a feeling of being fully alive. The word derives from *iki*, meaning life and *kai*, meaning the realisation of hopes and expectations. In the Japanese region of Okinawa, *Ikigai* is thought of as 'a reason to get up in the morning,' that is, a reason to cherish life. In the TED Talk *How to Live to 100+*, Dan Buettner, national geographic fellow, suggests that *Ikigai* is one of the reasons people in certain regions live such long lives. These regions have been called 'Blue Zones' and Okinawa is often cited as an exemplar of healthy longevity.

This is how you can delight and enjoy its benefits

If you wish take this process deeper and discover more of your purpose, consider the following four questions:

1. What are your skills, gifts and strengths? What are you good at? What do people compliment you on that they see comes naturally to you?

2. What do you love to do? How would you spend your time if you had no other responsibility?

3. What and who do you care about? What moves your spirit, lights your curiosity, and makes you feel enlivened? What causes do you care deeply about?

4. What do you consider the world needs? What are the problems that need to be solved in this world? What concerns you about the world, and that you yearn to find a solution for? How do you wish to serve the world?

This is how I optimise it and gain the most value from it

After a morning meditation, I start my day with the question, 'How can I be of service in today's world?' It lifts up my thinking towards a bigger picture of service and sets the intention for the day. It may be as simple as 'write, learn, and connect,' or something subtle, such as 'go to nature' or 'be love.' This becomes my over-arching guide and reminder how to be and what to move towards.

As an overall journey, my search for purpose has evolved through various stages of my life. Sometimes in transition it has been more elusive. These times have been frustrating and without clear purpose; I have, at times, been blown around in the wind! Then, I revisit the process using the four questions that I've shared with you. What is interesting is that while I think it might be something vastly different, it rarely is. What truly matters for me, has a familiarity of my own values and best wishes – a lifelong thread.

Where you can discover more

In *The Power of Meaning* journalist Emily Esfahani Smith reveals how people find meaning in life through 'four pillars' of meaning – *Belonging* (being recognised, understood by our family and friends and connected to community); *Purpose* (having long term goals that reflect our values and serve the greater good); *Storytelling* (crafting a coherent narrative that defines our identity); and *Transcendence* (finding experiences). Together these four pillars lift us above mundane habits and recursive patterns to live more rich, satisfying and meaningful lives.

> *Purposeful means that I want to approach every day and every activity with the highest of intentions to make my greatest contribution to the world. I want to be led by a higher purpose rather than by pride or fear or any underlying need to prove myself to anyone.*

Maggie Warrell, Author

5. Relieve and Restore

A strategy designed for being fully present.

Useful for: Generating mental relaxation and rejuvenation.

Future proofing: 'What eases my mind?'

This strategy is based on both ancient and modern-day meditation techniques that help you be and stay in the moment. Slow your breath, quieten your mind and be still for a few moments, as this changes your brain in positive ways. There are many ways you can meditate and the impact on well-being is similar. Whether it is ancient techniques of repeating a mantra, or modern techniques of flowing the breath, or putting thoughts on a leaf floating them away down a stream, they contribute to relieve and restore mental clarity.

How this strategy offers you an alternate coping approach

The evidence is unequivocal – meditation is good for your brain. Following neuroscience research we are now able to view the tangible benefits to our brains when practicing meditation. Brain scans show that meditation creates changes in brainwaves. These findings have triggered a new wave of research identifying many cognitive benefits, from greater attention and focus, a reduction in symptoms of anxiety and depression to improved creative ability and lateral thinking. Meditation works by increasing the grey matter concentration and density within the areas of the brain involved in learning and memory, this regulates emotions, and gives a sense of self and perspective.

The exciting news is that it doesn't take years of meditating to gain these neurological benefits. A study by Sara Lazar, neuroscientist at Harvard University, identified positive changes in areas of the brain involved in learning, memory and self-regulation after eight weeks of meditating on average for thirty minutes a day.

This is how you can delight and enjoy its benefits

There is a lot written about meditation and its many different forms. There is a saying that practicing yoga is about finding the teacher for you. With meditation it is more about finding the technique that best works for you. There are diverse meditation practices available that range from using your breath as a focal point, to repeating a mantra (a sound like *Om* or a word like 'peace' or 'love') or following a guided recorded meditation.

Whichever one you select, the key to its effectiveness is to commit to a regular practice. As journalist and author, Sarah Wilson, says about her journey of living with anxiety, 'When people ask me for the "one thing" that's helped with my anxiety, I tell them there's been no one thing. But if I am pressed, I concede that meditation has steered me to most of the good things that have happened in the past seven years.'

An effortless way is to establish a daily meditation ritual that works within your routine, like brushing your teeth or having a shower. Just as you take care of your physical hygiene, think of meditation as your mental hygiene.

This is how I optimise it and gain the most value from it

I've been meditating since I was twenty-one years old. At university, I learned Transcendental Meditation (TM) to enhance my ability to concentrate and settle my restless verve. This form of meditation uses a sound mantra to help focus the mind. Even though it is called 'transcendental,' I don't always experience a deep state of complete stillness. What I do notice is that my sessions at times can be busy and noisy, and the meditation becomes about disengaging from distraction rather than sinking down into it. Yet, when going about my day, I do feel calmer and more at ease, with the buzzy busyness in my mind having shifted. Through these experiences, I have come to realise that my practice makes a positive difference. Wherever I find myself in the world, the day starts with a formal meditation practice.

Where you can discover more

One of my favourite meditation teachers is Davidji. He spent over twenty years working in a corporate career and understands the pressures and stress of this lifestyle. Now he spends his life teaching and guiding people in meditation practices. In *Secrets of Meditation: A Practical Guide to Inner Peace and Personal Transformation*, he offers the latest techniques, research and resources to enhance your meditation practice towards the next level. On his website there are a variety of free guided meditations you can experience.

There are also many meditation apps available that offer a variety of techniques which can clear and calm your mind using guided meditation, breath focus or mindfulness practices. The Life Flow Meditation centre provides free guided mindfulness meditations on the soundcloud app (www.soundcloud.com/lifeflow).

Smiling Mind is an Australian not-for-profit organisation that provides children and adults with the mindfulness tools needed to develop a healthy mindset. It is a free app that works on iOS and Android. There are levels so you can start as a beginner and move to longer meditations as you become more confident with the practice.

Insight Timer is a free app for meditation and mindfulness practice available for iOS and Android. It has an alarm that times your mindfulness practice and lets you build a playlist of favourites.

> *Meditation opens the door between the conscious and subconscious minds. We meditate to enter the operating system of the subconscious, where all of those unwanted habits and behaviours reside, and change them to more productive modes to support us in our lives.*
>
> Dr. Joe Dispenza, Neuroscientist

6. Seeing Your Truth

A strategy designed to gain a deeper meaning and richer perspective.

Useful for: Asking better self-questions that seek out fresh comprehension.

Future proofing: 'What else sits behind the obvious, a deeper learning?'

This method is about getting to the core of 'What Matters' to you. This may be relevant with any issue you are facing – a choice about a new career, relationship or finding your larger life-purpose. The process involves systematically asking questions and listening deeply to gain broader, deeper and further perspective. This insight will assist you to gain an understanding about what might be important to you and your potential.

How this strategy offers you an alternate coping approach

Have you ever gone down a path on your journey and realised that you are following someone else's dream, not yours? In your desire to give have you inadvertently put to one side what really matters to you?

Finding your potential is an on-going process that requires that you move forward and expand in your awareness. Often this happens by defying and going beyond what limits you. Using this method can help challenge your reality and discover the edge of your own growth and awareness

By asking questions you start accessing the higher cognitive processes of your amazing brain and diffuse it from the grip of the emotional brain. If you are feeling confused, frustrated or even lost on your quest to find your true north, pause and ask yourself a question. In doing so, this will instantly aid you to think and shift towards a higher order perspective. It stimulates your brain to operate at a higher functioning and moves it away from just reactions driven by emotions that stem from the limbic part of the brain.

This is how you can delight and enjoy its benefits

When you seek to find the core of an issue or a larger quest you might be facing, a useful technique is to use the 'tripling down' sequence. The 'tripling down' sequence is a systematic layering of the questions to reveal a deeper meaning and purpose.

> *1. What matters really about this?*
> > *2. What is important about that?*
> > > *3. How is this significant for my future?*

Ask yourself the first question, then listen to your response. Next, based on this response, you ask the second question and find out what is important and again listen to your response. Then, the third question focuses on what is significant about the situation you are in.

You can use this 'tripling down' sequence to clarify issues or explore possibilities for yourself. You can also use it with others. By 'tripling down' with others you signal that you are actively listening, genuinely interested in their perspective and that you value and acknowledge their contribution.

If you seek a quick re-set, simply ask yourself, 'what matters' here, and listen closely to your inner wisdom. When with others who may be stuck in an old pattern or are confused, ask 'what matters?' and wait for their clarity to gently surface.

This is how I optimise it and gain the most value from it

I use 'tripling down' with my coaching clients and for myself. It is a fast way to get at the heart of what's important. Typically, I find that the first question, 'what matters?' gets me part way there, an unveiling of the real conversation. Often it takes until the third question, 'how is this significant?' before the real meaning can emerge. The skill is to hold this space, listen deeply and pay close attention to what is emerging as this is usually an insight for them.

The framework is also useful to discern another's perspective through active listening. As a modeller, my focus is to help others recover and make explicit their tacit know-how. I adore using this technique, as it allows me a drilling down into what matters and then assists those I model towards a better understanding of their own strategy and mastery. This for me is a worthy exchange.

Where you can discover more

Make Your Mark: A Guidebook for the Brave Hearted by Margie Warrell is about how you reset your inner compass, so you can live into your potential and purpose. It combines insightful advice with powerful questions which help you dig beneath your fears and re-discover passion for how you want to show up – in your work, relationships and life.

If you want a purpose for you and your team *Find Your Why* by Simon Sinek offers a practical guide to learn your why. An optimist who believes in a bright future, he declares 'fulfillment is a right, not a privilege.' He makes the case that people and organisations that know their *Why* have greater, long-term success and create deeper trust and loyalty with employees and customers.

The Matter model and tripling down questions were first published in *7 Days to Effective People Management*, Times Publishing 1996. It is no longer in print however it remains a core framework used in leadership development programs and in coaching.

Change the way you look at thing and things you look at will change.

Wayne W Dyer, Philosopher and Author

7. Your Best Friend

A strategy designed to bring out the best from your own thoughts about yourself.

Useful for: Lightening up on self-critique, befriending yourself.

Future proofing: 'How would I treat others I really care about?'

This strategy involves thinking about yourself in the same way you think about your best friends. It is the ability to afford caring, wise and positive thoughts and about being on good terms with yourself – as you would be towards one of your cherished relationships. That means to confront those thoughts that are judging and critical, so you can move towards what you want more of in your life, and avoid what you don't want.

How this strategy offers you an alternate coping and adaptive approach

Our brains have an ingrained negativity bias which is primed for survival. That means it focuses on negative experiences and tends to get stuck in conditioned patterns of thinking. This has the tendency to return you towards thoughts of events and experiences that have gone wrong, or to worry about what might happen in the future and to relentlessly pick at your own faults. It is like shining a big spot-light on yourself and saying, 'You're not good enough and I shall punish you by being harsh, uncaring and dismissive!' If you spoke like this to one of your closest friends, what impact would your uncaring words have on the relationship? It would probably sabotage the friendship and cause great pain.

Dr. Kristen Neff, pioneer in the study of self-compassion explains that being your own best friend is about being self-kind as opposed to self-judging. Her research shows that being self-critical and thinking we must beat ourselves up does not work for motivation or learning. In fact, it is counterproductive and can lead towards procrastination and depression. She says, 'It is a revolutionary idea that you can actually be kind unto yourself, accepting of your own faults and enjoy deep emotional benefits as a result.'

The science of kindness shows that being self-caring has positive effects on both your mental and physical health. When you are kind with yourself and others, your immune system becomes stronger, you are more creative, and have better social relationships and a desire to live life to the full. Corporate mindfulness trainer, Ramus Hougaard says,

> 'The first step in developing kindness is to show kindness to yourself. Give yourself a break. Don't beat yourself up. Instead, treat yourself how you'd like to be treated, with understanding and respect.' (*One Second Ahead*)

This is how you can delight and enjoy its benefits

The key with this technique is to focus on creating positive and empowering thoughts so you move towards what you want and create the best outcomes for yourself. Kindness experts say there is a quicker way to befriend yourself and become a positive influence on yourself and the impact you are having on others.

1. Start by observing your thoughts, and ask, 'What am I focusing on right now?' 'Am I being self-caring or self-judging?' This inquiry will bring you back into the present moment.

2. If you are being hard on yourself, gently pause, and self-soothe with an understanding and caring approach, acknowledging that you are struggling or suffering in this moment. Reminding yourself that you *are* your best friend.

3. Next, gently focus your attention on the thoughts you want to feel in that moment. It may be confidence, openness, self-assurance and being more capable.

4. Then, connect with how having those thoughts feels in your body. You may be aware that your body posture has now shifted in alignment with the new thoughts and subsequent feelings.

5. And lastly, ask yourself, 'Right now, what is the impact I want on others and is this adding to the situation?'

This is how I optimise it and gain the most value from it

In taking risks and trying something new, I sometimes doubt myself and feel a touch fearful. At times, this has led me to avoid risk and change, leaving me in a state where I am metaphorically 'treading water.' My learning is to alter my redundant thoughts. I focus on making a shift in the tone of my inner dialogue to find different ways I can reduce the negative impact on my desire to take a risk. In executing this circuit-breaker, I first acknowledge my fear as this takes the power away that it has over my actions and then I choose that it does not dictate my actions. On the way, I'll put my hand on my heart and gently say, 'I know this is scary and you are struggling, I'm with you. How do you want to be feeling and how can I help you?'

Where you can discover more

Self-Compassion: Stop Beating Yourself Up and Leave Insecurity Behind by Kristen Neff Ph.D. offers advice on how you can limit self-criticism and offset its negative effects, enabling you to achieve your highest potential and a more fulfilled life.

> *You, yourself, as much as anyone in the entire universe, deserve your love and affection.*

> The Buddha

8. Lean into your strengths

A strategy designed to build a solid self-foundation to work from.

Useful for: Establishing a sound default position.

Future proofing: 'What am I adding or building here?'

This strategy helps you identify all your positive strengths and to learn how you can build upon them. Your strengths are strong capacities within you that best describe the positive aspects of who you are. They are a combination of your skills, talents, interests, resources and character traits that shape how you are and how you show up in the world. Your strengths impact on how you think, feel and behave. They are important for you to be your best in the different domains of your life – work, home, personal relationships, community.

This constellation of strengths is distinctive, it gives you uniqueness.

How this strategy offers you an alternate coping approach

Countless studies show that we are at our optimal best when we use our strengths. When we regularly do so in new and diverse ways, we experience higher levels of happiness, improved relationships, feel more engaged and flourish at work and thereby promote higher well-being. In today's modern culture, there can be a tendency to focus on 'What's wrong?' – to hone-in on our problems, struggles and stressors and lose sight of what is good and functional within us and in the world.

Leaning into your strengths is a way for you to take a strengths-based approach to your life. It gives you resources to shift focus from 'What is wrong with me and how can I fix it?' towards 'What is right and strong with me and how can I use it?'

This is how you can delight and enjoy its benefits

There are two internationally recognised strengths assessments. The first is the *VIA Character Strengths Survey* and the second being the *Clifton StrengthsFinder.* Both provide evidence-based methods to identify your strengths and ways to leverage them for greater satisfaction and life fulfilment.

The *VIA Character Survey* is based on the research of Professor Martin Seligman, University of Pennsylvania. It is a free online diagnostic called *VIA Character Strengths.* It will assist you in discovering your best qualities and understanding your core character strengths. There are twenty-four-character strengths which are connected to six higher virtues. On your report, the top six-character strengths are called your 'hallmark strengths.' According to this framework, 'hallmark strengths' are your intrinsic motivators. When you use and have them active across the different domains of your life, they fill you up and give you satisfaction.

To identify your natural talents and abilities the *Clifton StrengthsFinder 2.0* is useful and insightful. It is an online survey that measures thirty-four different themes and tells you 'how you are talented.' It identifies what you naturally do best and provides customised results that name your unique talents.

This is how I optimise it and gain the most value from it

I first completed the *VIA Character Survey* in 2008 and have re-done it several times since. Consistently, I have found the same 'signature strengths' turn up. There may be a variation in the order they come in, however, the key strengths remain at the top.

My number one strength is 'Love of Learning,' followed by 'Appreciation of Beauty and Excellence,' 'Perspective' and 'Curiosity.' Knowing this combination has reinforced to me that being in the world is about seeking wisdom both through what I read, research through books and courses, and what I discover by modelling others – their mastery, skills and tacit know-how. These strengths motivate me to seek, explore and wonder.

Using a strengths-based approach is core to my coaching practice. It encourages clients to focus on what is working rather than what is not working, to harness their intrinsic motivators and build greater resilience and confidence.

Where you can discover more

Positive Psychology is the scientific study of the strengths that enable individuals and communities to thrive. If you are curious to learn more about Positive Psychology, the *Authentic Happiness* website at the University of Pennsylvania offers resources through readings, videos, research, opportunities, conferences, questionnaires with feedback and more. There is no charge for the use of this site.

Act Like a Leader, Think Like a Leader by Herminia Ibarra shows you how you can step up into a leadership mindset by making small but crucial changes in your job, networks and yourself. She offers advice to help you redefine your job, diversify your network and become more playful with your self-concept. This, in turn, allows your familiar and out-dated style an evolvement towards more of who you could be by utilising your inherent strengths and talents.

Your interests in life drive your character strengths and vice versa. Bring the two together and you have a recipe for success in life. Interests and character strengths are two natural energy resources within us.

Ryan Niemiec, Ph.D., Psychologist

9. Changing Your Mind

A strategy designed to remain open with what else you might learn.

Useful for: Reframing criticism and dealing with regrets.

Future proofing: 'Am I really open to new ways or approaches?'

This strategy helps you go beyond your unconscious biases and programming to find new perspectives and learning. It assists with being open rather than feeding into the jumble of information already sorted by the influences of your own likes and dislikes. It shows you a way to allow the possibility to find a new or different perspective. In other words, you are re-shaping your brain by being mindful of what you accept as feedback or criteria of success.

How this offers you an alternate coping approach

Typically, our brain's default is to judge people and situations and to judge quickly. Left unchecked, your brain will automatically judge things as good or bad, right or wrong, like or dislike, fair or unfair, important or not important and so on. Appraisals happen very fast, and often. Part of the brain's survival programming is to scan for difference and potential threats. It does this so fast that our experiences are shaped by it and most of the time we are completely unaware of what's happening.

Judgement and meaning are assigned based on how we interpret an event or person. Behind every thought is a 'frame of reference' which is determined by underlying beliefs and assumptions. Most of the time this frame operates at the subconscious level. To change your mind about anything requires you to start with reframing your previously held judgements. This involves identifying unhelpful thoughts and replacing them with more positive or adaptive ones. In the book *Breaking the Habit of Being Yourself,* Dr. Joe Dispenza says:

> 'If we want to change some aspect of our reality, we have to think, feel, and act in new ways; we have to be "different" in terms of our responses to experiences. We have to "become" someone else. We have to create a new state of mind … we need to observe a new outcome with that new mind.'

This is how you can delight and enjoy its benefits

The key to change your mind is to bring awareness into the present moment and to notice your thoughts by being aware of when you have made a judgement, albeit implicit or explicit. If you can pause, hold your judgement lightly rather than jumping towards an easy conclusion, labelling or evaluation, it allows you to be open with what else there might be. Often, the first explanation that we go for is not the most valuable to pursue.

When you notice that you have made a judgement for whatever reason or are in the process of doing so, pause and ask yourself one of these questions, 'What's another way I can view this?' 'How much am I stuck in my own likes and dislikes right now?' 'Could there be something here that I am not seeing or understanding?' 'What is useful about this judgement?' 'Is there another possible meaning?' If you look for a simple phrase to use as a generalisation it could be 'How useful is this judgement?'

By asking these types of questions, you are questioning your brain to 'reframe' either the context or the meaning. In doing so, you open other choices for yourself and potentially will be able to find a new perspective.

Become mindful of what you are accepting as a measure of success or what you inherently value. First, discern are they yours or someone else's judgements? What helps is to know the time-frame you place upon a situation and its reference points asked by placing a relevant check, on the task faced. It is best to keep these two separate - the person and the task. Remember we can all have less than optimal behaviours or performances which don't detract from us as human beings. For example: *She is a great person yet lacks an aptitude for this or has an issue with timing. She will need more time, so she can practice this skill further.*

This is how I optimise it and gain the most value from it

When I meet someone for the first time, rather than focusing on, 'I'm not sure about you,' I go with the positive intention, 'This is a lovely soul with beautiful values.' I connect to this one aspect and follow it as a core thread about the person. This is how I stay open. When I make a choice to focus on worth and value and connect with that aspect it is amazing what shows up!

Where you can discover more

The Now Effect: How this Moment Can Change the Rest of Your Life by Elisha Goldstein Ph.D. offers practical ways to cultivate non-judgement awareness, to calm your mind, transform negative emotions, reframe thoughts and facilitate greater self-acceptance, openness and inner peace. The techniques allow you to connect more in the present moment by making the changes in the now and then align these with what really matters as you go forward with your life.

Mindset: The New Psychology of Success by Carol S. Dweck reveals the power of mindset. How we think about our talents and abilities will govern success in all aspects of life. People with a *fixed mindset* — those who believe that abilities are fixed — are less likely to flourish than those with a *growth mindset* — those who believe that abilities can be developed.

> *Beyond anything else that we may actually do in our lives, the beliefs that precede our actions are the foundations of all that we cherish, dream, become and accomplish.*

Gregg Braden, Author and Pioneer

10. Resonating Positively

A strategy designed for how best you can communicate your message and its intent.

Useful for: Empowering change or giving feedback which results in greater effort.

Future proofing: 'How can I add to their day and ease their way?'

This strategy concentrates on how you can keep yourself resonating positively. Your vibration reflects your overall state of being. Your thoughts have a frequency and being mindful of what you are transmitting to yourself and others via your thinking will help you stay in a positive flow and to be at your best.

How this strategy offers you an alternate coping approach

Everything in the universe is made up of energy vibrating at different frequencies. Even things that look solid are made up of vibrational energy fields at the quantum level. This includes your body – especially your heart.

Research by the HeartMath Institute in the USA has found that the heart, like the brain, generates a powerful electromagnetic field. Director of Research, Rollin McCraty explains 'the heart's electrical field as measured in an electrocardiogram (ECG) is about 60 times greater in amplitude than the brain waves recorded in an electroencephalogram (EEG).' It has been detected and measured to expand around our body for about three metres and connect with others who are in close proximity. This means we are in touch with each other more than we realise and that what is happening to us, impacts on others in profound ways.

We are interconnecting with each other at an energetic level through our heart fields and affect each other far more than we appreciate. New discoveries have found that the heart field transmits emotions – both positive and negative qualities. The emotions we experience on the inside are expressed in our heart field. The frequency of love, gratitude and serenity puts our hearts into a state of coherence and balance. Emotions such as anger, frustration, sadness and grief, put our heart field into discord and erratic patterns. The heart's resonance is transmitted throughout our body, in turn affecting all the body systems. It also transfers externally onto people around us and can alter their resonance.

This is how you can delight and enjoy its benefits

What we think and feel has a direct impact on our energy and those around us. Positive thoughts and good feelings create high, buoyant vibrations, while sad or depressing thoughts and anxious feelings create low, negative vibrations. Your thoughts affect your mood and this has a frequency. If you are feeling optimistic, more than likely the people around you will catch it! If you are in a funk, then watch how others start to also feel flat and out of sorts. It works both ways, you affect others, and they affect you.

Research indicates that every living thing has a frequency (measured in megahertz, Mhz) and, moreover, we are all affected by the frequencies around us. Dr. Bruce Tainio found that the human body has a frequency that sits in a range between 62-68 Mhz. Positive and negative thoughts have been found to impact frequency. Negative thoughts were found to lower the human frequency by about 12 Mhz, while positive thoughts such as appreciation and gratitude raised the frequency by 10Mhz.

To keep yourself in a positive resonance requires you to move from auto-pilot and to pay attention to the shifts and changes in your state of mind. As you think choose what works and tilt towards 'the good.' Fear is one of the most potent emotions and left unchecked it can become all consuming. The more you choose a different thought, one that empowers and that is positive, the more you will start to build a new neural pathway. The more you engage in stepping beyond the fear and being courageous, the braver you will become.

This is how I optimise it and gain the most value from it

I am very aware of my natural frequency. When I'm there, the experience is one of being light, easeful and joyful. There is a wonderful appreciation and love of life and connection with people. Each day, I involve myself in rituals to strengthen and sustain my own frequency. The most important thing is to notice when it's off and to ask the question 'What do I need?' Sometimes it's as simple as going for a walk in a park, having a rest, having a quick chat with a close friend, or sitting quietly in meditation. Prayer and meditation have been found to raise frequency by 15 Mhz.

Being around people who are not generous or kind in manner also drops my frequency. Therefore, I limit the amount of exposure and time I give to these types of dynamics. It is to know when the energy exchange is no longer positive and to choose to set up clear boundaries or move away.

Where you can discover more

Two resource books by Doc Childre and Deborah Rozman of the HeartMath Institute, Ph.D. with strategies to resonate positively with yourself and others:

Transforming Anxiety: The HeartMath® Solution for Overcoming Fear and Worry and Creating Serenity.

Transforming Anger: The HeartMath® Solution for Letting Go of Rage, Frustration and Irritation.

> *For the seeker of positive change, the fact of energy as vibration is exciting.*
> *In a nutshell, if you alter vibration, you alter reality.*

Cyndi Dale, Author

11. Press Self-Pause

A strategy designed to build healthier habits, so you can live by example.

Useful for: Mental recovery and to prioritise what's important.

Future proofing: 'What else can I do to refresh my mind?'

This strategy involves purposefully pausing to gain more clarity by using your brain in smarter ways. It explores two aspects for mental recovery and refreshment: how to stop activity that consumes excessive fuel and taxes your brain, and how to bring in more activity that refuels and replenishes your brain.

How this strategy offers you an alternate coping approach

The brain consumes about 20% of the body's total energy. Making decisions, planning, controlling impulses and solving problems chews up metabolic fuel (glucose and oxygen). With high energy demands, the brain needs the right fuel in the form of high-quality nutrition and hydration. It also requires smart management, so not to have over-use, fatigue or burnout due to excessive processing.

The Energy Project study of twenty thousand employees world-wide identified a struggle to find focus and prioritisation as a primary source of pain in organisations and technology was found to be the primary cause. The research highlighted that never before have we been subjected to so much incoming information, so continuously, and with so much expectation to respond instantly.

For many of us, the way we have adapted to the 'always on' culture is to continually scan our environment for the latest information and ways to multi-task. This way of operating by being fully open-minded and scanning multiple data feeds, burns up a lot of mental energy and reserves. A study by the University of London found that constant emailing and text messaging reduces mental capability by an average of ten points on IQ tests (five for women and fifteen for men). This is equivalent to missing a night's sleep. The result of being continually alert is a mental fatigue which, in turn, splits one's focus and stimulates higher levels of distraction.

This is how you can delight and enjoy its benefits

According to Tony Schwartz, CEO of *The Energy Project* there are practical options available to build your mental stamina and to counteract the 'attentive deficit tendency.' To manage the multi-tasking dilemma, mark out designated times in your day to respond to voice mails and emails. Try to do your emails in dedicated sprints for thirty minutes, rather than ad-hoc through the day. This is more productive and a better use of your brain. Concentrate for intense periods of time, ninety minutes at the most; then take a break. Ideally pause for twenty minutes in which you are doing something different, without pulling on more mental energy.

Providing moments in the day to intermittently 'press pause' is an effective way to renew and recharge your mental energy. The act of pausing and using reflective thinking enables your brain to shift perspective and re-gain focus. Take a pause between meetings without skidding constantly from one meeting to another all day. Even if this a brief moment to catch your breath, be still, and reset for the next meeting. Micro-moments like this give your brain a rest, and build in recovery as you move through your day.

Schedule at least one hour a week for doing nothing other than pondering. This gives you an opportunity to reflect, look at the bigger picture, and to think strategically about your circumstances. Your brain loves this! Pause through your day, shut your eyes for two minutes or simply stare out the window and look at the sky. Take slow breaths and soak in the presence of where you are.

This is how I optimise it and gain the most value from it

When I'm writing or designing innovative ideas I go off line for chunks of time. These thinking tasks require high concentration and therefore more brain power. To keep my focus strong, I reduce interruptions by doing it away from email and phones. Sometimes, I forget to switch off my email and ping an email pops in, and immediately my attention is split. If it is too noisy or distracting around me, I'll move to a quieter space. Sometimes, I do the opposite; I take my note-pad and go to a coffee shop and sit with no interruptions to think and create.

Where you can discover more

The Energy Project involved research of twenty thousand employees across twenty-seven countries to examine what people need at work to maximise their capacity. The white paper *The Human Era at Work*, is a free download available on *The Energy Project* website. You will find options and techniques to take care of your energy at work.

Your Brain at Work: Strategies for Overcoming Distraction, Regaining Focus, and Working Smarter All Day Long by David Rock, offers ways to manage mental resources, overcome distractions, focus to solve problems and collaborate better with other people.

Your ability to make great decisions is a limited resource: conserve this resource at every opportunity.

Dr. David Rock, CEO Neuro-Leadership Institute

12. Down-time

A strategy designed to sustain mental agility and keep future dreams alive.

Useful for: Easing one's intensity of focus and performance tension.

Future proofing: 'What does my mind enjoy playing with – creativity?'

This strategy is about giving your brain down-time as a way to help you recharge and replenish your cognitive energy. It asks you to step outside your routines and mental focus for a period, to allow yourself a non-focused moment (without any specific goal) and to let your mind relax or daydream.

How this strategy offers you an alternate coping approach

From his studies David Rock found that 'down-time' really matters to the brain. It is the time the brain uses to integrate and provides insight to give us those 'ah-hah' moments. To disconnect from deliberate and conscious thinking gives the space to sort through many disparate elements of our mental life. Down-time is more about 'being' rather than doing pre-planned activities with goals and outcomes. This opens the space for insight and connection.

Research shows that any period of down-time that allows the mind to rest but still is awake, increases productivity, replenishes attention and motivation. The brain doesn't slow down or stop working when we are relaxing or day-dreaming. Studies show that down-time replenishes the brain's store of attention and motivation together with memory consolidation and learning. These processes are essential to both sustain mental performance and form stable memories from our everyday lives. The opposite, however happens if concentration goes on for too long without a break or relaxation, the restorative mental processes do not occur. This can lead to mental fatigue and exhaustion which limits learning and reduces quality performance.

This is how you can delight and enjoy its benefits

To replenish and recharge mentally, take a break from thinking and doing. Build into your day moments where you can experience a down-time. One of the quickest ways to move your brain into a down-time is to be in nature. As quick as five minutes in a natural space, or sitting under a tree, will lower your cortisol levels and relax your brain. If you're not physically able to go outside, even standing up at your desk and looking out a window at the sky will help. Studies show that even taking a few minutes to look at a nature scene on your computer screen has a positive effect.

Exercise is another effective way to replenish and recharge and even better if you do this within a natural environment. The trick to get the most benefit when you exercise is to take your brain 'off line.' Listen to music, look around you, or simply be present with your body moving and limit the amount of time you spend problem-solving in your head. Disconnect from your linear, external environment and for a period of time rest in a state of 'being' without having to do or go anywhere. Just be!

This is how I optimise it and gain the most value from it

In addition to utilising the strategies, I take mini breaks through my day. When I'm writing, I get up and move every forty minutes. Where possible, I go outside and stand in the sunlight to rest and get my Vitamin D hit. These micro breaks replenish my cognitive energy and spur me on to physically move, so I'm not sitting for hours. In between my coaching sessions, I take a thirty-minute break and go for a walk, followed by a short meditation. This way I am fresh and recharged for each new client.

I have a colour light unit called Bioptron light therapy which is an advanced light technology. Often at the end of the day, or during the day if I need to recharge I'll lie under it for ten minutes. Before doing it, I set an intention to find an insight into a specific issue or dilemma. It is as though I am 'incubating' the solution without consciously thinking about it. The light clears my energy and often an insight or learning will emerge either under the light or sometimes shortly afterwards.

Where you can discover more

The Upside of Downtime: Why Boredom is Good by Dr. Sandi Mann, explores the causes and consequences of boredom in a fast-paced twenty-first century. It tells the story of how we act, react and cope when we are bored, and argues that there is a positive side to boredom. It can be a catalyst for humour, fun, reflection, creativity and inspiration. The radical solution for the 'boredom problem' is to harness it rather than avoid it. Allowing yourself time away from constant stimuli can enrich your life. We should all embrace our boredom and see the upside of our downtime.

Wired to Create: Unravelling the Mysteries of the Creative Mind by Scott Barry Kaufman and Carolyn Gregoire, shines a light on the practices and habits that promote creative thinking. They show us how we can tap into our deepest creativity by incorporating into our daily lives practices such as daydreaming, imaginative play, passion, solitude, intuition, mindfulness and openness to experience.

Down time is more about 'being' in the moment with spontaneous emergence of whatever activity may or may not arise rather than 'doing' a pre-planned activity with a goal or pre-set agenda.

Dr. David Rock, CEO, Neuro-Leadership Institute

13. Deprogramming Self

A strategy designed to gain insight into your established patterns of thinking.

Useful for: Seeking a fresh approach or way forward.

Future proofing: 'What will be tomorrow's differences that matter?'

This strategy is about going beyond and moving past your preferences and prejudices to live more into your potential and promise. Your preferences are your 'likes' and they influence what you move towards. Your prejudices are your 'dislikes' and effect what you move away from and avoid. Together, they shape your predisposition towards life and your mindset. This strategy invites you to become aware of your orientation, explore if it needs an 'upgrade' and learn ways you can expand your preferences and limit your prejudices.

How this strategy offers you an alternate coping approach

We all have our likes and dislikes. They are tendencies to think in a certain or set way. There is a comfort and ease about them, like favourite friends. As a filter, they serve a function as they allow us to accept our world as 'sane.' There is one less thing we can think about or be concerned with. It's like operating on automatic pilot.

Our preferences and prejudices give a sense of order and familiarity and provide a sense of comfort. For example, when you put yourself in a foreign environment, everything can feel out of kilter; it is subtle and can be uncomfortable. That is because your reference points of what you know have shifted and you can feel unbalanced.

Preferences and prejudices are important. The vital question is 'To what extent are they working for you or are they a way for your world to shrink?' Perhaps, consider pulling up what you like and don't like and ask 'Are my likes and dislikes still relevant?' 'Have I grown as a person and do my preferences need updating?' 'Do I need to evolve and better align them with who I am becoming?'

One way is to add a new preference and take one of your prejudices away. Make a list of what you prefer in life. Then find something else you might like, for each preference held, and then add this to your list. This way, you are making your preferences broader, rather than narrower, to expand your world. Have conversations about what people like: ask them 'What lights your candle? 'What floats your boat?' In other words, what makes you happy and stimulated? Others might have some different likes that you wish to include into your preferences. This is an effective way to broaden the edges of your world and your comfort zone.

This is how I optimise it and gain the most value from it

A friend of mine has an effective and simple strategy to expand his preferences. He has an interest and a passion for roses. Over the past few years, he has replaced all the flowers in his garden with roses, to create a sensually fragrant garden. He calls the roses 'his girls' and tends them with care and this gives him a sense of contentment. His preference for roses has taken him out into the world. He now travels the world exploring roses found within different gardens, finding the great rose collections and visiting flower markets. He learns about the diverse varieties of roses and spends time in nurseries chatting with horticulturists about hybrid varieties and old rose types. His preferences are allowing him to anchor onto a broader perspective. It draws him out from a small view and demands it be bigger. Now he is even making multiple 'garden-teas,' varieties of comfrey, sheep's manure and seaweed for his beloved girls (roses) and has a menu of 'different delights' to nourish them. In doing so, he has found people with a similar passion and asked them how they tender their little darlings. His passion has called him out further into the world and he is going beyond just his own garden of pleasure and charm.

Where you can discover more

What is it for you? Perhaps for you it is pottery, art, food, collectibles, wine, chocolate or exploring sacred sites?

Whatever your preferences are consider how you can use them as a process to travel and find the best or alternatives on a global scale.

For example, if you are into culinary street food culture every year there is a *World Food Congress* that specialises in this type of food. You may want to find the top restaurants that make your favourite food and travel the world to experience them. There is a businessman in Singapore who travels the world so he can taste the best char kway teow (stir fried rice cake strips). It is considered a national favourite in Singapore and Malaysia and his endeavour is to explore and find many places in the world that produce the best taste sensation so he can then share this with his friends when they themselves go on holiday.

One of my preferences has been Australian Aboriginal art which has taken me into galleries across Australia and the remote parts of the country such as the Red-centre, Uluru and the Kimberley in the North West region of the Northern Territory, and to explore the stories behind the art-works. Authentic Chinese snuff bottles have been another preference which has pulled me towards markets and antique shops across Asia. I learned to discern authenticity from counterfeit pieces and found other people who also had a passion for these small porcelain collectibles. My latest preference is crystal orbs, particularly the unusual and rare crystals and learning about their healing properties and where I can find them internationally so I can discern true quality.

Our brain is continuously being shaped - we can take more responsibility
for our own brain by cultivating positive influences.

Richie Davidson, Founder and Chair of Centre for Healthy Minds

14. Standing Up for Self

A strategy designed to self-sustain and to flourish.

Useful for: When feeling overwhelmed and uncertain.

Future proofing: 'How will others respect my mind's ability?'

This strategy is about having a clear sense of self and what you will stand up for. It concerns what is okay to you, and what is not okay. Standing up for self is what happens when someone crosses the line with you. Metaphorically, you get up out of your chair and stand up, hold your ground and give voice to what's important. The key to be able to stand up for yourself is to have boundaries in place.

How this strategy offers you an alternate coping approach.

Family therapist and author Sarri Gilman states 'Your story is being shaped by what you say "yes!" to and what you say "no" to.' Your boundaries reflect your tolerances. They are your guidelines and limits that convey reasonable ways for others to behave towards you, and how you will respond when they transgress. Shaped by what you are prepared to tolerate is where tension will exist for you.

There are distinct types of boundaries. Your primary boundary is your personal space that exists around you. It is there to protect you and support you. Your personal boundaries enable you to decide who, what, where and when you let others into your space. Your mental boundaries are about your thoughts, values and opinions. This is about knowing what matters to you and standing into your own point-of-view, while also being open to other points-of-view without being defensive or rigid. Time is another boundary. The more you juggle in life, the more likely you will have additional boundaries around time limits. This will mark out for others (and you) what is tolerated in relation to your commitments, contribution and involvement.

This is how you can delight and enjoy its benefits

In her TEDx talk, *Good Boundaries Free You*, Sarri Gilman describes her most essential boundary tool as a compass, with Yes and No on it. Her advice is to place boundaries where you need them most and let them do their job by listening to your 'Yes' and 'No.' Your boundaries are your collection of your 'yes-es' and your 'no-s.' She says:

> 'When you ignore your Yes and No, you will get symptoms. You will have stress, feel overwhelmed, trouble sleeping, depression, thoughts about running away, high-risk behaviour, addiction, relapse, perfectionism – whatever happens to you when you don't listen to yourself. Because of the dynamic nature of boundaries.'

A key part of boundary setting is to tolerate stormy emotions from others as a reaction with you showing up differently. If you are being pushed into making a rushed decision, or doing something you are not sure of, buy yourself some time. A friend of mine will say, 'Can you give me twenty-four hours and I'll let you know my answer.' He sets a time limit as a boundary mainly so he doesn't immediately commit himself without first thinking through what his future energy needs might be.

The energy boundary ensures he safeguards his natural rhythms while not feeling obliged or later disappointing another because of a hasty reply.

Thoughts are energy. Over-thinking issues or concerns; both yours or others, can encroach upon your mental boundaries. Mark out clearly what is 'enough' for others is a gentle way to push back. If you notice that you are thinking too much about something, you can put some limits on yourself. Give it a name, notice and kindly say to yourself (out loud if that helps) 'It's time I let this part of my life go.'

This is how I optimise it and gain the most value from it

A big shift for me was to review why my boundaries did or did not exist and if I caved in on a boundary what was my motivation behind this. After doing this a few times I noticed that there was a pattern. When I made decisions based on wanting someone else's approval, I would feel a resentment because I was either taking on too much responsibility, by doing something I did not wish, or juggling too much. I have learned the technique from Social Scientist, Brene Brown that has been useful for boundary setting. In her compelling book, *Rising Strong*, she uses the acronym BIG which poses:

> 'What boundaries-(B) do I need to set in place for me to stay within my integrity-(I)
> and make the most generous-(G) assumptions about you?'

Where you can discover more

In Braving the Wilderness: The Quest for True Belonging and the Courage to Stand Alone, Brene Brown sets out a clear road-map based on four practices of true belonging that challenge the way we think about ourselves, show up with one another, and find our way back to courage and connection. She highlights that the key element of trusting others, and self-trust, is to have respect for boundaries, being clear about what is okay, and what is not okay.

Transform Your Boundaries, by Sarri Gilman reveals the process for letting your boundaries play their part in your resilience and health. It will give you skills to deal with the emotions and extreme challenges to your boundaries and how you can adopt self-care.

> *I'd rather be loving and generous, and very straight forward with what's okay and not okay.*
>
> Brene Brown, Social Scientist

15. Speaking to Yourself

A strategy designed to be kinder with a self-talk critique.

Useful for: When being too harsh to yourself or when you want fresher ways to progress.

Future proofing: 'How can I be my best friend and stand in a fairer truth?'

This strategy is about being deliberate and positive in how you speak towards yourself. Language acts as a sentencing process which means that your sentences can either limit or enhance the way you phrase them in relation to yourself. What is the literal language, messages and expectations that you give yourself? Without realising, it can be easy to be flippant or self-effacing by calling oneself dumb or stupid.

How this strategy offers you an alternate coping approach

Literal words, sometimes referred as 'organ language' is a process where you locate your expression in your body. Your words refer towards an organ or body part. There are different ways this occurs. For example, 'the hairs on the back of my neck' is about where instincts such as knowing and foreboding are found in the body. It is felt as a body sensation, a signal for when you should become more alert. A different type of self-sentencing is to locate an expression in a specific body organ. Such as, 'I can't stomach this right now,' 'I can't breathe,' 'I haven't got the heart for this,' 'It's too hard to swallow,' 'I must put my foot down' and 'It's breaking my heart.'

Often this happens because we are unconsciously transferring aspects of our anxiety onto different parts of our body. In doing so, we place our generalised anxiety within a location in our body. Through time, this can become an expression of that organ. By speaking to our body this way, it hears the message, and takes it as literal and then it becomes an actual physical problem. If you are saying, 'I am weighed down,' your ankles and knees might get tight and stiff from literally carrying too much of a load. Expressing that you are 'carrying the world on your back,' your shoulders will lock up with the heaviness. Feeling that you are 'gutted' by someone's behaviour could cause your gut to tighten and ache. Feeling angry with a partner or someone close to you and voicing, 'I'm pissed,' could show up as a bladder irritation. Wellness activist Kris Carr explains:

> 'Our minds can make us sick and they can make us well. Our feelings and beliefs impact our every cell. How we speak to ourselves matters. Whether or not we feel and express love affects our well-being. The very notion empowers me. It fills me with hope and curiosity.'

This is how you can delight and enjoy its benefits

Think of what you want more of, or how your body feels when it is thriving. By doing this, you can give yourself words you wish to dwell in, rather than just endure. For example, you can give yourself delightful, pleasant and lovely calibrations, which add rather than detract from how you respond. 'I have a thirst for knowledge,' 'I have a hunger for learning,' 'I am replete, full and satisfied,' and 'I am full of contentment,' 'I am filled with gratitude,' 'I am brimming with joy.' Remember your thoughts can sentence you, but as to 'what' is the question, whether it be unwitting or not.

This is how I optimise it and gain the most value from it

An associate of mine consciously set up a series of attractive calibrations for his business. I would hear him use sentences such as 'I have a gnawing desire to achieve,' 'I seek out a whiff of success,' and 'I have a hunger for satisfaction.'

For myself, I have noticed how I talk about my yearnings for travel and discovery. Over the years this has translated into experiencing restless legs, sometimes to the point of almost walking out of bed. Taking magnesium and then being mindful of my own words and self-sentencing has really helped. 'Rest up and rest more' instead of saying 'less as in restless' are my newer self-descriptions used when my mind wanders off. I now have a foot support and ask my legs to ease upon the leg rest while on planes or lounges, giving them permission to rest up, before we can go walkabout.

Where you can discover more

In the book *The Healing Power of Water*, Japanese Scientist Masaru Emoto, shares his research on the effect that words have on energy and form. Capturing the structure of water at the moment of freezing and through high-speed photography, he has shown the direct consequence of destructive thoughts and the thoughts of love and appreciation on the formation of water crystals. Given that the human body is about 70% water it suggests that the way we speak to ourselves has profound implications for our health and our relationships.

The Secret Language of Your Body: The Essential Guide to Healing by Inna Segal is a guide to healing and wellness. She unveils the secrets to understand the messages of the body and the underlying energetic influence of different symptoms and conditions. You can use this resource as a lens to gain insight on how 'self-sentencing' may be contributing to what is showing up in your body.

Language creates reality. Words have power. Speak always to create your joy shared.

Deepak Chopra, M.D., Wellness Advocate

16. Nurturing Tomorrow

A strategy designed for your mental balance and motivation.

Useful for: Graciously giving and receiving better praise.

Future proofing: 'How can I acknowledge their true worth?'

This strategy looks at how you reduce the expectations of tomorrow and the next day, week or month. It highlights how you can set up your present future by creating different moments of contentment, joy and replenishment. It offers simple methods, so you can pace yourself into tomorrow and foster gentler experiences that nourish and nurture you.

How this strategy offers you an alternate coping approach

When we have something we can anticipate, or look ahead to, or something worth celebrating such as an event, we feel more optimistic. When we are optimistic, we view the future as positive where we can create or have positive outcomes. Professor Martin Seligman, referred to as the 'father of positive psychology' identifies optimism as key to cope with life's trials and setbacks. He says:

> 'Optimism generates hope ... hope releases dreams ... dreams set goals ... enthusiasm follows.'

Optimism is a state of mind that has been highly correlated with life satisfaction and well-being. Creating experiences to anticipate, means that you can generate a pleasurable experience tomorrow. This could be activities with others, such as lunch with your friends, doing something on your own where you appreciate some solitude, or a healing experience like having a massage, a facial or going walking in nature. There may be important things in life that you can also look forward to. For example, changing jobs, completing a six-week gym 'boot-camp' or finishing a degree or other study.

This is how you can delight and enjoy its benefits

To nurture your tomorrow, design different experiences and activities that help you enrich your coming weeks, months and years. Treats, celebrations and anticipation are three methods that will contribute more to your optimistic state and create a positive future. If you know you have a tough day or week ahead, pre-order your joyful experiences to give yourself a boost. This means arranging some time ahead so you know it is there for you waiting in the future, on the other side of the demanding period.

Treats are a fantastic way to give yourself different moments of contentment and pleasure. Build yourself a big 'treats menu' that you can draw from in advance for your joy and pleasure. It could be as simple as having a hot chocolate sitting in the warm sun, spraying yourself with essential oils, buying flowers for your home, downloading some contemporary music, or watching a great television series. It all depends on what it is that lights you up or ignites your inner celebration.

On a smaller scale, if you have an intense day, build yourself a gap, just for you, and do something that gives you a moment of pleasure. Put on your favourite music, pick up a novel and then disappear into it for a while; buy a fresh juice or eat some delicious dark chocolate and just close your eyes for a few minutes and savour it – these are just some ideas for your 'treats menu.'

The other method is to build celebrations forward. To celebrate your accomplishments reinforces what you are doing well. It is a form of positive feedback that reinforces your brain with the message 'You've done well, this is working, keep doing this.' When you celebrate, your brain releases endorphins (feel good chemicals) and you feel wonderful. When you take the time to celebrate you, it creates fulfilment.

Without celebration, you are training your brain that what you are doing is not important and life can easily feel mundane. If you don't put treats, celebrations and pleasures out there, you can't expect to find them there in the future. It is about valuing that you are worth it, you deserve it and that, more importantly it works to keep you optimistic and positive in your life.

This is how I optimise it and gain the most value from it

I have a lot of enjoyable things on my 'treats menu.' They range from getting in my car and going to my favourite café for breakfast, taking the afternoon off and watching a movie, sleeping in, lying on my bed and reading a novel on a winter's day, having a massage, buying a new novel, or getting my hair blow dried. They all give me delight. I have at least one treat a day and I relish it and call it a 'treat' or a 'treaty.'

The key is to find treats that support your well-being, rather than those you feel addicted to and allow yourself an occasional naughty treat. I used to eat a treat called 'bounce balls.' They were made of almond and whey and I thought they were delicious. The other thing was they had over twenty grams of sugar in them, and I was eating one or two a day. They were my 'I deserve a treat' treat because I was feeling deprived. I've reduced them by now eating roasted cashews, dark chocolate and fruit as my treats. They are better for me, and more nourishing.

Where you can discover more

If you realise that you want to build new habits to nurture tomorrow, you can learn about the process of making and breaking habits in the book *Better than Before* by Gretchen Rubin.

Whoever you are … the world offers itself to your imagination, calls to you like the wild geese.

Mary Oliver, Poet

17. Making a date with Yourself

A strategy designed to generate enduring future memories.

Useful for: Building anticipation when feeling bogged down or in a rut.

Future proofing: 'What am I looking forward to achieving and doing?'

This strategy is about building future memories and setting out your own sign-posts to ensure that you focus on a future worthy of looking forward to. It also has the added benefit to ensure that you take what you need to remember into your tomorrow. In other words, it offers your future the rich gift of living in the now. With your future memories anchored to, or by certain dates, this is useful to live learnings knowing when next you will need them. Placing them on a calendar in your future ensures they are not just a repeat pattern of the past.

How this strategy offers you an alternate coping approach

It is useful to take yourself out of the intensity of a moment and to transfer your attention into a plausible future. This technique allows you to shift your state, so that you do not become bogged down by the mundane. It propels you into a probable future rather than a dream state. It is different from mindfulness practice which brings you consciously into the present. Here you go out into the future, three months, six months out, take the positive from that experience, and bring the feeling back to the present. The benefit is that by going out into the future, you have placed a sign-post of experience, so when you get there you can have it for a second time. It creates a sense of anticipation and future wonder about how you will show up a second time. It makes you consider to what extent your learning will be remembered and how much more can you expand upon it now that it is known; rather than facing a new and unusual experience.

This is how you can delight and enjoy its benefits

This strategy is about living your future experiences in the present. You can visit seasons, people and events in the future, and then bring the goodwill found there back into the present. If you like gardening, when it's cold in winter you can see how things will grow in the spring, and that you will be appreciating the first fragrances. You may live in a place where the summers are very hot. You can connect with the coolness of winter months and the pleasure of sleeping under a blanket and snuggling. Seasons are a fantastic way to use this process. Within nature there is a repetitive change. Within the change there is always an aspect of loving bits from each season. Something to relish in the moment and to anticipate forward.

This is how I optimise it and gain the most value from it

At night before I sleep, in my mind's eye, I get on my metaphorical magic carpet and go off travelling around the world. I visit the places and people I wish to visit in my future. It's wonderful going off to see the pyramids in Egypt, the Grand Canyon in the US, and Glastonbury in the UK. I find myself literally there in-situ, hearing, seeing and experiencing the sights and sounds.

I also travel to places and see what people I might meet in the future; strange sights and sounds, full of odd, yet quirky, characters from all over the world. Sometimes, I might have read about someone who I would like to meet one day, so I envisage a conversation with them sometime in the future, what would I like to ask and share. For me, it creates a sense of connection before I meet them. It can be fun to seed both your future with your present gifts, and to bring back into your now anticipated future joys.

Where you can discover more

Nature is a wonderful way to discover more about future pacing. You could choose to follow the moon cycles. For example, organic farmers and gardeners plant above-ground plants between the new moon and the full moon when there is increasing light. This increases the sap flow in the plant and enhances growth.

Lunar and Biodynamic Gardening: Planting your biodynamic garden by the phases of the moon by Matthew Jackson is a guide as to how to take advantage of the natural rhythms of the moon, by planning your gardening activities to coincide with the lunar cycles.

Another area to explore are Pagan Festivals which are governed by seasonal cycles.

The Pagan Book of Days: A Guide to the Festivals, Traditions, and Sacred Days of the Year by Nigel Pennick, contains information about rituals and celebrations that have for centuries been associated with the changing seasons of the year. Included are the observances of the ancient Greek, Roman, Celtic, Anglo-Saxon, and Norse traditions, as well as Wiccan traditions and worship of Feminine. It provides informative ways to integrate these ancient cultural and nature-based practices into your daily life.

My interest is in the future because I am going to spend the rest of my life there.

Charles Kettering, Engineer and Inventor

18. Playfully healthy

A strategy designed to assist the mind's overall calm and balance.

Useful for: When just feeling under the weather and not knowing why.

Future proofing: 'What does my mind need from me to feel healthier?'

Our mind is amazing in its capacity to just 'power on' regardless of not functioning at its optimum condition, albeit often with lower energy levels. Sometimes, we may feel slightly off as it may be diverting resources to ward off an underlying bug, *I think I am coming down with something,* or a pre-existing condition, *It is getting on top of me.* Our bodies know what is going on or what is off in its interlinked systems and sends signals about what it needs, invariably a desired rest and change of routine in order to recuperate.

How this strategy offers you an alternate coping approach

Your body is a highly efficient adaptive mechanism, changing its level of functioning based on your circumstances and treatment of its basic requirements. Sleep, nutrition, exercise and peace of mind are its four pillars needed to fully fuel mental energy. On the other hand, we can push our body past its resources, so it must compensate by taking from other areas to deliver upon our need to cram more into our time-poor day or to drive us towards a fixed deadline. We usually view being productive with a time measure by how much and when. Whereas the body simply charges up on energy until it is drained, which will vary depending upon many factors. Being in a constant state of stress and seriousness can lead you to push yourself and you will just keep going, and your body will keep delivering for you. Without reprieve, this tight state slowly inhibits and debilitates your body's optimal functioning.

Actively thinking about how our body works and what it needs is half the battle won to become healthier. If we look closely at how we treat it or take it for granted, then we wouldn't. Obvious mistreatment such as substance abuse (legal or otherwise) have been shown to affect our capacity to live life to the full. Less obvious are run down states of exhaustion and stress which impacts upon our long-term health.

This is how you can delight and enjoy its benefits

Simply imagine yourself being healthy and then overlay this image across your body and see how it is fairing in relation to your demands. First, notice the difference between where it could be and where it is. Then, ask your body what it needs in the moment so it can return towards its original baseline, a daily homeostasis and a natural time for healing. It will tell you and you do have to listen; this is not a task of perfection, for bodies can't be this, and cannot sustain themselves at a higher level of functioning for extended periods of time.

This is how I optimise it and gain the most value from it

Playfulness is the key request from my own body as it signals its wants. If it could speak it would say 'Lighten up, Sally. Don't take this too seriously,' or 'We have had enough, we have other things we can enjoy, rather than just doing more of this, and a change is as good as a rest.' I know my body is designed to tell me when it has pain or when it wants pleasure and if I listen it also tells me about its other needs.

When fighting an infection or feeling a bit under the weather I activate my body's natural defences. I have an imaginary army of good guys who go off and fight those yucky germs. T-blasters, suckers and scrubbers are the names I give to my body's own T-cells and immune responses. Walt Disney himself would delight in my imagination of these odd-shaped characters. 'Sally go forth and do my bidding. First we have a briefing then they charge off and complete their heroic deeds of defending my body's health.' This is an active process with me getting regular updates from the frontline. Each team have their own voice and tonality. The T-blasters are tenaciously strong and sound like little mini-marines as they move through light blazing any foreign threat in their way. They are very savvy at spotting sneaky bugs that hide behind other cells. The suckers are quieter and follow in the wake of the blasters tweaking out what is showing up.

Sometimes, my body's needs are subtler and without a clearly defined threat. This is where I use light and its spectrum to scan my body's energy and then flood it with an energetic vibration. Rose gold is my first scan, sent out to ease my body back into its resting state. When this passes through my body, it notices discolorations and then I bathe these areas with different coloured lights until I find the one which assists in restoration. Pink is for healthy tissues, blue for cooling down hot areas, green is for a verdant plushness, red is for strengthening, yellow is illuminating and full of lightness. Usually, these five swathes of colour scan and caress my inner body and seem to alter my body's own response.

When I am feeling fragile for no specific reason, I change from scanning colours and apply a range of exquisite coloured silk fabrics which I then imagine wrapping around my whole body to create a self-caressing pleasure.

Where you can discover more

Dr. Gerald Epstein, a Psychiatrist who has written a book, *Healing visualizations: Creating health through imagery* is a good reference source.

Pixar with its animation of characters gives a playful representation of emotions and healing in the movie *Inside out*.

Any physical ailment or disease can be cured or significantly improved by the use of mental imagery.

Gerald Epstein, Psychiatrist

Your Emotional Energy

CHAPTER FOUR
Emotional Moisturisers

The sun gives spirit and life to the plants and the earth nourishes them with moisture.

Leonardo da Vinci

Emotional You is about how you psychologically cope and adapt in today's world. Emotions can cleanse, soothe, buff and nourish you within a world that can sometimes be dramatic and volatile. These are gentler touches we all wish for more of, a reminder of your own sensuality and liveliness, to assist you to become more resilient, and to have emotional maturity. To take care of your own responses, means that you remain open and responsible for your own emotional journey whilst living in a complex and trying world and will better assist you in your relationships and expectations. In today's modern world of virtual and instantaneous relationships, we can all feel under pressure with others demanding and needing our attention, which in turn increases pressure on what and how we will feel about ourselves.

A healthy emotional energy can be viewed as taking charge of your own emotions and clearing away those feelings which deplete and drain you. It is considered as openness with one's experiences and the orientation to explore different ways to respond without manipulation or prejudice of others. Grace or charisma are the hallmarks to ensure others grow in your company and with an increased range of feelings explored than the usual twenty or so common emotions experienced. There are over three thousand descriptive words for emotions in the English language that invite you to live a breadth of experiences, both positive and negative.

In a rapidly changing and expanding digital world we are losing some of the more familiar ways to socially interact. Digital speed is hitting us with such force that it is shifting the way we relate to each other and ourselves. We have more connections, yet they come at us fleetingly and they can cause us to react. There are more ways for people to pull on our energy and for us to respond with their different needs and wants. What creates intensity is the constancy of external demands which means we don't have time to just think.

Coping with this 'pull to react' requires that we adopt strategies such as distancing, distracting, deflecting and self-destructive behaviours. There are, however, other ways to cope with these tensions that work in a more positive way. What is important is to understand why they work and to find better, alternative ways to respond and act.

Behind the scenes, our tolerances are becoming wired because so much around us has the tendency to be intrusive. We can more readily walk into another person's 'trip-wires' and have others deflect and project this onto us. In Western culture, we live in a blame society where it is easier to accuse first, rather than take personal responsibility. This state is a precursor to denial. We tend to overlook our own part in this emerging equation because we lack the energy or skills. The world seems crazy so it is about survival in a less than perfect world. But there are better ways to reconnect and that is what the following techniques are all about.

Our bodies are hard-wired to respond with positive emotions of love, kindness, gratitude, curiosity, amusement, contentment, calmness and compassion. These emotional moisturisers momentarily give you an increase in the essential brain chemicals and hormones, such as oxytocin, serotonin, dopamine and nitric acid. They are crucial players to our well-being and openness to living life. Without them, the research shows that we can experience anxiety, depression, sleep problems, lack of motivation and indifference to connection. The way you nourish yourself with emotional moisturisers can become a key factor in your own happiness.

All emotions are temporal as they simply indicate where we are located at any point in time. Most emotions are either past or future orientated, with the exception of anger and boredom which are located in the present. Guilt and shame can run as a thread through our lives as both these emotions draw us back into something from our past. They are, however, expressed in the present and in doing so they direct our body's sensations e.g. feeling guilt in the moment. Yet, guilt and shame are actually connected to the past.

Neuroanatomist, Dr. Jill Taylor Bolte, proposes that we employ a ninety second cycle to handle our emotional reactions. When we think a thought or have a memory, the brain releases certain chemicals. These messengers make your body feel exactly the way you were thinking. If we allow this process to run, it will complete in about ninety seconds. What tends to happen, however, is that we recreate the story in our heads about the situation, and the emotions re-run over and over on repeat. If we let this run for long enough it can start to re-shape who we are.

Neuroscientist, Dr. Candace Pert, in her ground-breaking research on the molecules of emotions, found emotional memories are stored on receptors throughout the body. Emotions ranging from grief, fear, anger, courage, joy, bliss, love, compassion and happiness, produce a specific pattern of change in the body and run every system of the body:

> 'When you experience an emotion the cells in your brain release hormones, peptides.
> The reality is that when you experience an emotion so does your body at the same
> time. And if that emotion is held for too long, the body will hold it and start to

complain … Don't underestimate the power of emotion to contribute to health and disease.' (*The Molecules of Emotion*)

From an emotional energy perspective, life can be viewed as a series of upswings and downswings as we move through our days, years and stages of development. The upswing of everyday life is about 'go-go-go,' getting things done and having a sense of purpose and achievement. Inevitably there are times when we come off the upswings in life and as this happens the energy shifts to the downswing and can feel more difficult to handle. On the emotional side, we can be left with feelings of emptiness, flatness, sinking and sense of feeling slightly overwhelmed. There can be the tendency to want to avoid these feelings and 'kick back' into another upswing. Mindfulness teacher, John Burston from the Lifeflow Meditation Centre in Adelaide says:

'We are not trained for the downswing. Culturally we don't value doing the down resting phase and it can be seen as a waste of time. Yet it's restorative. It's about learning to find periods to sink and being less afraid of leaving an open space and letting go. The emotions we experience on the downswing, such as dullness or anxiety can be a mismatch between the upswing and the body needing to come down. This split creates the emotional conflict.'

Developing the ability to sink into a downswing can be a powerful means of self-care. In a meditation retreat, John asked our group, 'How far do you sink?' What we learned that weekend was to come down properly is about moving into the body and resting there. This is the first step to regaining emotional balance and a calm inner mental state.

Examining the role of emotions on our state of mind, Joe Dispenza believes that it helps to be mindful of how we feel and think in a moment, as this shapes who we will become. He proposes:

'If thoughts are the vocabulary of the brain and feelings are the vocabulary of the body, and the cycle of how you think and feel becomes your state of being, then your entire state of being is in the past. In this way your past becomes your future.' (*Breaking the Habit of Being Yourself*)

To change your emotional state of being, it is preferable that you alter how you think and feel towards or about something or someone. Patterns of likes and dislikes tend to lock your emotional energy in place as emotional states or moods. At one end of the continuum the emotional energy is agitated and chaotic and the other end is rigid and dull. Our emotional habits can set us on a path to be stuck at one end of the emotional continuum, either way both are stuck states. In the middle is balanced states of being open, interested, curious and having a sense of lightness.

Learning to become aware of your emotional state when you are caught in the grip of chaos or rigidity is a key to freeing yourself up from being taken on an emotional ride.

Emotional energy issues of imbalance; these are five of the most common effects found when lacking a positive response:

1. Mood swings, recurring ups and downs

2. Being trapped or stuck in an emotional state

3. Lack of socially acceptable responses, such as empathy

4. Becoming numb, through disconnection and disassociation

5. Vulnerability, not being able to hold it, live with it and be with it.

These issues related to our emotional energy are being exacerbated by the complexity of the world we live in, with extraordinary rates of change.

In her clinical work and research, Susan David, witnesses how people tend to lock down into rigid responses with their emotions. Categorising emotions as 'good' or 'bad' creates emotional rigidity and pain. Default coping mechanisms such as brooding, bottling and false positivity are tight responses and build rigidity. In the face of complexity, what is needed are greater levels of emotional agility, a quality of suppleness, nimbleness and aliveness. She says 'research now shows that the radical acceptance – of all our emotions, even the messy, difficult ones – is the cornerstone to thriving, resilience and true authentic happiness.'

The ideal for the emotional realm is to resonate emotional breadth and emotional availability. It is having the balance between breadth and depth. If you have a personal preference for breadth, you may want to expand your emotional repertoire of responses. There are many different emotions you can explore, giving you diversity of your interactions, and more scope and freedom of expression. If your preference is for emotional availability, you may seek a deepening of your emotions, drilling down on subtle nuances required by intimacy with yourself and others e.g. making finer distinctions of pleasure and pleasuring another.

The Emotional Realm is the way to create psychological flexibility:

Quotient of Expressions	Expand the number and scope of emotions in your general repertoire to increase your emotional range and experience from the six primary emotions – Anger, Disgust, Fear, Happiness, Sadness and Surprise.
Response to Others, Contexts, Situations	Emotions enable you to interact differently in your environment. They create physiological effects in your body which help you to cope and adapt with the situation.
Create a Dynamic Interaction	Emotions allow other people to understand you and for you to understand them. They give clear non-verbal cues through body language or facial expressions.
Frequency of Attraction	The rate of occurrence of emotions that move you towards something (attraction) and feelings that move you away (repel). Breadth to stay with feelings creates a mood.
'Pure Moments' of Contentment and Joy	Positive emotions in comparison with negative emotions are short-lived and less intense. Sadly, we hold closer what hurts or is painful, so as not to repeat.

Healthy Relationships, Loyalties and Legacies	Being open and honest about your feelings and allowing others to do the same in a good-natured way creates respect. Loyalty is built on positive attachment.
Caring and Nurturing	Emotions such as kindness, compassion and tenderness increase a higher mood, satisfaction and quality of life for self and others and improve overall well-being.

When your emotions come under stress and pressure, reactions can get condensed and hardened and this can result in a state of emotional fatigue, tiredness, restlessness and depletion. At this point of weakness, you are not functioning at your best.

The strategies in the section I have called 'Emotional Moisturisers' are the soft and gentle caresses that you give yourself to feel vibrant, alive and buoyant. They are the moisturisers that can replenish your emotions by adding a plumper and plusher response.

The purpose of Emotional Moisturisers is to primarily create an emotional space to give you enough time to cope and adapt in your world. They allow you the chance to be in touch with yourself and your deeper feelings without competing needs and forces impinging upon you. They also allow you to regain your flow and remain fluid by offering a protective barrier that buffers you from becoming weathered by harsher reactions (by yourself or others).

The following eighteen emotional moisturisers provide resources and strategies to assist you in answering the following questions:

How do you manage your state?

How do you move through a range of emotions?

How do you clear your state and regain a sense of calm and balance?

How aware are you of your own dramas and the reasons you get pulled into them?

How do you grace yourself with soft 'self-caresses' that nurture and replenish you?

Emotions are tagged with blended feelings. It is rare to experience single emotions in isolation. They usually come in clusters, such as feeling good and at the same time feeling guilty because you are feeling good. It is also rare to have pure emotion because impurities get in the way, for example, worry, guilt and shame are multifaceted emotions and involve significant cognitive processing. Shame, for example, informs us of an internal state of unworthiness, inadequacy, regret and disconnection. It can take some mental effort and awareness to discern what is happening in our inner world and then shift this state.

Daily we can experience numerous feelings or sensations without any recognition of its state. Most of us tend to generalise with fewer common emotions: love, hate sadness, anger, boredom and joy. Some collect the negative and dwell more in this type of despair, a 'woe is me,' state which they find difficult to escape. While others only respond with positive emotions which at times can be an annoying bonhomie if it is just a social nicety of approval seeking.

103

Social settings and graces require a display of empathy, a human condition of walking in another's shoes. It is a caring act of kindness towards others which is why we tend to move away from those with constant negative feelings who tend to bring our own mood down and to seek out those with a lighter positive feel. People in love or parents with their first child can be overflowing with their state and can pass this on to others and positively affect their emotional state. The same can be said of grief and loss. These powerful positive and negative emotions can linger over time and either enhance or flatten life's moments. We can become consumed by a single state and this acts as our filter for how we show up and engage with others.

The inherent value of emotional moisturisers is to offer a gentle hydration to your senses with each asking the body to engage and secrete different hormones to affect your overall well-being.

Emotional Moisturiser Strategies

The following eighteen strategies have been found useful to change state and to access more pleasurable moments. They nourish your natural verve and sway.

Emotional verve; a pick-up response of energy, to describe the intensity of feelings felt, a condensed expression, a charged moment, an acute feeling. This concentration of sensations alters one's perception of time. Being fully associated can move swiftly and yet it can leave the body feeling exhausted from the intense feelings.

Emotional sway; a slow-down response of energy, to describe the sensitivity of feelings, a lighter moment, a languid breather, a sensual take, a dreamy quality. This easy-going feel of emotions stretches time, and allows one an escape from daily reality.

These moisturisers are the substance of what successful individuals use to move past a sense of being stuck and stagnation. Each has been selected based on its ability to replenish an emotional self, and to enhance an inner grace and emotional maturity.

Moisturiser	Description
1. Hydrating	Finding enriching connections that smooth and plump you up to create a sense of fullness. Relating with people who uplift you with their energy and good conversations.
2. Nourishing	Bringing in more laughter and smiling to relieve emotional tensions and discomfort. Stimulating the release of positive hormones into the body that make you feel good.
3. Revitalising	Moving into a neutral state through deep breathing and presence. Metaphorically taking your foot off the accelerator to feel rejuvenated and refreshed.
4. Absorbing	Using inquisitiveness to shift your emotional focus from the current state, so you can absorb something different. Focus outside yourself and create a fresher state.
5. Savouring	Celebrating, cherishing and treasuring positive emotions, moments and experiences. Savouring 'the good,' so it becomes part of your positive memories.

6. Sensualising	Being sensual by taking your senses out into nature's world, to fully notice what is different around you and to experience gentler pleasures and subtleties.
7. Spicing up	Find your tantalisers and bring them into your life, adding zest, colour and zing. Revel in what excites and entices you as a way to enliven and motivate yourself.
8. Smoothing	Using music as a quick way to shift your state and trigger different emotions. Utilise rhythm and harmonies to find your inherent rhythm of ease and improve your mood.
9. Plumping	Using truisms and convictions when in overwhelm to create a sense of reassurance. Going for simple ones such as 'the sun comes up,' 'I can breathe,' 'I can walk.'
10. Protecting	Visualising yourself in an emotional bubble for protection. Throwing out out-dated reactions from the inside of your bubble and placing a bubble around it for containment.
11. Buffering	Using positive emotions to build a buffer and then drawing upon it in times of adversity to meet a challenge, to recover quickly and being more resilient.
12. Flowing	Releasing tension in your body and mind. Tapping on key points on the body to let go of emotional disturbances and to restore a natural energy flow.
13. Exfoliating	Shedding difficult emotions and sensations to create more openness and glow. Use acceptance and diffusion to unhook from difficult emotions and to rebalance.
14. Tendering	Giving tenderness and compassion to soothe your frayed moments of tension, helping to build a strong resilience and inner strength and self-acceptance.
15. Nurturing	Taking care of, validating and protecting yourself. Embracing your vulnerability and letting go of the story, 'I'm not good enough' and having a new one, 'I am worthy.'
16. Appreciating	Recognising, cherishing and loving the goodness in others, your life and yourself. Feeling grateful for what is – to boost joy, optimism and satisfaction and to be less self-absorbed.
17. Softening	Easing and alleviating protective emotional shells that have been built around your heart and body. Removing the barrier so you are more available for intimacy.
18. Luxuriating	Creating filters of joyfulness by using coloured lens and frames to capture moments of sheer joy and then overlaying them into the future for a joyful tomorrow.

Emotions can be fleeting, persistent, powerful, complex, and even life-changing. They can motivate us to act in specific ways.

Kendra Cherry, Author and Educator

1. Hydrating

A strategy designed to increase connections and a sense of belonging.

Useful for: Feeling stressed and drained, warding off loneliness.

Future proofing; 'What would my best friend say about me doing this?'

This strategy is about fostering and strengthening our internal sense of belonging. Relating with other people is one of our fundamental needs just as water hydrates the body and keeps it functional, so too, does having multiple connections with others as these keep us emotionally functional, healthy and balanced.

How this strategy offers you an alternate coping approach

Social connections comprise the people we know, the friends we confide in, the family we belong to, our tribe of like-minded individuals and the community we live in. These relationships contribute to our physical and mental health. At a fundamental level we need each other for survival and to thrive as a community.

Studies confirm that interacting and relating with others strengthens our immune system. Having social support with people who evoke positive emotions also helps us to recover from disease faster. People who feel more connected with others have lower levels of anxiety and depression. When we are surrounded by loved ones, the feeling of being cared for and loved releases a flood of powerful hormones into our bodies which not only make us feel better, but also significantly bolster our immune system and its effective responses.

From her research Dr. Emma Seppala found that individuals with strong social bonds and close relationships have higher self-esteem, greater empathy for others, are more trusting and cooperative and others are more open to trust and cooperate with them. The good news is that we can do this even if we are not able to physically be with the people we care about. Research shows that a sense of connection is internal. The benefits of connection are linked with a subjective sense of belonging. If you feel a part of another's life in your mind you will also obtain the benefits irrespective of whether you are physically in touch with them or not. It works the same way as being in their company.

This is how you can delight and enjoy its benefits

Under pressure from the busyness of life, friendships can be one of the first things that can be put to one side. However, they can be a source of strength and a place of nurturing when we are feeling vulnerable.

How do you foster, strengthen and build your internal sense of connection? One way is to be with people who uplift and nurture you and leave you feeling emotionally hydrated. Who are the people in your life who give, make you smile, bring a positive energy and share in an interesting conversation and create an enjoyable shared space? You will know who they are. Having spent time with them you will leave feeling lighter, alive and renewed. These are the friends to spend your precious time and energy with, for they unwittingly hydrate your emotions.

Being with your 'tribe' is another way of re-hydrating yourself. A tribe is described as people with whom we share similar values, passions and interests. For women, close friendships are shown as being very powerful. Researchers have established that the hormone oxytocin is, for women especially, the panacea of friendship and by extension health. Scientists now suspect that spending time with our friends can counteract the impact of stress induced by anxiety and depression.

A landmark UCLA study on *Friendship Among Women: An Alternative to Fight and Flight* suggests that women respond to stress with a cascade of brain chemicals that cause us to make and maintain friendships with other women. The research has found that women have a larger behavioural repertoire than just fight or flight. In fact, says Professor Laura Klein, it seems that when the hormone oxytocin is released as part of the stress responses in a woman, it buffers the fight or flight response and encourages her to tend children and gather with other women instead. When she engages in this tending or befriending, studies suggest that more oxytocin is released, which further counters stress and produces a calming effect. This soothing response does not occur in men, says Dr. Klein, because testosterone – which men produce in elevated levels when they are under stress – reduces the effects of oxytocin. Estrogen, she adds, enhances it.

This is how I optimise it and how I get the most from it

When I am not physically with my close friends, I have an internal dialogue with them and connect that way. If I want to talk through an issue, I say to myself 'What would Jan say?' (she is a wise soul with a pragmatic attitude) and then I listen to the response. I will hear her give voice and say something affirming that she has said previously. The other strategy I use is based on the matrix re-imprinting technique. In my mind, I will go back in time, or forward in time, and speak with the younger or older me. I ask for help and listen to their sage advice.

Where you can discover more

Matthew Lieberman in his book *Social: Why Our Brains Are Wired to Connect* explains how we are wired to reach out and to interact with others and why this is central to our human ability to socially adapt with change.

Dr. Emma Seppala shows in *Happiness Track: How to Apply the Science of Happiness to Accelerate Your Success* that taking care of ourselves is the most productive thing we can do personally and professionally.

A deep sense of love and belonging is an irresistible need of all people. We are biologically, cognitively, physically, and spiritually wired to love, to be loved, and to belong.

Brene Brown, Social Scientist

2. Nourishing

A strategy designed to increase positive hormones.

Useful for: Reducing emotional discomfort and distress.

Future proofing: 'How can I bring a smile to another?'

This strategy gives you a way to find and have more emotional nourishment. You have probably heard the saying 'a smile can light up a room.' The simple act of smiling and laughter can change your physiology. Even if you don't feel happy, the mere act of smiling or having a chuckle will initiate changes which can uplift your energy.

How this strategy offers you an alternate coping approach

Smiling has a positive effect on our happiness and physical health. It releases pleasure hormones called endorphins, natural pain-killers, such as serotonin, which is a natural anti-depressant. Physically, it boosts our immune system, reduces our stress, lowers our blood pressure and helps the heart recover more quickly after stressful events.

Psychology Professor Marianne La France of Yale University says 'There are few compliments more flattering than being told that one has a great smile.' Socially it makes people want to be with us because we look and feel more attractive and open. Smiling has also been shown to help people get over loss and bereavement faster as it facilitates the recovery process and protects the heart.

While smiling is a wonderful antidote, even better if you can laugh at the same time. A good laugh relieves tension and stress in your body and the subsequent relaxation in your muscles can last upwards of forty-five minutes. The science also shows that laughter boosts the immune system and keeps you feeling well.

Research by neuroscientist Dr. Robert Provine found that laughter is not primarily about humour, but about social relationships:

> 'Laughter establishes – or restores – a positive emotional climate and a sense of connection between people who take pleasure in the company of each other.'
> (*Laughter: A Scientific Investigation*)

This is how you can delight and enjoy its benefits

The Dalai Lama acknowledges 'Smiling can be more valuable than meditating.' His practice when he sees someone is to smile. While he does this, it is an act of kindness helping to lift people's spirits and he admits that it makes him feel happy too. It is what he calls 'wise selfish behaviour.' He also engages in the practice of laughter and has a reputation for sharing a joke with his audiences so they can laugh along with him.

Want to enhance your mood? Try walking down the street and smiling. Find yourself in a bad grumpy mood, force a smile on your face and notice the shifts. Instantly, your body will release chemicals that will make you feel good. By activating your smile muscles your heart rate will start to drop and you will feel more composed.

Play with experiencing the difference between a genuine smile and a forced smile. Notice how you feel. A genuine smile is called the 'Duchenne Smile' named after the French Physician Guillaume Duchenne who studied the physiology of facial expression. This smile involves the movement of the muscle that opens and closes the eyes and uses both the eyes and the mouth. A 'fake smile' only uses the mouth area. Either way they both evoke positive emotions, but the genuine smile is a more powerful connector to others. That is why according to Marianne LaFrance it is called the 'Smile of Merriment' because it produces the most positive effects in others. Let your eyes sparkle when you smile and watch how others react.

The more you smile, the larger the positive impact on your mood, health and even longevity. You don't even need to feel like smiling to gain the benefits from it. Merely putting a smile on your face will shift your state. The body will respond with this non-verbal signal and release the chemical reactions that make you feel happier. When feeling flat 'put a smile on your dial.' The more you practice the easier it will become.

This is how I optimise it and how I get the most from it

I smile at people wherever I go and let my eyes sparkle. I look for the humour in situations and chuckle to myself as I move through the day. Young children make me laugh because they are so cute and funny. Any opportunity to play and have fun with them is very nourishing.

If I'm feeling flat I 'dial a friend,' there are certain friends that I know will make me laugh and they do! Sometimes just hearing them say 'hello' is enough to bring a smile on my face and a chuckle.

Where you can discover more

Smile: The Astonishing Powers of a Simple Act by Robert Gutman explores how smiles convey an enormous amount of emotion, and how grins carry different meanings across cultures.

If you would like to know more about the important role smiles play in human interactions *Smile*, by Marianne La France, offers a fascinating research and insight into why smiling is so powerful.

We are hard wired to connect.

Dr. Fiona Kerr, Scientist and Thought Leader

3. Revitalise

A strategy designed to rejuvenate your emotional state.

Useful for: Reducing mild or underlying anxiety levels.

Future proofing: 'How do I keep myself stress-free and my emotions healthy?'

This technique is about using the breath to revitalise your emotions. Breathing is considered the 'super stress buster.' Breathing techniques are simple to learn and can be used anywhere, anytime. It is the most natural thing we can do. However, in our busy lives, most of us tend to take shallow breaths and do not get the benefit from taking a slow, deep breath. Once you develop this technique, it can be a useful tool that you will always have with you.

How this strategy offers you an alternate coping approach

We can change how we feel by using our breath!

Studies show that different emotions are associated with distinct breathing patterns. For example, when we are feeling anxious, scared or apprehensive we take quicker and more shallow breaths. In contrast, when we are feeling calm, centred and refreshed, we breathe more slowly and deeply.

Slow, deep breathing activates what Harvard Cardiologist, Dr. Herbert Benson coined as 'the relaxation response.' This is a state of deep rest that changes our physical and emotional responses to stress. The relaxation response is a counterbalance to the 'fight or flight' stress response and evokes significant physiological changes in the body and promotes a state of calmness and replenishment. Further research has found that regular elicitation of the relaxation response can prevent and compensate the damaging effects that stress has on the body; and goes even further, to promote a healing mechanism that prevents and treats disease.

One of the most efficient ways to elicit the relaxation response is through breath-work. Pioneer in integrative medicine Dr. Andrew Weil has long promoted the benefits of working with the breath to affect both physical and emotional health. He comments:

> 'Practicing a regular, mindful breathing exercise can be calming and energising and can even help with stress-related health problems ranging from panic attacks to digestive disorders.'

This is how you can delight and enjoy its benefits

This particular strategy is called *Breath Counting* and is used as a mindfulness practice. It is useful to settle the nervous system and to create more emotional space to recover from stress and tension.

Begin by sitting in a comfortable position with your spine straight and head leaning forward slightly. Close your eyes and take a few deep, slow breaths. Let this flow naturally without trying to force the breath in or out.

Then count 'one' as you exhale.

The next time you exhale, count 'two,' and continue up to 'four.'

Then begin a new cycle, counting 'one' on the next breath out and repeat through to four again.

Count only when you exhale and if you find you're counting higher than four, your attention has wandered. Gently bring your awareness back and start the count cycle again.

This is how I optimise it and how I get the most from it

Practicing slow, deep breathing is what I do while doing other things, such as sitting on a plane, waiting for appointments or outside walking. When there is tension in my body, particularly in my shoulders I take three slow deep breaths and my body starts to unwind. At night, it is useful to quieten my mind. If I am struggling with sleep and a busy mind or scrambled emotions, I use a Kundalini Yoga breath technique to settle my mind and soothe my nervous system. Using my thumb, I press and block off the right nostril and with long, slow, deep breaths, I gently inhale through my left nostril. Then I exhale, slowly and completely through the left nostril. This I repeat to the count of ten breaths, as I feel my body relaxing deeper on each exhale.

Where you can discover more

On his website located at www.drweil.com Andrew Weil M.D. offers are range of different breath details. One of his favourites to settle internal tension or stress is called 4-7-8 or relaxation breath. He recommends that it be used whenever anything upsetting happens to bring down your reaction and create more emotional choice.

The informative book *And Breathe: The complete guide to conscious breathing – the key to health, well-being and happiness* by Rebecca Dennis, shows how letting go of unhealthy breathing patterns, clears restrictions, thus empowering emotional freedom. As a qualified breath coach, she believes that conscious breath-work is the ultimate key to thriving, health and inner peace.

> *There is one way of breathing that is shameful and constricted. Then, there's another way: a breath of love that takes you all the way to infinity.*
>
> Rumi

4. Absorbing

A strategy designed to quickly shift your emotional state.

Useful for: Not being overwhelmed - a pattern interrupt.

Future proofing: 'What else is of interest to pique my curiosity?'

To absorb is to take your focus and attention outside yourself and to become captivated by your surroundings, in doing so you will instantly shift your emotional state. It requires bringing to the fore your inquisitiveness and curiosity, so your senses can explore something new and captivating. This effectively shifts your attention towards being captured elsewhere. When you are focused on your surrounds you can no longer be preoccupied with internal issues, doubts or unnecessary worries.

How this strategy offers you an alternate coping approach

By placing your attention outside yourself you create a space between you and the uncomfortable emotion or sensation. Hopefully, when you focus on something unusual or new your brain engages with something different, rather than your emotional state.

Absorbing has an underlying technique called a 'pattern interrupt' which is designed to change a state of mind, thought or behaviour. Behavioural psychology and Neuro Linguistic Programming (NLP) use this method to alter emotional states, thoughts and habits. It intentionally transports you into a different orientation by jolting you out of your current emotional preoccupation. In doing so, you gain a fresher perspective.

The brain likes novelty and difference. By choosing to focus externally and get interested, the brain releases dopamine. This neurotransmitter will instantly lift your emotional state and keep your mind interested in learning new things and to seek out new discoveries. Dopamine is more commonly associated with the 'pleasure system' of the brain, providing you feelings of enjoyment which reinforce a motivation to do, or to continue with certain activities and learning.

In going external, take care of what you absorb from those around you, as a negative environment or comments can have a subtle, yet real effect. If you choose to take your attention in this direction, become a curious explorer as this will give you some distance between you and other people's dramas.

This is how you can delight and enjoy its benefits

This technique is a way to shift your focus outside of yourself. Begin by placing your attention on the outside and select something novel you can focus on. It could be an object, situation, animal or person. Then find yourself becoming extremely curious about this, its origins and its evolution.

Shift your focus around the situation by viewing its past, present and future shape. How did it evolve into its current state and where will it end up as it progresses? Is this something you wish for your tomorrow? Then be observant of both the foreground and background, notice which aspects could provide you with a richer source for you and how best you can frame yourself going forward i.e. do your past traditions define you or do you present an uncluttered openness?

You might also try observing it from left to right and vice-versa to shift your point-of-view What do you perceive that is different? Allow yourself to soak in all these differences as a dry sponge would water. What are the colours, shapes, textures, sounds and sensations that you are aware of?

Notice how each of these differences affect your mood. With practice you will be able to discern your own background influencers, those that subtlety shape your underlying mood. This will help you to be informed about where you can go and how you can readily find your own unique form of solace and tranquillity. For some, this might be a busy street-scape and for others it may be a stroll on a beach to look at the vastness of nothing, a sea-ward horizon.

This is how I optimise it and how I get the most from it

Absorbing is a technique that I take for a walk in the park when my focus has gone too far internal. Being outside with the trees makes it easier to put my attention on what is around me. As I stroll I select a tree and inquisitively look and notice all of its detail. I imagine what it looks like from above, side-to-side, up close and far away. Then I take my attention out wide and notice all of the trees around it and ask myself:

> *What is different about this tree from all the others in this parkland? If this tree could tell its story, I wonder what would it say about the passing of the years as it stands here?*

These types of questions are not necessarily prompting for specific answers, but they engage my imagination and I wonder in awe. This simple activity takes me beyond myself and helps me to re-centre.

Where you can discover more

If you're interested in learning more about dopamine and its impact on your brain *Habits of a Happy Brain: Retrain Your Brain to Boost Your Serotonin, Dopamine, Oxytocin and Endorphin Levels* by Loretta Breuning will help you to choose healthy ways to stimulate your happy brain chemicals.

Stop and smell the roses.

Walter Hagen, Golfer

5. Savouring

A strategy designed to build a repertoire of good emotional experiences.

Useful for: Overcoming negativity and a sense of failure.

Future proofing: 'What else can my mind relish?'

Savouring is a technique that shows you how you can take in more of the good things in life. It is a way to maximise the positive experiences and impacts in your life. Neuroscience shows that savouring changes or freshness in perspective activates parts of the brain that amplify positive emotions such as optimism, delight and joyfulness.

How this strategy offers you an alternate coping and adaptive approach

While savouring sounds attractive, it takes an active conscious effort to do it. Why? Scientists believe our brain has a negativity bias and is wired to preferentially scan and hold onto unpleasant experiences. It is neurologically designed to keep us safe and alive and that means tracking for negative experiences that may be a threat, even if the positive experiences out-weigh the negative ones. Studies have revealed that our brain will store the negative ones faster than positive ones. This in turn forms our implicit memories which sit in our subconscious mind below our conscious awareness. These memories are very powerful because they shape our emotional outlook, expectations, models of relationships and energy.

Savouring is about going against our neurological programming. It means actively looking for 'good news' and noticing positive events for long enough to convert them into memories. Studies about the way in which people react to positive events have shown that those who share positive feelings with others are happier overall than those who do not. In her research Professor Barbara Fredrickson found the long-term benefits of positive emotions: They lift your mood, increase optimism, resilience and resourcefulness; and help counteract the effects of painful experiences, including trauma. Savouring good feelings today increase the likelihood of good feelings tomorrow.

This is how you can delight and enjoy its benefits

The good news is that savouring positive experiences is a skill. This means that with effort and focus on your part, it is possible to develop your ability to achieve more. Below are two strategies to maximise positive experiences based on the research from Psychologists Dr. Rick Hanson and Dr. Fred Bryant.

The first strategy is to turn positive facts into positive experiences and then into good news. Often when good things happen in our lives we momentarily notice them and then let them slip by. They may show up as 'flirts in the field,' shimmers of good vibes that disappear quickly if we don't take hold of them. On the other hand when we have a negative experience we hold onto it, ruminate and turn it over in our minds.

Savouring can be applied with simple things in your day, like a gesture of kindness, the smell of delicious coffee, laughter, a lively conversation or stunning sunset. The key to build a positive landscape is to first notice and grab the experience. Then, to really embed it, share your good feelings with others. Tell someone who cares about you when you're having a positive experience.

The second strategy is to extend the experience. Consciously stretching the experience is another way to convert it into powerful memory. Make your positive experiences last for as long as you can. Stay with them for five, ten or even twenty seconds without letting your attention wander towards somewhere else. While you are doing this, capture the sights, sounds, feelings and smells. Call them up and reflect on them after the event. Go fully into how wonderful the hug felt or the moment of laughter you had with your friend; the gentle words from your partner or playful joy with your children. Let it sink in, intensify it as this enriches the experience and builds a stronger trace of the experience in our memory.

This is how I optimise it and how I get the most from it

I savour moments of contentment throughout my day, experiences of happiness and satisfaction. They can be big or small events such as sitting outside with the sun shining, walking early morning through a park, feeling alive and vital, eating something completely delicious and sipping on a cup of coffee first thing in the morning. I note them and acknowledge them out loud 'This is wonderful!' If it is a big moment I dial a friend and share the positive news in a very up-beat way.

Equally, if someone calls me with big (or small) moments I ask questions which help them to savour it. All too often, we can move from joy and onto the next thing. Hold the space by asking questions and centre them within the experience for longer, inviting the brain to transfer and place the experience into long-term memory.

Where you can discover more

Hardwiring Happiness: The Practical Science of Reshaping Your Brain – and Your Life by Dr. Rick Hanson, shows how we can make good feelings last. Drawing on recent scientific breakthroughs that reveal how we think and feel changes the brain, he explains how to overcome negativity bias and get good experiences into the brain to promote lasting health, contentment, love and inner peace.

> *Our brain works like Velcro for negative experiences and like Teflon for positive experiences ... We can savour and celebrate these experiences by consciously pausing when they occur, exploring them curiously and letting them sink in and fill our being.*

Dr. Rick Hanson, Neuroscientist

6. Sensualising

A strategy designed to extend and expand your world view.

Useful for: Overcoming frustration by seeking out subtleties to delight.

Future proofing: 'What else captures my desire?'

This technique is about pleasing or fulfilling all your senses to create more pleasurable moments and richer experiences. We invariably rely on one sense more than others. In other words, we have a preferred way of viewing or hearing the world. Sensualising is to take all five senses out into the world and then pay attention to the rich tapestry of sounds, smells, flavours and energies around you. It is simple and you can use it as you move through your day. As the poet John Keats says, 'O for a life of sensations rather than of thoughts.'

How this strategy offers you an alternate coping approach

When we sort for difference we avail ourselves of the capacity to learn new things. The key to enhance our world view is to sense rather than think; one allows you to remain up-beat and external while the other is internal and allows for the processing of retrieved learning and meaning. Just being and inputting new sensory data is a joy. Your unconscious mind will process this later, rather than seeking an instant insight. Wonder, joy and awe are the three major states of sensing. Each is important to create a sense of flourishing and ensure freshness of mind and perspective. Author of *A Delicious Life,* Gary Yardley invites us to explore our sensual side:

> 'Being sensual is engaging with all your six senses ... first notice the inherent beauty found within everything around you, what do you find an attraction for, and then how this in turn fits within its surrounds. Notice how it caresses and interacts with those things which support its presence.'

Sensualising is also a powerful form of diffusion as it takes you out of your inner dialogue and shifts the focus externally. This brings you into the present moment. One of the easiest ways to stop your thinking and to just sense is by interjecting sounds and not thoughts in your head such as: mmm, wow, aha, haaah.

This is how you can delight and enjoy its benefits

You can take your senses out in a variety of ways. The first way would be to choose one of your senses and notice four things you haven't noticed before. This may be in a familiar environment or an activity that you do on a regular basis. What do you notice that is different? Another option, is to take each of your senses and to notice something new for each of them: ask yourself 'What am I seeing, hearing, feeling, smelling and tasting that is new or unfamiliar?' Alternatively, you could emphasise a sense you don't use very often within a given context.

If it's visual, seek out and add assorted colours into your day. What different colours can you add to your wardrobe that will lift your energy?

If it's sound - what are three diverse types of music you can add to your play lists? If it's feeling, you could add a variety of sensations and textures. Is it time for a massage or to wear a fabric like silk and satin which heightens your sensuality?

If it's smelling, experiment with adding essential oils into your home or on your body. There are many diverse types of oils - explore which ones open you up and lift your energy?

With the sense of taste you can focus on flavours. What new spices and herbs can you add into your cooking or even try in a new cuisine?

This is how I optimise it and how I get the most from it

I take my senses out when I'm walking through airports. It's easy to get stuck in my head thinking about the day and all its pieces. This technique brings me into an external focus and piques my curiosity. As I walk through the terminal I ask myself 'What am I seeing that I have overlooked before?' I look for four things I haven't seen, heard or felt before. In doing so, I presume that novelty exists everywhere. I repeat this process in the baggage claim area and in the taxi-ride home. Apart from keeping my airport trips and travel interesting, I arrive home feeling relaxed and at ease.

I do a lot of walking in nature. Softening my ears and allowing myself to absorb sounds is a refreshing way to walk through familiar tracks. The sound of the rustle of dry leaves, the whirling of the wind through the gum trees, the creek babbling and dogs barking. Tuning into the different sensations is another way I sensualise, feeling the breeze against my skin, the warmth of the sun, my feet treading on different types of surfaces and rubbing dog's backs as they come up and say hello.

Wandering around local food markets is also a wonderful place to sensualise. I find they are rich in texture with colour, different sounds, pungent smells and exotic flavours to tempt and taste. They are a smorgasbord for the senses, uplifting and invigorating.

Where you can discover more

Looking to expand your sensual range? *The Kama Sutra* is an ancient Indian Hindu text written by Vātsyāyana. It is widely considered the standard work on human sexual and sensual behaviour in Sanskrit literature. More famous for its positions of lovemaking, it also has over eleven hundred pages dedicated to being sensual and its practices.

> *Beauty is to recognize how full of Love you are. Sensuality is to*
> *let some of that love shine through your body.*
>
> Nityananda Das, Divine Union

7. Spicing Up

A strategy designed to enliven your future and to spice it up.

Useful for: Overcoming boredom and weariness of mind, motivating a desire.

Future proofing: 'Hmm, now what tickles my fancy?'

This strategy is about using nature's tantalisers to excite your senses and liven up your whole disposition. It shows how life's many subtle fragrances and flavours have the ability to engage your different senses and bring little moments of desire and desirability into your daily routine. Spice markets are evocative of a once great trade across the unknown world and brought fresh discoveries to those that couldn't travel to far off exotic places.

How this strategy offers you an alternate coping approach

Scents actively change the biochemistry of your nervous system. A certain fragrance can evoke memories and emotions before we are consciously aware of it. That is because it goes straight into the amygdala, the part of the limbic system within the brain which is responsible for emotions, survival instincts and memory. This process bypasses the logical brain. You may be uplifted by the aroma of a freshly made cup of coffee, ginger biscuits or cinnamon cake cooking in the oven, the smell of clean linen or freshly cut grass. That is because what we smell immediately affects how we feel.

Aromatic spices have been shown to have healing properties for the body and positively impact upon our emotions. Science is now proving what traditional cultures have benefited from for centuries. While spices have been used to add colour and zest, certain spices are a powerful source of mood-boosting nutrients. Not only do they add tempting flavour to our food, they also stimulate the natural brain chemicals such as dopamine and serotonin which help create a positive mood. Spices make us feel good and invigorate our experiences.

This is how you can delight and enjoy its benefits

Ever thought that some of your most tantalising foods are sitting in your spice cupboard and they patiently wait for you to use these culinary pleasures?

Turmeric, a popular herb in South Asian food has been found to possess healing properties. The curcuminoids in turmeric regulate neurotransmitters, dopamine and serotonin. Keeping these brain chemicals in balance alleviates depression and makes you feel at ease. You may try and add some into your smoothies or juices, to provide an early morning non-caffeine zing.

Eating hot spicy foods like chilli peppers releases endorphins, chemicals that can relieve pain and cause a feeling of euphoria. Chilli contains an active ingredient called capsaicinoids which produce an uncomfortable burning sensation in your mouth. Your body reacts to neutralise the pain by producing endorphins. The side benefit is a boost to your mood which stays stimulated for an hour afterwards. Definitely a spice up!

Saffron is well-known and valued as a spice. Currently, research has found saffron is not only tasty, but it also helps to alleviate the symptoms of premenstrual syndrome and depression. It assists in the release of serotonin into the brain which is a natural antidepressant. Try adding this into or on your salads, curries, desserts and soups.

Cinnamon is one of the oldest spices and has been traded for many centuries around the world. It is known to reduce inflammation and improve memory and attention, all of which can support a positive mood. Simply smelling cinnamon will improve mood. Try this with your morning porridge or latte.

Cardamom can be effective as a drinking tea and has been known to relieve depression and make your mood feel lighter. It also helps to protect the brain from free radical damage which causes memory loss and brain fog. Having clarity will contribute to you having a positive state of mind. It is wonderful in curries and chai tea drinks.

This is how I optimise it and how I get the most from it

Recently, I have started drinking chai tea. For many years green tea has been my hot drink of choice. Friends have introduced me to this delicious beverage and it has been a pleasurable discovery. The authentic version includes black tea with cinnamon sticks, cardamom pods, whole cloves and ginger. It is a rich source of flavour and at the same time, it both heals and nurtures the body and mind.

Where you can discover more

If you are interested in exploring more about the healing power of culinary spices, *Healing Spices* by Bharat B. Aggarwal Ph.D. and Debora Yost is a useful resource. It explains how to use 50 every day and exotic spices to boost health and beat disease.

All the things that have ever deeply possessed your soul have been but hints of it, tantalizing glimpses, promises never quite fulfilled, echoes that died away just as they caught your ear. But if it should really become manifest - if there ever came an echo that did not die away but swelled into the sound itself – you would know it. Beyond all possibility of doubt, you would say 'Here at last is the thing I was made for.'

C. S. Lewis, Poet and Novelist

8. Smoothing

A strategy designed to replicate your own unique frequency, emotional harmonic.

Useful for: Overcoming sluggishness and uncertainty.

Future proofing: 'Hmm, time to engage my groove?'

This strategy is about intentionally using music in your life to smooth out your emotional fluctuations and take advantage of its mood-boosting benefits. Music you like gives voice to some of your own inner rhythms. It makes you feel good and moves you physically and emotionally. Also, at times, it can stay with you – an endless ditty – which is why it is so powerful.

How this strategy offers you an alternate coping approach

Music affects our mood and it does so quickly which is why it makes it a simple and easy coping strategy. It can shift our state, depending on what we listen to. We can use music and rhythms daily to create different effects or moods we want, either to enhance or reduce our energy at different times of the day.

Research shows that music affects our emotions and moods in several ways. The core of what makes the impact is the music's rhythm, melody and timbre (tone quality). When we listen to certain rhythms, our heart's pulse can actually get into sync with it. The beat of our heart sends a signal to the brain which affects our mood. A slow heart-beat with a strong diastolic pressure (when your heart rests between beats) tells our brain something sad or depressing is occurring. A fast beat is usually associated with excitement or alternately it could be anxiety. A dreamy rhythm can signify love and peacefulness.

Tones are as important as rhythm as they affect the brain. A 'major key' piece signifies upbeat and optimistic communication to the brain. Whereas a 'minor key' closely mirrors an expression of grief and mourning.

In studying the healing properties on our minds and bodies, neuroscientist, Dr. Candace Pert explains that music, like our bodies, is structured of vibrations of energetic patterns and it has been proven that the molecules of our bodies, not just our ears and brains, can literally resonate the music we hear. In the meditation recording, 'Healing the Hurting, Shining the Light', she clarifies:

> 'Beautiful music literally creates good health as the harmonious vibratory integration of the whole, inside and out.'

This is how you can delight and enjoy its benefits

Make music work for you with its mood-changing qualities. You can do this in a couple of distinct ways. The first is to build seven different play lists that align with your most familiar emotions or moods. Design it so you can use some songs to enhance your mood and others which actively help shift your mood and create more emotional balance. Here are some suggestions:

Soothing music lowers the stress hormone cortisol and elevates mood. This music will help you feel serene, peaceful, calm and patient.

Upbeat dance music will help boost your immune system. This is because it activates the alpha brainwave which signals the body to release endorphins. This music will help you to feel excited, upbeat and cheerful.

Sad slow music will help you connect with feelings of melancholy, loss, grief. This will take you deeper into the experience. While it may be useful to connect with these feelings, it may not shift them. Your soothing soundtrack will be more effective here.

The other strategy is to make music work for you through the cycle of your day. The hormones related to the 'get up and go' energy you feel in the morning peak around breakfast time. In the morning choose upbeat music. Get yourself into alignment with your body by putting on some light, easy, positive music after you wake up.

In the field of music tones and mood, one of the latest trends is called 'directed tones.' This is music that speaks with the brain and directs it towards achieving the changes you want to experience. An example is binaural beats which are tones played in each ear individually. This produces rhythms that the brain starts following and this creates a shift in brain frequency, towards the mood you want.

At night, as you get ready for sleep, you may choose something calming and peaceful. For example, listening to music with binaural beats that induce delta brain-waves (the very slow frequency that happens with deep sleep) so you can fall asleep and stay asleep. Or if you want to calm your body and mind, binaural beats that evoke alpha brain waves (the relaxing frequency) will help to access this state.

This is how I optimise it and how I get the most from it

When doing exercise, I can maximise my workout with my own gym workout play list. The science shows that there is a correlation between upbeat, fast paced music and the effectiveness of an exercise workout. The notion is that my heart will sync up with the beat of the music and make it easier to pace strenuous exercise with loud and fast music because the heart falls into sync with the tempo. It works for me!

Where you can discover more

For binaural beat music the website www.I-doser.com offers many binaural beats for different effects in CD and MP3 format. Their products are used to help achieve a simulated mood or experience through the use of special binaural audio.

Music is the universal language. Humans are hard-wired to appreciate and need music – so find some music you enjoy and let its good vibrations stimulate your brain in wonderful ways.

Om-Harmonics, Mind-valley

9. Plumping

A strategy designed to enrich your world.

Useful for: Overcoming feeling down or unfairly treated.

Future proofing: 'Hmm, I wonder where I shall find my next lucky break?'

A truism is a statement that is so obviously true that it doesn't require a discussion or thought to comprehend it. It is a self-evident truth, a kind of vague notion when talking about supposed morals or the way life sometimes works for and against us. Some common ones are 'life isn't or wasn't meant to be fair,' 'you can't win them all,' 'just need a lucky break.' These statements have many examples piled up as proof that life sometimes sucks and is just plain unfair. We can all relate to them. However, if we accept their truth then the reverse of these statements is true, 'you can win most times and life has fairly given us many gifts.' This strategy shows you how to use truisms to plump up your attitude and emotions.

How this strategy offers you an alternate coping approach

When you are feeling overwhelmed or lack confidence, stating a truism will create a sense of reassurance for yourself. It will take you out of the immediate sense of not feeling safe or in feeling sorry for yourself by recognising that some things are consistent and they don't change. For example, 'The sun will rise in the morning,' or 'I can walk,' or 'I'm alive and breathing for another day.' It normalises what is happening and reinforces certainty. While your world could feel like the wheels are coming off and you are not able to cope, a truism brings you back into the realisation 'Some things don't change' or 'You can count on that.' It helps to shake off flat feelings and plumps up your disposition.

Truisms can also be used as a form of motivation. If you procrastinate, the truism 'A journey of a thousand miles starts with a single step,' could help you start regardless of how long or difficult the task ahead may be, by breaking it down to just placing one foot in front of the other.

This is how you can delight and enjoy its benefits

Create your own set of truisms ones that you can draw upon when needed. We all have sayings based upon our life experience, nuggets which buoy us when we are feeling down or disheartened. Have a conversation with people you know and explore what truisms they use to bolster themselves up.

A death of someone close or a major illness brings these truisms closer to mind … shifting our focus to what matters and how fortunate we really are. Using these strengthening sayings helps to sustain our energy in difficult times:

> 'I am lucky to be alive'

> 'One's true wealth in life is their health'

> 'Money can't buy happiness.'

A friend of mine buys a weekly lottery ticket not to win any jackpot or to fulfil his own wishes, rather to participate in a larger dream. He just smiles each week as he loses and says *I have aided in making another's lifelong dream come true.*

This is how I optimise it and how I get the most from it

If I am having a pity party and feeling sorry for myself I use a truism to shift my state. I say out loud 'You are in the 10% of the world that sleeps safely in your bed, a safe and comfortable night's sleep without fear of what lurks in the dark.'

A friend of mine uses the truism 'Every seven seconds a baby dies on this planet from malnutrition, an unnecessary death.' That is dramatic and because he sees the image at the same time it is virtually impossible to remain hard done by or to stay with feeling like poor me. Another one I use is 'All that glitters is not gold,' if I find I'm being swept along by a quick get rich quick offer or deal.

Where you can discover more

By talking with those who run not-for-profit organisations. These organisations bring relief to those less fortunate and value their own altruistic worth. Check out their values and mission statements of intent, do they live in their truisms?

Then read stories of those who have overcome unsurmountable odds who mostly see themselves as fortunate or not hard done by. These people embody a perspective for living and finding meaning in everything they do despite hardship and suffering and seek to make the most of life. Biographies of athletes and adventurers who have triumphed over disability to reach extraordinary achievements are a wonderful source of inspiration.

In the biography *Find Your Inner Gold: A Gold Medal Paralympian's Secrets*, Carol Cooke AM shares her strategies to overcome adversity, accept change, find hidden courage and create a winning mind-set. Living with Multiple Sclerosis since 1998, she has won a gold medal at the 2012 London Paralympics and two gold medals at the 2016 Rio de Janeiro Paralympics. She believes 'If you dare to face your fears and believe in yourself, you can overcome anything.'

Seek not greater wealth, but simpler pleasure; not higher fortune, but deeper felicity.

Mahatma Gandhi, Pacifist

10. Protecting

A strategy designed to clear away your emotional baggage.

Useful for: Letting go of life hurts and disappointments.

Future proofing: 'What do I wish to surround myself with?'

We can experience unpleasant feelings and sensations that can make us feel anxious, jittery and distracted. This technique is a quick and effortless way to contain these feelings so we feel protected and safe. What we hold near and dear we choose to hang onto. Sometimes we keep our fears, doubts and worries close, fearful they might just get out of hand if we let them out of our sight. To let go of our hurts and disappointments frees us up so we can gather new or fresher experiences.

How this strategy offers you an alternate coping approach

Using an emotional bubble is a quick way to erect a protective boundary and cover around you. When we experience emotion, they are translated into chemical expressions or 'codes' by our bodies and then this information is communicated through, and, subsequently, affects our various bodily systems. The science of emotional biochemistry has discovered that these chemicals occur not just in the brain, but often simultaneously in virtually every system of the body.

Research by Molecular Biologist Dr. Candace Pert, discovered that when we are experiencing an emotion the cells in our brain release hormones called peptides. These peptides play a significant role in connecting both the mind and body in a network of shared information. This discovery shows how intricate the connection between mind and body is. She found that if we continue to experience an emotion (for instance, anger, sadness, guilt) and hold onto it the body is affected. In her book, *The Molecules of Emotion: The Science Behind Mind Body Medicine*, she explains:

> 'When you experience an emotion so does your body at the same time. And if that emotion is held for too long, the body will hold it and start to complain.'

Creating a feeling of safety, refuge and shelter activates a code in our bodies that switches on the parasympathetic nervous system, a counter-balance to the stress response of 'fight-flight-fright.' It creates the pathway for emotional re-generation and healing in the body. Doc Childre, Founder of the *HeartMath Institute*, states:

> 'You can emotionally regenerate in three ways: building emotional energy reserves, stopping energy drains and clearing old emotional accounts.'

To make a sanctuary and harbour of protection is one way to provide deep caring to yourself, as it facilitates the chance to restore and replenish your emotional energy. Nature is the most conducive for this and ensures a stress and tension-free environment. Mother Earth offers an invitation to find your quiet place, to just sit and to draw from her natural energies.

This is how you can delight and enjoy its benefits

This technique is about creating a feeling of safety and choice. Sometimes we inadvertently keep our hurts close so we learn from them while not wishing the same mistake twice, thus allowing a hurt to dictate and direct our life choices. When discarded or ejected we can place another bubble around us to ward off a reoccurrence – a safety buffer or zone.

Simply visualise yourself in an emotional bubble. Imagine you are throwing out the rubbish from the inside. As you are doing this clear out, ask that anything that is not relevant leave and not return.

Remember this is your personal space, you decide what you fill it up with and, more importantly, what others must wade through to get to meet the real you rather than working through all your surface collections of mis-steps and trust issues. Avoid holding onto your hurts and disappointments, distance them from yourself. Send your concerns off towards one side freeing up your space for other more pleasurable things you could share. Find your joy and hold this closer. Why should new people in your life pay the price for your previous mistakes; a hidden trail and obstacle course that they must navigate before they can find if they are worthy or can breach your defensive perimeter of pre-judgements?

This is how I optimise it and how I get the most from it

I use this strategy when I am working and need a quick containment option. I visualise the emotional bubble and spot where the feelings are located. The first thing I do is ask 'Who does this belong to? Is this mine?' If it's not mine, I say 'I return it to sender.' If faced with another's entrenched opinions, I ask myself 'Why bother?' if this is too hard or there isn't an opening for me to exist in this world-view, then I move on. Because I like to give and if my giving has heavy demands placed upon me or I have to jump through hoops, suspicion and trust issues, then I can easily give to those who welcome an open exchange.

For extra protection, I imagine chain-mail around my body, extending out at arm's length around me. Unlike the chain-mail of medieval knights, this material is made from thread that is super strong but very light and fine. It allows me to be open in my own space while protecting me from other people's emotions and energy.

Where you can discover more

In the book *A Delicious Life, One Moment at a Time* by Gary Yardley, the protagonist talks of two bubbles; one of potency and the other of impotence. This is where she takes charge of her own emotional availability, to ensure others don't face her unsorted stuff or life baggage. She in-turn can stop another's baggage from intruding by placing their issues into a bubble of impotence, reducing their neediness.

> *Emotional Bubbles may give us time and space to feel safe, to think*
> *things through, to just be, to re-charge our batteries.*

> Karen Sieger, Psychotherapist

11. Buffering

A strategy designed to build an enriched emotional intelligence.

Useful for: Resilience and robustness in the face of adversity.

Future proofing: 'How do I wish to be noticed by others at a meeting?'

This is a simple practice to create positive emotions and to strengthen your resilience. Positive emotions create a buffer, so you can recover more quickly from difficulty and hardship. Furthermore, it is less likely that you will find yourself in emotionally stressful situations because you are working from a more secure sense of self.

How this strategy offers you an alternate coping approach

In studying the science of emotions Dr. Barbara Fredrickson, leader in the field of positive psychology, has found emotions such as love, kindness, compassion, awe and joy help us to become more resourceful, creative and healthier. She posits:

> 'Positive emotions can set up upward spirals in your life, self-sustaining trajectories
> of growth that can lift you up to become a better version of yourself.'

Even though we may experience positive emotions in subtle, brief moments, they ignite a flood of body chemicals that serve to shift our outlook. Feel good hormones, oxytocin and dehydroepiandrosterone (DHEA) uplift our mood. When they are high, we feel more energetic, vital and optimistic about life. These micro-moments accumulate over time and help build resources to deal with life's challenges.

Positive emotions awaken powerful forces for growth in our lives. The shift in our biochemistry literally expands our mind-set to become more open, broader and encompassing of the world around us. In the book *Positivity*, Dr. Fredrickson says:

> 'You can put positive emotions to work as you navigate your days to overcome
> negativity and thrive … they are a means to broaden and build.'

The greater openness that positive emotions create, shifts us out of a state of self-absorption and makes us more attractive to be around. The emotions of gratitude and loving kindness nourish our relationships and help them grow stronger and closer. They are also an essential buffer to stay well, and even alive. Dr. Kelly Turner's research into prevalent factors involved in radical remission from cancer revealed positive emotions as one of the key factors that can unlock pathways to healing.

This is how you can delight and enjoy its benefits

A simpler way to activate the elevated feeling of loving kindness is via a meditation practice. It is a technique honed over many years in Buddhist traditions and is designed to condition your heart to become more open and loving. Although this meditation is Buddhist in origin, it has become a popular mindfulness practice. As with all phrase-based practices, it is not the words you choose that matter, but rather the feelings these words evoke. The key is to really connect with those feelings as they change your body's chemistry and open your heart. Practice this daily for a few weeks and notice the difference in your openness and appreciation for life.

Following is a shortened version of the *Loving Kindness* meditation. The complete meditation has been recorded by Dr. Barbara Fredrickson and is available from www.love2.0.com as a free download.

Begin by sitting comfortably and close your eyes. Bring your inner awareness towards your heart. Breathe in and out as if you were breathing from the heart. Rest in this awareness for several breaths, soften and relax. Now in this moment, visualise someone for whom you already feel loving, tender and caring feelings. This could be your child, your spouse, best friend, mentor, even a pet – someone whom the mere thought of, makes you smile. Let her or his smiling face surface in your mind's eye.

As you take in the image, call into mind this loved one's good qualities. Your goal is to awaken warm and tender feelings naturally, by visualising how connecting with this loved one makes you feel. Once these tender feelings have taken root and created genuine warmth and kindness in you, gently repeat the traditional phrases of the *Loving Kindness* meditation, silently to yourself. The traditional phrases go like this:

> *May you feel safe. May you feel happy. May you feel healthy. May you live with ease.*

Say this several times and notice the feeling it generates in your heart and body.

This is how I optimise it and how I get the most from it

My intention is to be in the world with a loving kindness, cultivating micro-moments of connection with others, even strangers each day. The *Loving Kindness* meditation increases my capacity to make joy and love my prevailing desire in all domains of my life. It helps me see, recognise and value each person I interact with and to add to the energy exchange between us.

Where you can discover more.

The Myths of Happiness: What Should Make You Happy, but Doesn't, What Shouldn't Make You Happy, but Does, by Sonja Lyubomirsky offers practical lessons to build vision and mindset to have a healthy and satisfying life.

> *Positive emotions don't just make us feel good, they transform our minds,*
> *our bodies, and our ability to bounce back from hard times.*

Professor Barbara Fredrickson, Scientist

12. Flowing

A strategy designed to increase your own personal resonance, a balancing harmony.

Useful for: Releasing the accumulation of tension and stress.

Future proofing: 'How do I wish to feel by the end of this?'

This strategy is useful to release built-up tensions in your body and mind. It incorporates *Emotional Freedom Techniques* (EFT) which work on the premise that the source of an emotional disturbance is located somewhere in your body, not just held in your mind. Emotional disturbances cause a block to the body's natural energy flow. By restoring the energy flow and shifting your attitude, the emotional problem is resolved.

How this strategy offers you an alternate coping approach

EFT is an approach used to improve emotional energy and balance. It is often referred to as 'acupressure for the emotions.' The method focuses on shifting internal states of body experience where emotions are held. By tapping on energy points on the skin while focusing the mind on specific emotional issues, the brain's neural pathway can be shifted quickly to help you. International leader in functional medicine Dr. Mark Hyman says:

> 'Tapping is one of the most directed and powerful ways to peel those layers away of chronic stress. It's very effective for very difficult problems.'

Tapping provides a pattern interruption on the stress response and gets the amygdala in the limbic brain (our 'emotional brain') to settle down. The immediate benefit is a release of tension and a relaxation effect in the body. Other benefits include clearing traumas, negative experiences and emotions that have become stored in the limbic brain. Tapping is useful to reduce worry and anxiety and to increase confidence and self-esteem. It has also proven effective for handling conflicts, criticism and tension and thereby improving relationships. Long-term use of the technique has been found to create more resilience and optimism.

This is how you can delight and enjoy its benefits

Australian energy pioneer Steve Wells adopted many of the early energy psychology approaches to create Simple Energy Techniques (SET). His approach is 'simply tap and follow where the energy goes, focus on what comes up and go with it.' That means notice where you have tensions, put your attention there and start tapping on the key energy points (shown in the diagram on the next page). It's important to keep your attention on the tension area until it shifts. It may go somewhere else in your body or some other sensation may show up; simply go with it and keep tapping.

Start by becoming a curious observer and focus on where the tension is showing up in your body. Next calibrate what score you would give the tension, where ten is extremely tight and zero is no tension. Observe closely the tension in your body. Where is the sensation located? Is it showing as a colour, shape or even a sound? Put your attention towards the tension and it will present itself. What do you notice?

Now, start tapping. Tap reasonably firmly on the key points using the tips of your index and middle finger. The points are inside the eyebrow, under the eye, on the top lip, below the bottom lip and just under the inner end of the collarbone. Keep tapping and pay attention. How is the tension changing? Keep tapping and focus on the tension until the energy completely shifts and you feel better.

Diagram of key tapping points:

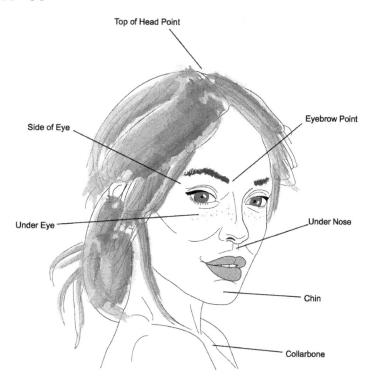

This is how I optimise it and how I get the most from it

I incorporate tapping techniques with my coaching clients. It has helped them to resolve conflict, stress, emotional overwhelm and anxiety. Often, someone will come into the session extremely tense from their stressful jobs and leave having reconnected with their serenity and gained fresh perspective.

Where you can discover more

100% YES! The Energy of Success by Steve Wells shows you how to use revolutionary SET to free yourself from the emotional blocks behind self-sabotage, procrastination, inertia and false starts.

If you want to know more about the science behind these techniques *The Promise of Energy Psychology* by David Feinstein, Donna Eden and Gary Craig provides a good introduction and overview.

> *If we spent our energy focused on getting into the flow instead of fighting our way up the river we'd be so much happier, have more energy and in the end, I believe get more of what we want. But we humans are stubborn.*

Christine Arylo, Transformational teacher

13. Exfoliating

A strategy designed for self-acceptance and to make the most of self.

Useful for: Shedding difficult or intense emotions.

Future proofing: 'Who do I wish to give a gentle caress of energy to?'

This technique is about shedding and getting rid of old emotions to create more emotional vulnerability, a softness with an inner glow. As with exfoliating the skin, we can reduce the layering of emotions that have built up over time. It is not about scrubbing harshly as this is too abrasive and leaves one feeling raw and tender. It is about consistently peeling away the layers of emotions to create a smoother emotional quality. Exfoliating is a way of reducing the weary edge and harshness of life's many knocks and tribulations.

How this strategy offers you an alternate coping approach

Emotions can accumulate and become baggage that we carry around. They can be a heavy burden that gets carried forward in our lives. They act as a filter for how we engage in the world. Without regular exfoliating, the dry, old emotions accumulate. There needs to be active cleansing to slough away the old residue. Just like the skin, emotions can undergo renewal, but it is an active process. You can easily peel them off. The more you do it, the more emotional renewal you will achieve.

According to Dr. Todd Kashan, people who lack the capacity to withstand strong feelings, frustration and uncertainty are at a disadvantage in life. When faced with a difficult life dilemma, they react with greater emotional distress. Instead of dealing with the challenge, their energy gets diverted into worry, procrastination and the pursuit of harmful activities, such as drugs and alcohol to take away the pain. They spin their wheels trying to rid themselves of the emotional discomfort and pain rather than fully living their lives. In his book, *The Upside of Your Downside* he explains:

> 'There is a not so hidden prejudice against negative states, and the consequence of avoiding these states is that you inadvertently stunt your growth, maturity, adventure, and meaning and purpose in life.'

Rather than avoid discomfort, the task is how to lessen the grip of old emotions and reduce the intensity that has built up over time. Otherwise, we can get bogged down where our emotions are too big, too hard to handle and there doesn't seem a way to peel away the layers.

This is how you can delight and enjoy its benefits

A powerful way to consistently peel away the layering of emotions that have built up over time is through the power of love, moments of warmth, respect and connection that we share with ourselves and others. Love is a powerful emotion to shed old emotions and to re-gain a soft glow within.

Love itself comes in many forms. There are three powerful states you can seek out to enrich your dynamic. They are 'Loving,' 'Having a love for,' and 'Being in love.' How many have you explored and enjoyed or does life hold only one true love?

'Loving' is the minimum basis of all friendships and relationships because without it these attachments are not worth the angst. 'A love for' speaks about a deep-seated respect, a reflection of your own self-respect. Spend time with those who share this with you for without it your sense of worth will wane. Lastly, 'In love' is a rare commodity to be treasured, but remember it isn't the 'be all and end all' of living a great life. If you have been blessed to experience its warm embrace, draw daily from its presence as a subtle soothing. If not, act as if you are open to its desired caress from those you wish and want in your life.

This is how I optimise it and how I get the most from it

One of my techniques is to release my attachment with old emotions. There have been experiences in my life that have left a residual hurt, guilt and even shame. To peel them away I bring into my mind's eye the experience and then notice what sensation is happening within my body because this is where the emotional residue will show up. Sometimes I find it lodged within the muscles, other times in my heart or different organs. It's always there, deep if it's intense and has been there for a long time. Once located I name and acknowledge the emotion, for example 'I acknowledge this sadness.' Then, I use the following phrase 'I release all of my emotional attachments to this sadness,' and notice the intensity ease off, and usually dissolve away. I learnt from Energy practitioner, Steve Wells who calls it the 'Intentional Energy Process' (IEP). What seems to be a simple process, works quickly and effectively to 'exfoliate' difficult and intense emotions.

Where you can discover more

If you have a strong auditory preference, an emotional healing technique called *Logosynthesis* may suit you better. To learn more of this energy psychology technique *Self-Coaching with Logosynthesis* by Willem Lammers, shows you how to apply the model and move beyond limiting memories, fantasies and beliefs. In doing so, you can stop the emotional suffering and take more control of your life.

In *How to Love* Zen Master, Thich Nhat Hanh talks about developing self-acceptance and self-love. He distils that we can only love another when we feel true love for our self; love is understanding; understanding brings compassion; deep listening and loving speech are key ways to show our love.

Life appears at times like an onion. You peel it off one layer at a time and sometimes you weep.

Carl Sandburg, Poet

14. Tendering

A strategy designed for self-forgiveness and compassion.

Useful for: Letting go of the past and renewing your future promise.

Future proofing: 'How can I be a kinder person?'

Being tender with yourself is a powerful emotional moisturiser, it speaks of an inner forgiveness and self-acceptance. Compassion is to treat yourself with the same type of kindness, support and understanding that you would show with anyone you cared about. We have all grown up with an inner voice, one which is more of a naysayer, where its inherent and repeated message can easily blunt our fine edge and take away our ability to live fully.

How this strategy offers you an alternate coping approach

Most of us can make incredibly harsh, cruel self-judgments that we would never make about a total stranger, let alone someone we cared about. It seems easier to give love and compassion towards others than ourselves. For many of us, we have grown up in cultures that admire toughness, strength and resolve. These three elements are viewed as admirable leadership qualities, shoring up uncertainty and a way to build confidence. Caring for self is actually the cornerstone of resilience. Knowing that one's strengths are also one's blind spots and can be weaknesses. Self-flagellation may drive the moment, but does little to install a self-sustaining worth.

Tendering doesn't have to be soft or mushy or be perceived as weak. It can be seen as good preparation to ensure optimal conditions for growth, as found in gardening and growing healthy and robust plants. Consider for a moment how you give tenderness towards yourself. How are you expressing and receiving gentle and caring feelings?

How do you forgive yourself when you make a mistake – laugh and learn?

How do you reward and pamper yourself with a celebration – share and give?

How are you sensual to your gentler needs – ease up and just enjoy?

How do you refresh your playfulness and curiosity – seek out daily joy?

For Dr. Kristen Neff of Berkley University, self-compassion is about self-kindness, as opposed to self-judgment. A lot of times when we suffer, we just take a very cold attitude toward ourselves. She says 'self-compassion involves being warm and supportive — actively soothing ourselves — as opposed to being cold and judgemental to ourselves.' Mainly, it is how we talk to ourselves on the inside, and how we talk about ourselves to others on the outside. It is also what we do with ourselves when we are feeling vulnerable or out of balance.

This is how you can delight and enjoy its benefits

Harbouring feelings of resentment, judgement and harshness about yourself not only burdens you, it also ripples out and enters into all of your other relationships. The first step to move towards self-tendering is to take a moment to acknowledge your difficulties, challenges and suffering. Use softer tones when speaking to yourself a gentler voicing of what you can shape.

A simple technique is to be caring, gentle and self-soothing. When you are feeling insecure, uncertain or even disappointed in yourself about some action you have or haven't taken, put your hand on your heart or stroke down the outside of your upper arm to calm yourself. Gently say to yourself, as if speaking with a child who is hurting 'I know this hurts you, but you will be okay, I'm here' or something similar that works for you.

This technique is called 'How would a friend treat you?' Recall someone who cares about you and imagine that this person who cares about you is feeling and expressing compassion for you. Imagine his or her facial expression, gestures, stance and attitude toward you. Let yourself receive this compassion, take in its warmth, concern and goodwill. Open to feeling more understood and nurtured, more peaceful and settled. The experience of receiving care primes circuits in your brain to give it in return.

This is how I optimise it and how I get the most from it

I pay close attention to my inner dialogue and the tone of its message. The first thing I notice is the shift in the tone of my voice. The inner critic talks at me in a cold, harsh, dismissive and demanding tone. I now recognise this tone and identify it as my 'inner critic.' I listen to what she is saying with a purpose to listen for what's behind her words. She sees her role as keeping me safe by taking control, so I look for what is triggering her need to be harsh. What is it I need or want from life? Maybe in that moment I'm feeling unsafe and uncertain. Once I know and acknowledge this, I put my hand on my heart, and say very gently to myself 'You're okay. You are safe' and breathe.

Where you can discover more

To learn more practices for developing greater self-tendering *Self-Compassion: The Power of Being Kind to Yourself* Dr. Kristin Neff offers exercises and an action plan to stop beating yourself up, to leave insecurity behind, and to step into your potential.

With self-compassion, we give ourselves the same kindness and care we'd give a good friend.

Dr. Kristen Neff, Researcher and Teacher

15. Nurturing

A strategy designed to embrace your vulnerability.

Useful for: Finding your daily joy to live an enjoyable life.

Future proofing: 'When is enough, enough?'

Nurturing is the ability to care for and protect yourself as you would a young child who is growing and developing. It is about helping and encouraging you to be the best version of you and to cherish your hopes and dreams. It is vital to your own well-being that you know how others could inadvertently destroy or reduce your happiness by their insensitivity. Your innocence, naiveté, openness, trust, curiosity, kindness and intuition all must run the scrutiny of cynics, naysayers or so-called previous life experience. Each of these elevated emotional states are conducive to fast-track learning and should be protected at all costs from dismissiveness and fully cherished.

How this strategy offers you an alternate coping approach

Being gentle and kind with ourselves is the start of truly taking care and looking after our promise and potential. It requires an ability to let go of the need to be perfect and to always get it right. This pattern is fundamentally about 'Not Enough,' 'Not enough money,' 'Not enough success,' 'Not enough perfect body weight,' 'Not enough beauty.' Underlying the pattern is anxiety stemming from a relentless pursuit of flawlessness and self-imposed high expectations. It is usually accompanied by harsh self-critical evaluations and the need for approval from others. It is the opposite of being nurturing.

The pursuit of perfect, is encoded in the cultures we grow up in. Social psychologist, Geert Hofstede, widely known for his cross-cultural model, identified a dimension called 'Masculinity versus Femininity.' He states:

> 'The Masculinity side of this dimension represents a preference in society for achievement, heroism, assertiveness and material rewards for success. Society at large is more competitive. Its opposite, Femininity, stands for a preference for cooperation, modesty, caring for the weak and quality of life. Society at large is more consensus-oriented.' *(Cultures Consequences)*

For those of us who have lived in cultures with a strong 'Masculine' side that rewards toughness; learning, self-nurturing and tendering can feel at odds with our unconscious programming.

Nurturing is protecting the essence of who you are and being compassionate with yourself. However, it is normal to want to let ourselves be deeply seen and be known. For this to happen, walking beside our vulnerability is required, not being a hostage to it.

Social researcher Brene Brown found that there is one variable separating people who have a powerful sense of self-love and belonging and the people who really struggle with it – they believe that they are worthy. This translates into a keen sense of self-love, belonging and a belief that they are worthy of love and connection.

On examining this quality of worthiness she found that these people have the courage to be imperfect. They let go of 'Not enough.' At their starting point they are kind and gentle with themselves which then helps to be compassionate with others. Their strength comes from letting go of who they thought they should be and embracing who they truly are.

This is how you can delight and enjoy its benefits

The strategy starts with you believing that you *are enough* and owning your imperfections. Changing the 'I am not enough' belief can be testing because you are re-programming a deep-seated pattern that has been there from a young age. Whenever you feel the cringe of shame or the insidious 'I'm not enough' enter your inner world, spot it; pay attention. What is it saying? What's the tone? (probably it's harsh, cold and critical). Now, name it and say, 'That's the *I'm not good enough* story.' Now, feel where it has lodged in your body. Where is the tension? What has happened in your physical body? Has it crunched in on itself? Gently, pull your shoulders back, put your hand on your chest and say gently 'I am enough.' What shift do you notice?

This is how I optimise it and how I get the most from it

There are four actions I do every day to self-nurture. I learned these from mentors and life experience. The first is to let go of exhaustion; this is about releasing the drive to push myself and instead to stop for a rest, take a nap, read a novel and simply be. The second is to find my joy; and to know what gives me joy and doing more of it. The third is to practice being calm and to access moments of stillness. The fourth one is to make time for play-time when I am entertaining myself and being spontaneous.

Where you can discover more

If you are interested in changing unconscious cultural programs neuropsychologist Dr. Mario Martinez explains in *The Mind Body Code* ways to break through ceilings of limiting cultural beliefs and how to create new sub-cultures of wellness.

For more about cultural differences *Cultures and Organisations: Software of the Mind* by Geert Hofstede, provides insights into what drives people apart – when cooperation is clearly in everyone's interests.

To be beautiful means to be yourself. You don't need to be accepted by others. You need to accept yourself.

Thich Nhat Hanh, Buddhist monk, Teacher

135

16. Appreciating

A strategy designed to show gratitude and respect.

Useful for: Cherishing what you have.

Future proofing: 'Where is the inherent beauty in this moment or person?'

Showing appreciation and gratitude is a simple and easy practice even if you are feeling flat. It is recognising the beauty and appreciating the goodness in your life and in others. By doing so, it takes you out of a focus on yourself and, let's face it, we can all do with moving out of our own way and being less self-absorbed. It is a way that makes others feel valued and acknowledged, and in doing so, you are adding to their sense of well-being. All of this actually takes very little effort, it is more a state of mind.

How this strategy offers you an alternate coping approach

Latest research studies from the Greater Good Sciences Centre at the University of California, Berkeley, confirm that gratitude has many benefits in supporting us to better cope with life. Practicing gratitude has proven to be one of the most reliable methods to increase happiness and life satisfaction. It boosts feelings of optimism, joy, pleasure, enthusiasm and other positive emotions which contribute to feeling happier about life. On the flip-side, gratitude also reduces anxiety and depression by lifting our serotonin levels, the 'happy messenger' which works as a mood enhancer.

Studies by leading scientific expert on gratitude Dr. Robert Emmons found that gratitude has significant social benefits because it strengthens relationships. Practicing gratitude assists us in becoming more helpful, generous and compassionate toward others. By encouraging us to be more out-going, we feel less lonely being out in the world and find emotional nourishment in connecting more with others. He says:

> 'It's an affirmation of goodness. We affirm that there are good things in the world, gifts and benefits we've received. This doesn't mean that life is perfect; it doesn't ignore complaints, burdens and hassles. But when we look at life as a whole, gratitude encourages us to identify some amount of goodness in our life.'

This is how you can delight and enjoy it

A simple approach to use appreciation is to take on the habit of smiling and saying 'Thank you.' To make it even more powerful, be specific. You may add in, and acknowledge and recognise another person's actions and say 'Thank you, I appreciate what you did for me,' or 'Thank you, I am grateful to you.'

If you prefer structure, a gratitude journal could work for you. A ritual could be to write down each night what you are grateful for from the day. You may start by capturing three appreciations. They can be small experiences and acts; simple things like a beautiful sunset, a smile, a kind gesture and good things that happened to you and that created a heart-opening effect. Oprah Winfrey is well-known for her commitment to using a gratitude journal every night and acknowledges how much it has helped her through the years when life has been difficult and demanding.

If you prefer a less structured approach, a simpler way is to count your blessings on a regular basis. Ask 'What am I grateful for?' Then reflect on the three experiences that you are grateful for from the day. To make a deeper feeling, recall the experience and how you felt, savour that feeling and let it flow through your whole body. Alternatively, first thing in the morning before you get out of bed bring into your awareness the three things you appreciate in your life.

Some families I know practice this ritual around the dinner table. They each share an experience from the day and talk about what they appreciated about it.

This is how I optimise it and how I get the most from it

I start and end my day with appreciation for the experiences and connections experienced through the day, it opens and closes the day for me in a gracious way. Giving 'spot gratitude' is how I can show and share my appreciation for others. In the moment, I will acknowledge what I appreciate about them, what they are doing in the world and how it makes a difference to others, and to me.

Another ritual is to write emails, texts and cards (yes, I know it's an outdated method) to show my appreciation. I regularly write my mother notes and letters, thanking and valuing all the extra things she does for me. She loves it.

As I move through my day, I smile at people and say, 'Thank you, I appreciate what you have done for me.' Often people in service roles will say 'Thank you, you have made my day!' They feel appreciated while I leave feeling the vibration of a positive exchange.

Where you can discover more

To learn more about the science of gratitude *Thanks!* by Dr. Robert Emmons provides many steps to cultivate gratitude.

If you are curious about the power of gratitude and how it works, the book *The Magic*, Rhonda Byrne, (author of global bestseller, *The Secret*), shares *magic practices* for all aspects of your life. They all start with gratitude.

A thankful heart is not only the greatest virtue to have, but it is the parent of all other virtues.

Marcus Tullius Ciceromu, Statesman

17. Softening

A strategy designed to ease back your emotional protective shell.

Useful for: Removing barriers to intimacy.

Future proofing: 'How do I make it easier for others to share with me?'

This strategy is a way to gently relax our bodies and soften the shell we have erected around our hearts and bodies. When we are being swept up by the flow of our emotions, we can feel separate, lonely and disconnected. We can feel each other's protective shell in the form of tension and resistance. We can see it in each other's faces, the strain of holding life together safely constrained.

Shells form a hard, protective outer case. We can often put these shells around or in front of our hearts to form a wall with the intention of stopping us from being hurt again, or we put them around our entire energy field so we can feel sheltered from harm, which contracts our openness. It is a form of protection. If we can close off the world, then, perhaps, we will be safe and self-reliant.

How this strategy offers you an alternate coping approach

Shells shut us off from our openness and flow and can be created when we perceive our boundaries have been violated or pushed. Boundaries are a demarcation that says, 'This is within my bounds and acceptable, and this is out-of-bounds and unacceptable.' To maintain healthy boundaries is a useful way to preserve our sense of self. Although these shells of protection can be useful, over time, they can block us from truly experiencing what we deeply want – love and connection.

Neuropsychiatrist and medical intuitive Dr. Mona Lisa Schulz, has found that the domain of the heart field registers heartache, pain and misery that we experience in partnerships all through our lives. When trapped emotions lodge in the heart area it blocks the energy flow which can cause physical symptoms in the heart, lungs and breast areas.

In the book *The Emotion Code*, Dr. Bradley Nelson describes the 'Heart-Wall' phenomenon, when trapped emotions created in the body lodge in the heart area. He says 'Sometimes your subconscious mind will take that extra energy that is now in the heart area and it will literally make a *wall* with it.' Why does this happen? He explains 'The walls are there for protecting your heart from injury; keeping your heart from being totally broken.' Heart walls, however, can make it more difficult for the body to heal itself, and numb us from fully opening our hearts towards others and life.

By learning to listen for the intuitive signs from your heart and then releasing the trapped emotions, it is possible to unlock and soften your emotional shell.

This is how you can delight and enjoy its benefits

The secret to unfolding and softening shells is to recognise that they are there. The easiest way to find them is to hone in on where the tension is lodged in your heart and around it. Set an intention to make any shells pliable and to dissolve the barriers blocking you from receiving and giving love.

Gently close your eyes. Set an intention that you are softening and releasing your emotional walls. Place your attention around your heart. Feel into your heart field, ask that you be shown any shells that are there. You may see or sense or feel them as tension and tightness.

Start with the shells furthest out from your heart. What do you notice? How does it feel? What are you seeing, is there a shape, texture or colour? It may present as a symbol, like a shield, edge or wall. Whatever shows up, just gently place your attention on it and say 'I release all my emotional attachments to the shells around my heart.' Notice what happens. Keep your attention around your heart. Just allow whatever becomes visible to simply be there.

This is how I optimise it and how I get the most from it

I use the above technique when I notice that tension has accumulated in my body or there is emotional closure and I'm shut down. The starting place is with the outer shells. When I place my attention there, the shell cracks in the middle and splits apart. Then shifting my attention to the next one, it does the same. I go right into the core of my heart field. Then imagine a vacuum cleaner, I use it to suck up the broken parts. Once this is done, I sit with the feeling of the edges melting and experience openness in my body.

Where you can discover more

You Can Heal Your Heart by Louise L. Hay and David Kessler discusses the emotions and thoughts that occur when a relationship leaves you broken-hearted, a marriage ends in divorce or a loved one dies. Together, their wisdom and experience can help you develop greater self-awareness and compassion. They provide you with the courage and tools to face many types of loss and challenge knowing that your heart can heal.

Sometimes we get lost inside our own shells of closure, and we don't allow our hearts to connect with love.

David Deida, Author

18. Luxuriating

A strategy designed to ensure one never loses sight and touch of the joys of life.

Useful for: Future memories and a reminder of delights yet to be experienced.

Future proofing: 'How can I bring more joy to those around me?'

This strategy prepares for strenuous times, like coping with a planned specific project, or when faced with a 'silly season' where excessive demands are placed or expected from us. In our busyness, we can miss out on simple joys and can take ourselves and the moment far too seriously. This is obvious by the way we are appearing somewhat stressed out and slightly uptight in our responses and interactions. Ease up and luxuriate for a moment or two. By placing these beautiful desired states into our future, we can then collect them as powerful reminders as we charge forward with a full head of steam so as to ease our whole body into a joyful tomorrow.

How this strategy offers you an alternate coping and adaptive approach

The body seeks a balance and deeply dislikes a 'one-tracked' use of its resources and takes from other areas to compensate. The body can do reparation well, but not for extended periods of time. An over-compensation throws out balance, with a cascading effect. For example, if you injure one leg, you will tend to favour the other leg. This, in turn, throws your spine out of alignment and affects your whole posture and brings forth new aches and pains. The same effect happens to the body when we pursue with resolute focus and no respite.

Making a provision for a moment of pure joy signals to the body your desire to care for it, rather than just depleting it by relentlessly working until you drop. It could be a joyful moment, a shared hug with someone else. A moment with yourself doing something that gives you pure pleasure, as simple as a cup of tea in the warm morning sun. Or a joyful moment in nature, playing, strolling or soaking up sunshine. Encouraging us towards finding joyful moments of play Stuart Brown of the National Institute for Play says:

> 'Playfulness enhances the capacity to innovate, adapt, and master changing circumstances. It is not just an escape. It can help us integrate and reconcile difficult or contradictory circumstances. And, often, it can show us a way out of our problems.'

This is how you can delight and enjoy its benefits

Emotional rest is a powerful form of recuperation which is why we adore a massage or a soak in a hot tub to ease and provide relaxation. Our mind also needs blissful distractions, a playful moment or two to distract itself from a single-minded pursuit. Discovery and appreciation are two effective ways to provide relief and to give yourself a moment of joy. Think of a child full of curiosity, awe and wonder, stimulating the mind to learn and grow. Bathing in your passion, an escape or something new that is not perceived as threatening, is a way to captivate your spirit. Joy is one of these, a bubble of wellness from within and affects our whole body with the glee of being fully alive.

We know when we are missing out on something intangible. We tend to become irritable and easily frustrated with an underlying dissatisfaction, with some of us experiencing a restlessness and yearning. This is why looking forward to a holiday is a powerful incentive, to either luxuriate or disappear and to discover something different. By placing these joyful memories into our future, we can then move into these reminders of what else we emotionally need to endure or survive a sustained workload.

This is how I optimise it and how I get the most from it

Whenever I find one of my joys, I take a snapshot of it, first as a single image photo and then as a mini-video. Both are valuable; the photo as a future reminder and the video to immerse myself in its memory. I seek them out when I become a 'serious-Sally' and no longer 'silly-Sally' just for the sake of it. My niece and I play with photos using FaceApp where we can transform images by adding different filters to create effects such as 'slow motion-Sally,' 'blurry eyed-Sally,' 'contrast-Sally' and so forth. It is a great tool to create and capture moments of enjoyment.

Do you notice how we never display grumpy or sad photos? Think about your joyfulness and have it as a future reminder for your emotional energy needs.

Where you can discover more

A conversation between his Holiness the Dali Lama and Archbishop Desmond Tutu about the pillars of joy is beautifully articulated in *The Book of Joy: Lasting Happiness in a Changing World* (with Douglas Abrams).

Discovering more joy does not save us from the inevitability of hardship and heartbreak. In fact, we may cry more easily, but we will laugh more easily, too. Perhaps we are just more alive. Yet as we discover more joy, we can face suffering in a way that ennobles rather than embitters. We have hardship without becoming hard. We have heartbreaks without being broken.

Archbishop Desmond Tutu, Theologian

Your Spiritual Energy

CHAPTER FIVE
Your Spiritual Fabric

Your spirit has its own presence, a unique vibration that's totally distinct from your personality. The best way to connect with your spirit is to start recognising what makes you come alive.

Sonia Choquette, Intuitive and Author

Your *Spiritual You* honours the connection with something larger than just yourself. Some talk about your being as your 'fibre,' your 'metal,' or your 'inherent truth.' While others describe it as your humanness and kindness. These are the essential qualities of being spirited, standing up for what you believe and going beyond your own comfort.

You were born with a strand of DNA comprised of two forces combining as one to create you. As life begins, so does your fabric, the essence of who you are. How or what you make of this continuous strand that is linking you from the past towards the future, is governed by your choices. Whilst fate provides challenges of a destiny, your early years are a journey to find you and your independence. How you relate to your life and its trials and adapt as a result, shows up in your life lessons and in capturing the wisdom of others, and this creates your own distinct character.

One's spirited health is often perceived as either a boundless energy waiting on a pursuit or curious questioning of the unknown and uncertain. Spirited individuals have a desire to explore and discover more from life, an edging towards and over their own boundary of what is possible. Nothing about their demeanour is staid or conservative. They exude an unquestioning thirst for what else life could be. Life for them is a gift, one which has at its very heart, a mystery for a spirited journey.

The journey of individuality is to overcome early patterns imprinted by others – by your parents, teachers, friends, community, technology and culture. They give you a template for your values and beliefs and this provides you with a framework for engaging the world around you. Your uniqueness or style, reflects your choices, how you wish to be seen, what you connect with and how you express 'you' as a distinct being. Your voice tone, fingerprints and mannerisms are more the physical you. Whereas, your attitude is shaped by your will-power which sustains your sense of what you stand for, your wilfulness which serves you to overcome obstacles, and your willingness to be open. This is your spirited self.

The journey of connectivity is heightened with the discovery of intimacy; a closeness to a loving relationship and its ultimate expression that is 'soul mates,' while also searching for the meaning behind one's purpose. Your spirited connections add substance and worth to life and the lifestyle you choose. This invariably goes beyond the more cognitive traits of performance, wealth, power and influence. Ultimately, it is about creating intimate relationships where your spiritual energy is a trusting exchange with someone up close and personal; a sharing premised on a give and take, to create a shared space of love and caring.

You have your own unique vibrations and together you create shared frequencies of being in tune with someone; families, friends and partners can share in this harmony. These energies are connected within a larger universe, a conscious sharing field, often referred to as the quantum field of all possibility. Science is now revealing the notion that we are not just individuals operating alone, but are a part of a larger set of frequencies sometimes called humanity or humaneness; that we care about the well-being of everyone; a larger inter-connected spirit.

Finding the unfolding of your potential in this lifetime relates to the journey of the spirit; its lifelong purpose, potential and promise. Some people follow a path of religion to explain the unknown, uncertain and unpredictable. Until explained, yours is to live within the grey areas and explore the substance of your very own character. Your own fabric has many qualities from smooth silkiness of kindness and fairness towards durability; a surge forward to weather life's storms. Stretched, pulled and battered for something better, for something enduring and worthwhile is the fabric of you being here.

The Spirited Realm is about having consciousness and awareness that goes beyond the self. It is a sense that there is a larger essence that exists between and beyond us. Aspects of humanity, kindness, and compassion show us that we are part of something greater than an individual life. To live a spirited life is to give credence to face the unknown and to accept a journey that goes beyond just living on 'terra firma.' Most would have a sense that we are connected as part of the human condition or consciousness. We feel and are moved by the plight of our fellow kind, usually felt and then expressed with notions of fairness, kindness and caring. Taking this a step further most of us have a spiritual side connected to something higher than just our daily life. It takes us towards belief in and acceptance of a larger force, purpose or design.

The spirited side of you that sits within you is expressed through your will, willingness and wilfulness. This shapes your energy, frequency and creates your own unique signature:

Will: equates to your purpose and promise to live life.

Willingness: equates to your openness and connections.

Wilfulness: equates to your struggle and challenges faced.

With each of our choices undertaken there are consequences, some intended, some not. The reverberations will create issues as one choice is rarely straight-forward, where a simple moment can unravel or undo one's life, a cruel accident or unfair loss being the most devastating to one's dreams and intentions.

Issues of imbalance to spiritual energy include:

1. Loneliness and a loveless life

2. Lacking purpose and worth

3. Giving life a 'go'

4. Inclusion and exclusion

5. Ageing, mortality and regret.

For some, connecting with the metaphysical energies requires openness to something larger than self and expanding the boundaries of what is real. Albert Einstein summed up the ideals of the spiritual realm as being the capacity to go beyond the self and experience being part of something larger and eternal. He saw measure of our promise and purpose being the extent to which we can obtain liberation from the self and embrace our compassion and humanity.

> 'We experience ourselves, our thoughts and feelings as something separate from the rest. A kind of optical delusion of consciousness. This delusion is a kind of prison for us, restricting us to our personal desires and to affection for a few persons nearest to us … The true value of a human being is determined by the measure and the sense in which they have obtained liberation from the self.'
>
> Albert Einstein, Nobel Laureate

Ways to live into our compassionate self could be as simple as extending the wealth of human kindness and little acts that brighten another's day. This could be shown in the form of giving others your 'benefit of the doubt,' 'goodwill' and 'generosity of your spirit.' Neuroscience tells us that when we are generous, caring and show compassion to ourselves and others, our brain rewards us with pleasure chemicals. This is referred to as the 'helper's high,' where that nature rewards us for kindness.

Doing acts of service or kind deeds speaks of an innate fellowship, what we refer to as human nature and kindness. At two distinct stages in our development cycle, this becomes more prevalent, almost a cornerstone of these stages.

Adolescence comes with an altruistic streak, a desire to assist those less fortunate than ourselves; and a tendency to be more idealistic, yet it is an important shaping part to differentiate self and to not make everything about you. Young people do offer some wondrous undying energy for the human condition. Sadly, most of their ideas gain little credence of support as being too large or idealistic and not immediately profitable.

Middle-age brings with it a larger civic contribution, a desire to give and to nurture those less fortunate, a community caring. For some, when their children leave home they still wish to care and do so by becoming involved in their local community. Lions, Rotary and charity groups look after those disadvantaged and may choose to contribute in some way shape or form. Others are more diverse in their caring approach and may wish to volunteer with animals, nature and the environment. Both are about expending energy and adding more to the larger dynamic, giving of themselves to create either a better experience or place. This energy signature is one of caring beyond themselves: a spirited verve where they participate.

The Spirited Realm seeks a daily woven thread of the following:

Consciousness	Having an awareness that transcends your physical reality and five senses. The brain is not the producer of consciousness, but is a receiver and processor.
Will and Willingness	Clarity about what you stand for, who you want to be, and engage with. Some of these aspects include dynamic energy, persistence, determination and purpose.
Connectedness	A feeling of belonging, a sense of affinity through having close relationships with a person, group, environment or energetic field to create connection.
Faith in the Unknown	Making sense of our lives and the many mysteries we face. An openness to the unexplained and unrevealed nature of life and that which cannot be readily reasoned.
Intuitive or Sixth Sense	Accessing extra-sensory ability to bring in information without using the five senses and then consciously managing this communication to create purpose and meaning.
Metaphysical World	Engaging with the exploration of reality and the nature of being, and in the idealistic sense, how such knowledge may benefit human life both individually and collectively.
Human Condition	Valuing characteristics essential to our human existence and development. Recognising compassion, benevolence and kindness as an evolved part of human nature.

Legacy, Create a Better Future for Others	Investing time and energy in the future for the next generation. Using delayed gratification, creating substance and meaning for future generations.
Mortality, Transcending	Coming to terms with, and achieving a state of comfort about the death of the physical body. Having appreciation of an existence beyond a physical level.
Your Promise	Making decisions based upon your dreams, hopes and musings, instead of wanting evidence, rationality or reality. Accessing your heart's intuitive guidance.

Our spirit is our expression and connection to a larger universal force that is part of every living being on this planet. It is our life force and subsequently our energy. When we are born, our spirit is open to creativity and moves across realms. At this point, anything is possible. Then, as we go through life, depending on our context, we are directed towards containing our spirit by conforming to cultural, familial and social norms and traditional beliefs.

A spirited life is about escaping your containments and being your exception. The way this happens is by challenging your restraints; going beyond the programming and trusting your spirit's guidance. Intuitive consultant Cyndi Dale, proposes that the spiritual truth that defines your purpose or destiny is really a belief. This belief is encoded into aspects of your being. If you access this core belief and only those beliefs that align with it, your psychic abilities and strengths will always reflect your highest and truest nature. She explains spirit as:

> 'Your core essence or self, that part of you that expresses a unique and well-defined spiritual truth. It's your job to express this truth through all that you do, in order to create more heaven on earth. This expression is your destiny … Your spirit, is always connected to the Divine, retains a pristine picture of destiny no matter what happens to the other parts of you.'

When we talk about spirit, and our sixth sense, this is a frequency beyond our five senses. The vibration travels too quickly to be readily perceived by our everyday senses. That is why we must access our psychic abilities. These are our extra sensory abilities to tune into higher and lower frequencies that already exist around us. Allowing ourselves an openness with what is already there requires a shift of mindset or what Einstein calls a 'leap in consciousness.' Our logical thinking offers little to develop these innate abilities. Rather than asking why, it requires us to be open to discover the viable solutions coming from our hunches. This frequency is already there, it exists only lacking our capacity to fine tune it. Once we match the frequency with what we wish as an experience, we can then move into its reality.

Your Spirited Fabric is a metaphor. It is a representation of the different aspects of the spirited side of you, that ability to push boundaries back, and to discover something different from reality. It is the spirited side of ourselves that desires to go beyond the confines of convention. When life presents extraordinary events, they challenge your spirit. It draws something else out of you a discovery of yourself, to find that extra something, a chance to lean into a different part of yourself.

The following eighteen spirited fabrics provide resources and strategies to assist you with the following questions:

> *How will you bring your spirit into the forefront of your world?*

> *When are you spirited? How are you being? What are you doing?*

> *When you are present, what shows up about your spirit?*

> *What makes you come fully alive and feeds your spirit?*

> *Lastly, what draws you out into life?*

Your spirited side exists and yearns for connection no matter how small or trivial it first might appear. At times, our spiritual energy is not clear-cut, it is subtle and full of nuance, unlike a physical pain or pleasure. Some would say it is a calling, others would say it is your tribe or others might talk in metaphysical terms of the supernatural.

Whatever it may be, it is real and an integral aspect of who we are. Some of us would argue it is the most significant and meaningful part of our life; parent, carer, provider, lover, all ask for more than putting our own needs first and foremost.

Humanity accepts all this no matter how small or insignificant one's contribution. Our collective energy speaks about us as a race and species. While we are the most indulgent and destructive of our planet's inhabitants, we are also much more and have the capacity for doing greater deeds. Yet for many, there is a lack of stewardship or a worthy cause to rally our energies pooled as an overwhelming force for doing good.

Governments and business leaders, invariably, have different agendas and fuel a world of 'woe is me' and run the paternal line of 'we know what is best for you,' but this is changing with transparency and we are becoming more aware of our own footprint, asking something more than just consumption and wastage of our resources.

> *I want you to get excited about who you are, what you are, what you have, and what can still be for you. I want to inspire you to see that you can go far beyond where you are right now.*

> Virginia Satir, Psychotherapist

Spiritual Fabric Strategies

The following eighteen strategies are useful to cope when your spirited self faces life's unknown mysteries and uncertainties. They nourish your natural verve and sway.

Spiritual Verve: describes an individual's life convictions, an inner drive, an intuitive urging; an imperative for life. Each of these relates to a journey of purpose and meaning to engage with living one's promise and worth.

Spiritual Sway: describes an individual's sense of faith, an acceptance of the unknown, something larger than life, an ethereal quality, an ethical and moral compass. Each of these aid in a collective connectedness and a lifetime pursuit of enlightenment.

These Spirited fabrics are the substance of what successful individuals use when exploring and discovering their spirited self. They are a calling, asking for something more than just living in the moment.

Fabric	Description of the Quality
1. Threads of Connectivity	Feeling part of something larger, overcoming isolation and loneliness. Connecting with the larger collective and spirit through prayer and putting goodwill into the world.
2. Threaded Dynamics	Connection with time passage, past, present and future. Recognising that we time travel. Using this ability to resourcefully go back and forth in time.
3. Silken Response	Finding and being in the flow with your truer nature and liking being authentically you. Seeking your true essence and character to reach your own natural frequency.
4. Satin Finish	Refining and improving what you are doing so you gain mastery. Continuing to grow and develop in the refinement of who you are, bringing through your quality essence.
5. Lacy Knit	Being sensual, warm and natural with others, a celebration of having a delicate and soft approach to living life. Balancing the hardness that can surround us.
6. Layered Textures	Embracing your whole character by exploring the layers of you – your values, substance and meanings which add depth. Aligning with values-based choices.
7. Embroidered Signature	Defining your identity, what makes you exceptional. Being acknowledged for your unique gifts and contributions and bringing these into the fore.
8. Cut of One's Cloth	Coming back towards your default when things get hard or tough, what you can be relied upon. Knowing where your spirit needs to reposition itself to be enlivened.
9. Rippling Movement	Increasing your awareness and response to external frequencies that can impact upon you and your energy. Harnessing the energies around you in a positive way.

10. Patch Working	Evolving and learning from others' journeys by asking questions and being inquisitive as a way of adding freshness and vitality to your life.
11. Cross Stitching	Accessing information from higher frequencies and subtle energy. Recognising and using your psychic abilities, gifts and talents to strengthen empathic skills.
12. Tailoring	Choosing an action that lifts your spirit when you are feeling overwhelmed and frayed by your circumstances. Feeling more connected with yourself.
13. Made to Measure	Maintaining your boundaries, knowing your fit and purpose. Not allowing people to drain your energy, or manipulate you, trusting your energy in letting you know.
14. Pleated Folds	Mirroring back other peoples' energy when they are in drama and stressed. Become a reflector and bounce the energy back onto them without taking it on board.
15. Off The Cuff	Connecting with your intuitive sense to explore and discover more from the moment. Paying attention with moments of spontaneity and following your joy.
16. Heart on Sleeve	Making an empathic connection towards other people. Being able to stay vulnerable within the moment and set limits on your own emotional state.
17. Coloured Threads	Knowing energy has colour and cultures interpret colour connections with different meanings. Distinctive colours cue the people you can connect with and for a reason.
18. Design Statements	Appreciating how your unique energy signature moves outwards and affects the mood around you. Your spirit influences the energies of others that you meet.

As mentioned at the beginning of this book – in our fast-paced modern world it is becoming more and more difficult to look after and nurture ourselves. Strategies have focused on the physical, cognitive and emotional, however equally important is the need to recognise and find time for the spiritual. It is the spiritual that seeks to honour the connection in our lives to something larger than ourselves.

1. Threads of Connectivity

A strategy designed to increase a sense of belonging.

Useful for: Overcoming isolation and loneliness.

Future proofing: 'How am I being part of something larger than life?'

This technique helps when you are feeling isolated, lonely or experiencing a lack of understanding with others. It will assist you in shifting your sense of separateness towards one of being more connected and open and considering the needs of others. Your own well-being is inextricably linked with the well-being of those around you.

How this strategy offers you an alternate coping approach

We can have the tendency to think of ourselves as separate. When we feel stressed and our negative thoughts get stronger, we can become more and more self-centred. Our inner world-view gets smaller and narrower. Dr. Craig Hassed, international mindfulness expert, says 'Unfortunately, the "me attitude" sacrifices our prosperity as well as our emotional and physical energy. This is of immense practical importance if we are to understand how intimately our individual and collective well-being are entwined.'

How do we create a sense of affinity when feeling alone? One way to connect with others is through prayer or spiritual intention. Whether you are religious or spiritual, prayer is a powerful way to expand our broader self-interest. Prayer comes in many forms. It can be a meditation, intention, structured verse, generosity of spirit or mindful positive thoughts that are directed towards someone else, or a larger consciousness. Dr. Larry Dossey, proponent of the healing power of prayer, cites that there are more than one hundred and thirty scientific studies showing that when someone adopts a loving, caring attitude to another living organism, human or not, that organism becomes healthier.

Teacher and peace activist Thich Nhat Hanh, says that when we send the energy of love and compassion towards another person, it doesn't matter if they know we are sending it. The important thing is that the energy is there and the heart of love is there and is being sent out into the world. When love and compassion are present in us and we send them outward then that is truly prayer. He emphasises that prayer can offer a beneficial way to reconnect with ourselves while satisfying the basic human need to make a connection with something larger than our everyday self.

This is how you can delight and enjoy its benefits

If there are times when you are in a negative spiral, a short prayer or intention may be the answer to regain your serenity. First, establish a relationship between yourself and the other you are praying for. Set your intention that you are making this connection. Become aware that you are connected, not separate. Second, be present in your body and mind and notice where your thoughts and feelings are in this moment. Third, visualise the person or people and send the intention that their suffering be relieved and ease be restored.

Another way is to set an intention and prayer to regain your sense of peace, strength and ease. Shut your eyes, take a few slow deep breaths and imagine a stream of white and golden light streaming down over the top of your head and around your body. Gently say 'May I be safe, May I trust the Divine flow, May I relax with ease.'

Poet Tosha Silver is renowned for her prayers of surrender and presence. From her years of teaching others to use the process of surrender she reflects 'People often say learning to surrender is easier said than done. And yes, they're right. The mind has to be retrained from its focus on pushing, grasping and fear. Sometimes Divine answers are immediate, sometimes you wait. But one way or another, you learn to trust that you will always be shown the Way.' In her popular prayer 'Change Me,' the final line 'I am Yours, you are Mine. We are one. All is Well,' is a reminder that we are not alone but connected on many levels.

This is how I optimise it and gain the most value from it

When I am feeling self-absorbed or over controlling with people or circumstances in my life I use prayer and intention. It dissolves the tight constrained boundary that I have set around myself, taking me towards a higher perspective. From this place, I regain acceptance for 'what is.' By coming back into my body and handing over what I am pushing or forcing to a larger presence, this serves in bringing me back into the present moment.

Where you can discover more

If you are interested in the healing power of prayer - *Prayer Is Good Medicine*, by Larry Dossey, explains ways to access the healing benefits of prayer.

Looking to have more trusting openness in your life then *Outrageous Openness: Letting the Divine Take the Lead* by Tosha Silver offers wisdom and fresh perspectives about life's big questions.

A Blessing

Blessed be the journey that has taken you so far along in your life. Blessed be the willingness and fortitude you have to face each day. And blessed be the goodness in you to want to rest on sacred ground.

Caroline Myss, Ph.D. Spiritual Teacher

2. Threaded Dynamics

A strategy designed to spiritually travel across time.

Useful for: Altering and reinterpreting one's perspectives and moods.

Future proofing: 'What else could be occurring out of my present awareness?'

This strategy provides ways to shift through time, back into the past, forward towards the future and even across into parallel realities. It is the realisation that you don't just live in the here and now. Your awareness is also connected with multiple frequencies and realities and you can travel across time to access the resources you need in this life.

How this strategy offers you an alternate coping approach

Engaging with the possibility of change is a powerful way to keep your openness available. Sometimes this can be hard to sustain as it may feel uncomfortable or uncertain. Going with more of the same may feel like an easier and safer way to live life. However, taking this path will most likely shrink your possibilities, in turn reducing your future. A willingness to be true to your spirited self means engaging with what could be different. An effective way to resource yourself is to move forward and back on your timeline. Both directions can assist you in being more resourceful and self-managing of your current circumstances.

This is how you can delight and enjoy its benefits

When leaning into the future, the strategy is called 'future pacing.' With notable events, such as a presentation, deadline, difficult conversation, our doubts and fears can become blown out of proportion. Issues and situations can appear and become 'larger than life.' Future pacing places you into the future after the event. Then you look back and see yourself on the other side of whatever is worrying you. Spend a moment to notice that the worry no longer exists afterwards, it is only before an event. Now, focus on how you will look and feel after you have achieved and gone through the event. Shift back and view yourself before the event. What can you offer and add to make it better and to ensure that you give of your best?

When collecting resources and experiences from the past, the strategy concentrates on shifting back in time. When faced with a challenge, go back and look at the last time you handled something similar. See how you successfully navigated it, coped and got through it. What resources are available to you from your past experiences that you can use now? How did you approach it? What were you feeling and saying about the situation and yourself? Who was around for your support? What advice can you give yourself to tackle your current situation? Now come back into the present with these resources.

When considering the potential impacts of the strategy, it is done by taking a sideways shift across into an alternative pathway or timeline. Here you can have more than one option, a fork in the road that you can determine for yourself. This can be done in two ways, either by taking a shift to the left, or, alternatively, shifting towards the right. On the left pathway, obtain all the things that could go wrong, these are your doubts, fears and worries. From this stance, you look at your reality through the lens of 'What If …' What if this happens, what if that happens, or this goes wrong? How will I cope? Being here, in this alternative path is about 'Doubting it could be.'

A shift on the right pathway is a different focus. This is where your wishes and dreams fall into place. From this stance you consider 'If Only …' It is where you are open to the possibility of your world being different. This is about a future in which you 'Dream it could be' and connect with the possibilities in this reality.

Typically, alternate paths tend be more negative than positive. We can become over absorbed by what could go wrong. This is the brain's inherent need for certainty and predictability. Both play a powerful role and have a significant impact on how you approach your future. The key is to flip into a positive parallel. If you could do this, how different would your world be?

This is how I optimise it and gain the most value from it

When I am faced with a situation that requires me to do something different and I'm either not skilled in that area or there is an elevated risk of failure, I use a technique called 'What If?' It involves creating three distinct images and placing them out into my personal space:

> The first image is *It is, with no repercussion, it just is.* This image is directly in front.

> The second image is *It could be doubt.* This image is on my left side. It represents my worst nightmare, of all the things that could go wrong. Where I can fail, look incompetent and lose face.

> The third image is *It could be a dream.* This image is on my right side and is my wildest outcome, it is beyond what I expected.

Then I step into each, noticing how it affects my stance, presence and sense of self. Before stepping back onto my original place, I decide on the three options in front of me. My choice is based on how I want my spirited self to show up, living fully.

Where you can discover more

Both the fields of Neuro Linguistic Programming (NLP) and Hypnosis discuss in some detail the process of time-lines and experiencing time distortions.

I could see the past, present and future all at the same time.

Nikola Tesla, Inventor and Futurist

3. Silken Response

A strategy designed to be authentic to self.

Useful for: Exploring the potential of your own character.

Future proofing: 'What else within needs to be liberated?'

A silken response is one that reflects your true nature and essence. It is a refined response which shimmers and ripples out with radiant luminosity. This strategy is about assisting you to reach your own natural frequency. It is designed to help you connect with what is authentically you, to embrace what is uniquely you, and to determine what belongs to other people.

How this strategy offers you an alternate coping approach

Everyone's frequency is inherently different and how we manage this variation creates disturbances within our own field of endeavour. Being aware of what is yours and what is another's is important to sustain self within relationships, rather than becoming lost or overwhelmed by another's will.

Finding what is authentic for you requires challenging both the content and boundaries of your world model and its reality. This includes your value judgements such as your preferences and prejudices (what you like and dislike), your 'deal maker' and 'deal breaker' values that act as tipping points when making decisions. The deal maker is what moves you towards life and the deal breaker is what moves you away. Is it possible to move beyond these boundaries? Typically, we don't question the edges of our world model or our frames of reference. Our point-of-view is part of a pattern that was established at an early age and became unconscious 'deal breaker' and 'deal maker' values.

Coming into what is authentically you can mean going against your natural reactions. Your spirit is being swayed as you travel through life. When you are weaving your future spirit, it is important to know the validity of your world model. Does it align with the essence of your true nature or is it a program you have picked up along the way? The spirited side of you is much more than a program or set of rules and beliefs. You have an option to push back, to discover something different, being plucky and spirited. Taking this approach will empower you to go beyond your confines and to take on conventions that may be constraining your natural flow.

This is how you can delight and enjoy its benefits

In Zen Buddhism the word *satori* means to awaken, the experience of seeing into one's true nature and essence. It is about acquiring a new point-of-view in the way you deal with life, a view that is empowering. The ability to let go of a fixed attitude and your frame of reference can serve to elevate your perceptions.

Most of us comply with our own conventions, often without knowing where they stem from. If you pause and choose to challenge, you may discover a new perspective. For example, notice your intention when you seek and take in information. Are you gathering information to feed and support your 'deal breaker' or 'deal maker' values, or do you want to explore them? How much are you aware of the choices you are making? What do your own language patterns tell you? What are you feeling about their impact on your spirit? Are you uplifting and enriching yourself or are you feeling constrained and contained by your frame of reference?

A silken response towards others is about supporting them in connecting more to their true nature and higher essence. In this context, your silken response is to find what is inherently behind someone else's intention and the value that drives them. Rather than listening to the words they place on the top layer of the conversation, listen for the deep layer i.e. what matters. Help them recover something; caress them into a new piece of information or way of perceiving themselves.

This is how I optimise it and gain the most value from it

Having a silken response can be a liberating experience. It begins for me by listening to and noticing the language patterns with others and myself. My endeavour is to pay close attention to the rules and judgements that sit inside my conversations with others, or within my internal dialogue. The next part is to challenge the unconscious program that is running and the underlying rules. Simple questions include: Who says? For who is this true? According to whom? Where does this come from? By whose rules should this occur? How is this useful?

Often, it is to realise that I have learned this program from what is acceptable in my family or from the culture I grew up in. It is an unconscious agreement about a way 'things are done around here.' The consequence of holding these rules and beliefs is that my model of the world can become out-dated. Defying this convention means that I can delete what is obsolete or inaccurate or expand my perspective by including some additional information.

Where you can discover more

Discovery of different fields of enlightenment and meditation are the basis to clear one's mind and then allow your character to come into the fore. Then it becomes a deepening process of self-discovery to liberate from old programming and expectations.

> *A silent velvet footstep filled me, unwelcome yet so needed. You finally found my hidden shore with grains of time and ocean of the most secret secrets, violet and red; left a trail of deep blue footsteps on my glowing beach of soul, and no matter how many times tides wash the golden sand anew, your prints can never be erased. Each one a shining star in my quiet Universe ...*

Oksana Rus, International Visual Artist

4. Satin Finish

A strategy designed for a sense of progress.

Useful for: Fine tuning your attitude and approach toward life.

Future proofing: 'What edges of my character need refinement?'

This strategy is about your elegance and grace, a journey of refinement of character. Whatever you are doing or becoming, you can always apply a finishing touch to your style for living life. A beautiful satin finish flows and shimmers, captures the light and attractiveness of its surface and exudes a hidden quality and depth. This is about a continual sense of fine tuning you and who you can become.

How this strategy offers you an alternate coping approach

The simple learning theory of cause and effect, along with conditioning, sets up a lot of our earlier responses and triggers. In our early stages of development, we learn a direct association between our behaviour and either reward or punishment. Typically, this is established based around cultural and family expectations, rules and preferences. How we show up in the world is modified as a way to fit in.

Sometimes, we need to undo poor habits before we can acquire our true talents. A simple early belief about trust can preclude someone from even considering trusting in their intuitive knowing. The same is true about your worth and more importantly, your contribution. Well wishes may not seem like much, but collectively they become a potent energetic force. What do you wish for your fellow kind?

We move in life from thinking about primarily ourselves towards caring for others and then the larger community and planet we live on. Adding the satin finish approach into your life, acknowledges that you have something worth offering and sharing with others. By continually refining 'you' and how you communicate your message will allow you to develop further and give a much-needed sense of progress.

A silken response of refinement taps into a 'quality' essence. You signal to yourself and the world your commitment to go that bit further. It is about a sustainable approach to life and a promise to further your personal growth and spiritual maturity. It becomes a form of life, a celebration of your good fortune.

This is how you can delight and enjoy its benefits

Satin finish appears more natural each time you do it. It is about taking something as far as you can go and improving each time by making small incremental changes and adjustments.

To enhance your character, focus on what you want to achieve or experience and then add a quality lens onto it. How can you polish this a little more each time you experience it? The focus is not to strive to make something perfect or to become perfect, as this will only create an inner angst, rather it is more about a flowing sense of evolvement. To take personal pride in how you connect with others and what you freely contribute and give back. The qualities of character to offer and add depth to your finishing touches lies with sharing a kind, compassionate or caring thought and touch, and by going out of your way towards being inclusive.

Although it might sound shallow, a surface polish, it is not the case. View a satin finish more as layering another level of caring on an expansive world. Such a soothing touch can only add spirited affection. Perhaps, in your journey to become more sustainable, you want to re-think, re-touch and re-surface your values about how you care about life, others and self.

This is how I optimise it and gain the most value from it

Probono Australia is a business with a social purpose mission. One of its contributions is *Volunteer Match* which is a platform where Not-for-Profit organisations can advertise opportunities that require a skilled volunteer. These opportunities can range from specific tasks such as book- keeping, graphic design or board positions, or guidance such as mentoring and business advice. Founder Karen Mahlab says 'Basically, we are a match-maker for people who want to help and organisations who need help. Nice isn't it?' If this interests you visit www.probonoaustralia.com.au/volunteer.

Not only does the sector benefit by accessing capability, the volunteers also benefit by their acts of service. Many studies have demonstrated that helping others kindles happiness. Researchers at the London School of Economics found that the more people volunteered the happier they were. Another study at Harvard School of Public Health identified that people who volunteered for more outward reasons – compassion for others – rather than self-interest 'I want to get away from my problems,' had a higher sense of purpose and better health.

Where you can discover more

Volunteering may be inspiring for you and a way to expand your character. There are many community groups and legions of silent volunteers who have a civic responsibility to care more about their larger surroundings. What is a worthy cause to you and a way of giving back beyond yourself? Find your own way to participate in a larger consciousness.

Be the author of your own life fully lived. And then claim who you are in all of your potency now.

Rebecca Campbell, Spiritual teacher

5. Lacy Knit

A strategy designed to find moments of being touched by life.

Useful for: Reducing the harsher realities from hardening your choices.

Future proofing: 'How can I ease another's day and ease up on myself?'

Lacy knit is a strategy where your natural qualities are constructed into a hefty weave. Its very essence is created by those moments that you find yourself touched by life. It is a celebration of a delicate and softer approach to life. What has moved you or called you towards acting outside of your normal routines? Sometimes it is a moment where you are incensed by the unjust or, at other times, by the act of a simple smile or decency received. These accumulated moments provide you with a structure for being kind, warm and natural, while still viewing the holes or gaps within your fabric. This delicate side allows you to counter-balance your inner qualities of strength and robustness.

How this strategy offers you an alternate coping approach

You don't want to become completely hardened by life's ups and downs. Living a life fully resolute, firm and staunch can be a hard life to live. This tendency will leave its mark upon you with a grimace of thin lips, steely eyes and tight energy. Most people pick holes in themselves and their failures and try to fill these up with victories or challenging successes. When drawing on these harder, robust abilities you are putting your body under tension. Your body is not designed to hold prolonged periods of tension while remaining healthy. You need the softening innate qualities for ease and recuperation. Constantly seek out the softer you and then balance out life with aspects of nurturing.

A gentler and kinder way is to embrace your vulnerabilities when faced with the unknown and uncertain. This acceptance allows others an opportunity to assist and care for you. How often do you allow others in? To what extent can you receive as well as give? How open are you to allow others the opportunity to enjoy giving to you?

Strong resilient people at times consider others worthier of care than themselves, as theirs is a life of sacrifice. A more sustainable strategy to contribute is when your spirit dances with a two-way connection, a give and take. In this way you both can share in the receiving and worthwhile feeling in giving something back. Be touching whilst allowing yourself to be touched by those who have a desire to share their appreciation and thanks.

This is how you can delight and enjoy its benefits

A simpler way is to be kind towards others. You can do this by seeing their vulnerabilities and giving them the benefit of the doubt and generosity of your spirit. It requires that you spend more energy looking at what is good and positive in someone than at what one thinks is bad or negative. When you engage with an open heart and mind, it forms a sensitive warmth that caresses others and allows them to soften their edges and take a breather. While there may be obvious flaws and 'holes in their weave,' they are still whole. Taking this approach, you consider that each person has a 'back story,' the part that sits in the past. Usually, we don't have access to someone's back story until there is a closer trust, as there is fear of judgement and perhaps feelings of shame.

At each of the developmental stages of life, we will all face different vulnerabilities. Some are easy to overcome, while some remain unfathomable, such as hormones or nutrient depletion as these mostly occur out of our conscious awareness. Simply put, sometimes people are not functioning at their best and they just need a helping hand or your generosity of spirit.

This is how I optimise it and gain the most value from it

My natural disposition is to be kind and generous. The implication being that at times I can be in situations where I find myself being taken for granted. Indeed this is a small price I am willing to pay, yet one I still have to manage. In these circumstances, I switch from lacy knit of a generous sensitivity onto the reverse side, a steely sensitivity made from a stronger mesh. This creates the energy and appearance that I am not weak or someone to be walked over. It also sends a signal, 'You may think you can manipulate me, but watch out! I'm not a weak person because I'm kind.' With this approach I can be steely with my personal resolve but not hard, harsh or lack caring because I might be hurt or manipulated. It requires knowing what is mine and what belongs to others and then being responsible for myself and my impact upon others.

Where you can discover more

For learning more about generosity of spirit *The Compassionate Life: Walking the Path of Kindness* by film director and author Marc Ian Barasch, explores the nature and practice of compassion towards others. He presents the argument that the driving force of our evolution is the survival of the kindest and simple shift in consciousness that can change everything.

And a building must be like a human being in its fabric
It must have a wholeness about it, something that is very important.

Minoru Yamasaki, Architect

6. Layered Textures

A strategy designed to find your truer purpose and promise.

Useful for: Gaining more from your potential.

Future proofing: 'How am I showing up and what do others see as my contribution?'

This strategy is about embracing the whole of your character, the essence of how you want to engage with the world. Your character is expressed through your traits, outlook and abilities. This is your substance. It is how you choose to show up in the world. The aim in life is to be aligned with your character. However, it requires you to update your authenticity. Has the world shifted and are you stuck?

How this strategy offers you an alternate coping approach

You are being shaped by the three powerful influences which speak to your values and need updating as you travel life's journey. The three Ps. The first 'P,' is for promise. This comprises your dreams, hopes and capabilities. Together they provide assurance to you and create an expectation of forthcoming satisfaction and goodness in the future. You may have created dreams and hopes early in life and are either still striving towards them or have not realised them because circumstances have changed. When losing sight and connection to your dreams, it becomes flattening to your spirit. Perhaps your dreams need updating. Maybe your hopes have taken a dive from one of life's challenges and need rekindling. Giving consideration in the moments of quiet reflection and pondering can show you what is important.

The second 'P,' is your potential. This is about giving voice to your hidden talents and unearthing the other aspects of you that have not been expressed or developed. It could be that in your early life your family saw you in a particular way that shaped the future you. Perhaps, you were called the 'smart one,' 'sporty one,' or 'creative one.' You may have been discouraged from doing what you loved such as dancing or acting because your parents thought you lacked the physical build or looks to make it on stage so you kept your love of acting close within your heart not telling anyone of your dream to be an actor. It wasn't until many years later you allowed yourself to step onto the stage and started using your voice and presence beautifully!

The third 'P,' is for Purpose, your reasons for what you do and be. It is your intention and motivation to the way you approach your life. Purpose can feel elusive. The message in 'find your purpose,' 'discover your calling,' 'live from your heart's desires' can be daunting, if you feel you have landed on it or you are still searching. The key is to focus on your heart and spirit, not the goal and outcome.

This is how you can delight and enjoy its benefits

Clarifying what you value will help you to embrace more of who you are. Your values are what matters for you in how you live life. They are your guiding principles for life, what you hold in high regard. They determine your priorities and they form the measure you use to determine if your life is turning out the way you want.

Values also change as you develop and grow. They will need a regular update for relevancy or a recharge to be sustainable. Some turn their values into a lifelong pursuit, say of happiness or caring. While others change them as they grow, shifting from more practical considerations such as providing healthy options towards growing their own produce.

For your three 'Ps,' time and energy will be your currency and your cost potential will be the other choices you have opted against in order to fulfil a spirited life. How you expend your energy and allot your time will avail you of different opportunities.

This is how I optimise it and gain the most value from it

Clarifying your three 'Ps' is a powerful way to find your own passionate verve and sway. I ask these questions regularly as a review of my life.

Promise – what are your hopes, dreams and musings? The timeframe could be – the next three years, the next decade, your 'golden years,' the second half of your life or whatever helps you towards generating a desirable future.

Potential – what do you want to develop, express and bring into the light? This could be using more of your strengths that give you joy and satisfaction. You may not actually be competent at them. However, when you are activating them, you feel a sense of fulfilment.

Purpose – what is your heart's desire? What is your most joyous and meaningful activity? What lifts your spirit and makes you feel alive and vibrant? What is your true vocation?

Where you can discover more

If you want your strengths and potential to be galvanised *Your Strengths Blueprint: How to be Engaged, Energized, and Happy at Work* by Michelle L. McQuaid and Erin Lawn shows ways to discover new and exciting pathways.

> *There is a vitality, a life force, an energy, a quickening that is translated through you into action, and because there is only one of you in all of time, this expression is unique. And if you block it, it will never exist through any other medium and it will be lost. The world will not have it.*

> Martha Graham, Choreographer

7. Embroidered Signature

A strategy designed to live your full potential.

Useful for: Overcoming self-doubt and becoming exceptional.

Future proofing: 'What else do I need to discover?

This strategy is about defining your identity and what makes you an exceptional human being. It invites you to be true to the essence of you and to fully own it. Being your own exception is about showing up in the fullness of your unique spirit. A myriad of intangible aspects and qualities make you exceptional. There is no-one else on the planet like you. You have been shaped by a combination of your genetics, energetic make-up, context and the results of daily choices made.

How this strategy offers you an alternate coping approach

Your embroidered signature is a recognisable and unique expression of your identity. For most of us, we live in cultures where people are hyper-aware of feeling a personal lack and not being enough.

We now have experts on everything who point out what we are not doing or should be doing more of to become a better person. This creates feelings of dissatisfaction, frustration and an incessant drive to find the missing piece and to get things sorted. This can manifest as a desire or yearning to become someone you are not, a sense of missing out and a feeling of not quite being there.

If you do not know who you are, then you are more likely to succumb and to conform to another's expectations of you. Knowing your true nature can give you autonomy to guide yourself from the inside out. Spiritual mentor Hiro Bogo calls this being the sovereign ruler of your life. Understand that your exception is a buffer against cultural and social expectations of how you should and need to be. It brings you back towards your core essence. From this place, it supports you to become more resilient and re-connected with what matters to you. Standing in her uniqueness and success Oprah Winfrey says:

> 'I sit here profitable, successful, by all definitions of the word. But what really, really, resonates deeply with me is that I *live a fantastic life*; *my inner life is really intact*. I live from the inside out. Everything I have, I have because I let it be fuelled by who I am and what I realize my contributions to the planet could be.'

This is how you can delight and enjoy its benefits

The starting place is to acknowledge the unique combination of strengths, gifts, talents and qualities that are distinctively you. The *VIA Character Survey* which identifies your character qualities and strengths or the *StrengthsFinder 2.0* by Gallup are assessments to identify your talents and capabilities.

Where in your life can you step up and bring into the world more of your innate gifts and strengths? What experiences in your life have shaped your substance and how can you build on this? What would happen if you were aligned with your purpose and values?

Then embrace and go with your differences, take pleasure in you and how you can offer a different take or perspective. Avoid being right or imposing your beliefs and opinions upon others, just smile and appreciate you as a contrast.

This is how I optimise it and gain the most value from it

I find myself going out of my way to find people from different walks of life, things I know little about or find strange and unusual to my own way of living. My curiosity wants to hear how each person has a story or a tale to be discovered. We all have a narrative ready to be shared if asked … my starting place is to show an interest in their choices taken and opportunities missed, not challenging them, just listening to the unfolding tale. Afterwards, in moments of reflection, I try and walk a mile in their shoes; what would I have done given their circumstances and without the aid of hindsight?

I highlight the many moments of delight in how my life would have been different if I had followed their path. The intention is not to compare where I could have done better. It is more about adding wisdom gained from their circumstances and restraints. I am left feeling mindful of the folly of not repeating another's mistakes and thankful of their learning which I can then share with others, making their choices a little easier.

Lastly, I sit and ponder in awe at their exceptions to the rule.

Where you can discover more

There is a plethora of self-help books or life coaches who can assist you to reach your potential for whatever your field of endeavour might be. A good starting place is to seek out those who already have years of experience in your interests and to simply ask if they would become a mentor to you.

You are the spark, the light … generate the flame from within you, this is who you are and can become.

Braco, Spiritual Healer

8. Cut of one's cloth

A strategy designed to fully know your inner strengths.

Useful for: Overcoming uncertainty and self-doubt.

Future proofing: 'What or who else can I draw upon to face this challenge?'

This strategy helps you to come back into your core strengths when life becomes tough and hard to handle. It focuses on identifying the default position for your spirit when you find yourself faced with life's ordeals. Extraordinary feats are borne out of necessity, some from survival and others from the reality that no one else can do it for you. The desire to push beyond the everyday trials requires spirit … what is yours when push comes to shove?

How this strategy offers you an alternate coping adaptive approach

Life can throw us some large obstacles mainly when we least expect them. It becomes about how we choose to engage with them or not. Larger than life incidences can come along and really test your resolve. It may be your health, wealth or a disaster that confronts you full on. When they come, it requires you to call upon your inner spirit to pick yourself up. It can draw something else out in you. You may find that these ordeals ask for something different, something else of you.

In January 2011, Queensland was experiencing massive flooding. The Premier at the time Anna Bligh showed the public another side of her character. Facing the media she was visibly shaken as she described the devastation and hardship that extended across the state. Close to tears she said 'We're the people that they breed tough, north of the border. We're the ones that they knock down and we get up again.' People hadn't seen that aspect of her before. The choice to show up as real and honest was powerful. Her courage in being open and letting herself be seen in all that she was ignited courage in others. Her vulnerability sounded like truth and felt strong. Her words and presence touched the spirit of the public to pick themselves up, and to draw deep on their own courage to face the difficulty.

This is how you can delight and enjoy its benefits

One way to find the default for your spirit is to consider the question 'What does your spirit crave?' It may be family connection, experiences, adventure, knowledge, learning, being of service, quality time with close friends or discovery. If your spirit is not being nourished you may feel a yearning for it. For one of my friends his default is loyalty towards his friends this is what he draws on when life gets tough.

Another way to find what your spirited self needs is to think about your overall life satisfaction. Ask yourself two questions 'What is the most satisfying thing that happened yesterday?' and 'What is the most satisfying experience of your life?' What do you notice about your answers? For most people the answers are quite dissimilar.

Typically, the first one is about achievement of an outcome, a positive interaction or doing something pleasurable. The second one has a different tone. Often this experience is about a life challenge that people have faced and overcome. It required them to draw their strength and grit to cope and adapt. Typically most feel tremendous satisfaction having made it through the experience.

This is how I optimise it and gain the most value from it

When facing a struggle, I take myself all the way down into my feelings and notice what is present and what is clamouring for attention. Invariably what is there is a need to find some stability through solving or managing the experience. When up against a difficult situation I know my strength sits within my will-power. Whether it be a willingness for something or a wilful response in nature, it just is and knows what I need to surge forward rather than becoming a victim of circumstance. Wilfulness means my approach to stand up and fight for something important, a spirited verve. Willingness means it is time to learn something completely new and ask me to move forwards and grow from this experience – a spirited sway.

Where you can discover more

Find stories of adversity and moments in history that depict extraordinary and compelling human endeavour.

Biographies of people that I admire are an enthralling source of inspiration; the chance to read about how others have lived life. Similarly listening to podcasts of 'In-conversation' with Richard Fidler on the Australian radio station ABC draw you deeper into the life story of someone you may, or may not have heard about. Usually this is someone who has seen and done amazing things.

Anita Morjani in *Dying to be Me* describes the journey of her near-death-experience and spontaneous remission from cancer. She explains 'Illness is a wake-up call telling me that I am living a life that is not mine so … what can I do for creating a life that *is* mine and live a life of passion?' Coming back into her body she made the choice to live a life that she is passionate about. She says 'The biggest determining factor in my health is my reason for living. What is my reason for being? Am I following my passion? Do I feel I have a purpose?'

Life doesn't give you much, but for the ones who want to learn, life teaches them how to be strong before they start living their lives instead of just existing within this world.

Auliq Ice, Singer and Songwriter

167

9. Rippling Movement

A strategy designed to appreciate external energies.

Useful for: Comprehending larger forces at play and their effects.

Future proofing: 'How can I fully harness the energy around me?'

This strategy is about increasing your awareness and response towards external frequencies that can impact upon your energy. Rippling around you are the frequencies of your external environment such as the solar energies emanating from the sun, the shifts in seasons and nature's cycles. Being aware of these vibrations can help you to support your energy and to keep mood and spirits high.

How this strategy offers you an alternate coping approach

The sun has a major impact upon our energy fields in multiple ways. Whether it is solar flares that explode on the sun and interact with the earth's magnetic field, the reduction in sunlight during autumn and winter or the shifts in temperature; the sun is a major external influence upon us.

Research has shown that over a 2,500-year period, elevated solar flare activity is correlated with increases in political unrest and upheaval. During peak activity it has been connected at an individual level with increased anxiety, depression and bipolar activity. Solar flares have been shown to upset our 'circadian rhythm,' the twenty-four-hour biological clock. In turn, this affects the pineal gland in the brain which governs the balance of melatonin (the sleep hormone) in our bodies and the sleep cycle. We end up feeling like we have jet-lag, yet haven't left home.

During the shift in the seasons, the sudden change in the amount of sunlight can also disrupt your sleep cycle and energy. Studies by the Mayo Clinic discovered that decreased sun exposure is associated with drops in serotonin, a hormone that is associated with boosting mood and helping you feel calm and focused. Decreases in serotonin can lead to Seasonal Affective Disorder (SAD) a form of depression that is triggered by changing seasons. It is more likely you could experience SAD in autumn and winter when the days are shorter and the nights longer.

The sun not only governs your sleep clock it also strengthens your Vitamin D levels. In autumn the lack of sunlight and being outdoors can deplete your Vitamin D stores which in turn creates fatigue.

Weather affects our body temperature. Warm weather promotes blood circulation. In the cooler weather you may find you experience fatigue because your circulation is not flowing as easily.

This is how you can delight and enjoy its benefits

In the winter and autumn months the key is to find ways to boost Vitamin D and exposure to light. One way is to find a warm protected spot in your garden, outdoor area or nearby park where you can sit in the sun for ten minutes a day and have the warmth on your face. This will boost your serotonin and Vitamin D levels. If daylight is limited, an alternative is to purchase a colour light therapy unit that you can use at home. These phototherapy devices are popular in Scandinavia where there is often only four hours of light a day.

When the weather is clear, rug up and go outside. Walk in nature, if you can. Research has shown that living in cities and being bombarded with constant noise and vibration is leading to increased stress levels and health problems. A ninety-minute walk in nature has been shown to slow the activity in the brain responsible for rumination and unhelpful self-reflection. Recent studies found that short micro-breaks spent looking at nature has a renewing effect on the brain and can help to counteract the unbalancing effects of sun activity and seasonal shifts.

This is how I optimise it and gain the most value from it

I am aware of my body's sensitivity towards the world around it. This means paying attention to how my body and energy is showing up and responding accordingly. Sometimes this means having a sleep or rest during the day or getting into bed early and having more sleep during the winter months. Moving in the colder months means being proactive when my preference is to stay warm and snuggly inside. This involves heading to the gym when it is raining, walking when it is clear and doing stretches and Tai Chi. Exercise is a great way to jump start the brain's production of powerful brain chemicals such as serotonin, dopamine and norepinephrine which are geared to shift our mood by creating a calmer focus.

Where you can discover more

As a way into exploring the benefits of light therapy for health visit Bioptron Light Systems which offer a clinically tested and certified light therapy system to fight SAD.

If you are interested in planetary and sun activity Astrologer, Elizabeth Peru based in Adelaide, Australia (www.elizabethperu.com) offers regular updates called 'Tip Off.'

> *We are all one Energy Stream, but what makes the separations or distinguishes the differences is perspective. You are a unique and individual perspective.*

> Abraham-Hicks, Group of Spiritual Beings

10. Patch Working

A strategy designed to enliven your spirit.

Useful for: Modelling what works.

Future proofing: 'Are there better ways of doing this?'

This strategy is useful to become more vital in your life. Initially it involves identifying people who you admire and their qualities that touch your very essence. Then, with each person pursue the 'how to' that sits behind what they do and how they show up in their lives. Ask and share these attributes along with their experiences, which serve to provide proven patterns of success. From here, you can instil what works from their approach into your own approach and outlook to enrich your spirited life. Over time you can combine these distinct aspects to create a larger design, expand your perspective and change tastes within the fabric of your own life.

How this strategy offers you an alternate coping and adaptive approach

Funnily enough giving 'self-permission' is one of the quickest ways to ignite your spirit. We all have rules and responsibilities about how we should be living life if we are to be clever with our wealth, equating this to our overall worth. What if there were a wealth of other resources available to enrich not only your material success but your spiritual wealth?

Modelling is the capacity to obtain both the 'what' and the 'how' of successful living. This involves asking questions and identifying the strategy that is being used and the sequence to achieve the desired or best result.

What if you could access another's wisdom about the way they live a spirited life? What would you want to know and how much would this accentuate your future? This practice involves learning *how* others are doing what they do. What is it about how they are thinking, feeling and acting that enables them to do it successfully? It is based on modelling the strategies of others to create a more fulfilling life.

There is no prize for you to re-invent the wheel. Most people have faced similar issues. There is no need for you to have all the answers or resources. What you do need is to access your resourcefulness to find them. Approach and chat with people. Listen to their stories and different aspects of what works and from this variety of sources build your own form of success.

This is how you can delight and enjoy its benefits

An easier way to do this is to become very curious and start asking questions of all you meet. If you are open and inquisitive you will discover 'gold.' These conversations will broaden your perspective and change your thinking and will offer you suggestions as to alternative ways for proceeding in your life. By being aware of a better way you can then take the path to change what you could do or become.

Review and make observations of your conversations by asking questions. How are they sensitive towards others or how do they take charge of their own energy? What gives them the capacity to be open-hearted, kind and compassionate? What makes someone happy and have a productive and healthy life? How does someone pick themselves up when they are lying face down after a failure or heart-break? How does someone hold onto a sense of purpose and retain hope in the face of life's challenges? How do they retain a sense of humour? What lights their fire? What is in their essence where they can do this?

This is how I optimise it and gain the most value from it

As a modeller I am fascinated by the 'how to': how someone knows what they do. We can see this implicit wisdom with most who are living a spirited life and they are generally unable to explain a natural talent or they don't see what they do as anything other than normal. For most people, it is simple and usually a single precursor which invariably says 'why not?' tapping into the adventurous side of one's spirit.

My mother loves playing bridge. Most of her bridge friends are in their 80s and 90s. Being younger than them I asked 'What advice they would give me about living my life.' Collectively, there was over three hundred years of experience sitting at the table enjoying their pastime. They unanimously said 'Don't put anything off. Do all the things that require you being active. Live your life today!' As a result I have booked a trip to visit the sacred sites I have yearned to see. It no longer became a decision based on the where or why, it just was what my spirit needed.

Where you can discover more

The Secrets of Being Happy by Richard Bandler and Garner Thomson is about taking control of your mind and your life so you can do more of what you want.

Jiyo (www.jiyo.com) is a comprehensive digital platform for well-being that lets you engage, learn, and interact with a diverse range of information, articles, videos and reminders that help you be your best self.

> *Your past may have gotten you where you are, but it is more knowledge and*
> *different strategies that will create a new and compelling future.*
>
> Richard Bandler, Trainer and Author

11. Cross Stitching

A strategy designed to find your intuitive gifts.

Useful for: Strengthening one's empathic skills.

Future proofing: 'What else can I notice from my surroundings?'

This strategy helps you appreciate your own subtle abilities, gifts and talents. Just as we have specific abilities and strengths in the physical world, so too, we have these in the energetic realm. We are all psychic which means we pick up and send off information that is hard to measure. The option is to understand what and how our specific gifts work. In this way we become intentional and develop them in a conscious way rather than being at their mercy.

How this strategy offers you an alternate coping approach

While we have no grasp on our subtle abilities we are not anticipating the information that comes towards us. To develop competence and confidence with our gifts gives us more choice in how we respond.

There are three common subtle abilities: clairvoyance, clairaudience and clairsentience. They can become reliable tools for everyday living as they provide access to information not available through our five senses.

Clairvoyance is the spiritual gift of clear seeing, the ability to see subtle energy. Individuals with this talent see colours, patterns and symbols in energy fields of others usually in the mind's eye. Clairaudience is the spiritual gift of clear hearing, the flair to hear things outside the normal scope of auditory awareness. Individuals with this ability hear messages internally. This may come in the form of words, phrases, music or sounds. Clairsentience is the spiritual gift of clear sensing, to feel the emotional states of others (past, present and future) without using the normal five senses. Individuals with this ability can feel energy that includes other people's feelings, inanimate objects and places. It can trigger emotional reactions and physical sensations within the body.

This is how you can delight and enjoy its benefits

Fundamental to develop these three abilities is having the awareness to recognise and not dismiss subtle information that comes your way.

Opening up your clairvoyance begins with paying attention to the signs which may come as visions in the form of pictures and movies, flashing subtly in your awareness. They may also show up as vivid dreams that foreshadow events. Accessing your inner clairvoyance begins by releasing any fears about seeing the future. Carefully word a question so it truly meets your needs. For example 'Will I meet my next romantic partner at the workshop tomorrow?' is stronger than 'Will I meet someone at the workshop tomorrow?' Now focus on your 'third eye' which is the area between your two eyebrows and breathe. This is a subtle energy centre which supplies psychic images. Notice any pictures that enter your mind. These could appear as a single image or movie. If you are unsure what these images mean ask either mentally or aloud 'What do these pictures mean?' You will receive an answer as a feeling, thought or sound. Sometimes it doesn't come immediately wait for a while. Trust what you see.

When developing your clairaudience try using automatic writing as it can be a fun activity. Get some blank paper and a pen. Settle somewhere quiet. Set a timer for five minutes. Open your intention towards connecting with your higher guidance. Put your pen to paper and start writing whatever comes into your mind. While tempting, do not filter the information just keep writing. You may find that it becomes hard to keep up with what is coming through; it can be downloaded very rapidly. When the time is up read what has come through. What messages are there for you?

To develop your clairsentience, shift your awareness into the changes in your energy and sensations in your body. Have you ever felt fabulous and walked into a space or connected with someone and started feeling off? More than likely you have picked up on the energy, mood or sensations of another. A quick way is to ask yourself 'Is this mine or is it someone else's?' If it is not yours the energy will start to lift and you will feel lighter. If you are continuing to feel burdened say 'Return this to sender.' Gently place your awareness on how your energy frees up and becomes lighter.

This is how I optimise it and gain the most value from it

I use all three abilities in my daily life. Regarding my clairvoyance I pay close attention to the visual images that come into my awareness. This could be a movie of what could happen or information about someone I care about. In my coaching practice I often receive downloads either as images or words that could be relevant to my clients. I will share what I am receiving and ask what is relevant to them? With my clairaudience I hear psychic information. My friend Shelley and I communicate telepathically. I will hear her voice in my head and will pick up the phone to call her. She laughs because she invariably was just thinking of me. With my clairsentience I am very conscious of the feelings and sensations I pick up. Managing my empathic boundaries is important as a way so as not to become energetically drained.

Where you can discover more

To learn more about your intuitive gifts Cyndi Dale has a questionnaire in *The Intuition Guidebook*. It will give you a score on each of your distinct intuitive abilities, identify your subtle gifts and provide more explanation on how to develop them.

> *Open a window to your soul. You will see so much more beauty in the world and will wonder why you missed seeing it in the past.*

> Richard Webster, Psychic

12. Tailoring

A strategy designed to lift your spirits.

Useful for: Connecting more with your inner self.

Future proofing: 'What else can I tune into that might be useful?'

This strategy assists you to handle feelings of being overwhelmed. It is for those times when there is not one piece in your life where you are feeling in flow. This approach will help you to let some pressure off so you are not feeling frayed and stretched by your circumstances. It will offer a variety of ways to restore and renew your frequency and will leave you feeling more connected to your spirited self. This process includes finding a space that is for you or if needed clearing a space so the energy feels more uplifted and clearer.

How this strategy offers you an alternate coping approach

Having all aspects of your life stretched does not work does it? What tends to happen is that sooner rather than later the fabric of you will start ripping or tearing because it is never allowed to relax. If the weave of a cloth is under pressure for too long it gets bent out of shape and frays. The same happens to your energy when it is stretched and pulled. When feeling overwhelmed you need one facet of your life suited to you. This works to reduce some of the intensity and pressure as it gives you a place to gain some respite. Finding some breathing space can enable you to better handle the other remaining aspects that are pulling at you.

This is how you can delight and enjoy its benefits

Make a point to find time in your day that is yours alone. This is where you choose something that lifts your spirit. Find options that are not expensive. These are little ways that ultimately when you do them you are absorbed in the pleasure rather than being stretched or pulled.

These breathing spaces could be having 'friend time,' a coffee, chat or hug with a friend. At night when the house is quiet it could be 'pamper-time:' a bath when you can soak and settle or ask your partner for a back massage. Sometimes it is choosing something fun that gives you joy such as having your nails done. Maybe it's 'moving time,' put on your active gear and go out for a jog, walk the dog, do pilates or yoga. For some people it is entertainment or 'chill-out time' to watch their favourite team play or sit in front of a fire on a winter's night, or to watch a movie.

When the energy in your home or office has become taut or frayed and needs to be more measured then clearing the space is a quick way to shift stuff and to lift your spirits.

This can be done simply by using a sage smudging stick or diffusing essential oils. Sage is helpful to clear yourself, others and spaces that have dense energy. Essential oils like cedarwood, lavender and frankincense are useful to purify and uplift the energy around you.

Another effective way to lift your spirits is to have plants in your home. Not only do they brighten up any space they remove chemicals in the environment. *Peace Lily* removes air pollutants. *Areca Pam* converts a lot of carbon dioxide into oxygen during the daytime to give a lift. A good one for the bedroom is *Mother-in-Law's Tongue* which converts carbon dioxide to oxygen at night.

This is how I optimise it and gain the most value from it

I find at least one time each day where I connect with my spirit through an uplifting experience. This could be going out for a delicious breakfast at my favourite whole-foods cafe, having coffee with a friend, listening and moving to upbeat music, going for a walk, or lying on the grass in the summer and soaking up the rays. All are simple ways to find a time of the day that belongs to me.

To keep the energy light and flowing in my office, home and personal space I employ different crystals. Not only are crystals beautiful art-forms they radiate different energetic vibrations. I choose them for distinct purposes. In my office I use selenite, as it is a very high frequency crystal and is best where clear-thinking is needed. It is known as the 'mental clarity' stone and enhances mental flexibility and decision-making.

In the bedroom I have rose quartz and amethyst. Rose quartz is a pink variety of quartz and is often called the stone of 'universal love' or the 'friendship stone.' Its frequency opens the heart chakra and serves to promote love, self-love, friendship and feelings of peace. Amethyst is named the 'spiritual' stone as it has a very high frequency. With calming and meditative qualities, it promotes a sense of calm, balance and peace.

Where you can discover more

To seek ways to give yourself a lift *50 Simple Ways to Pamper Yourself* by Stephanie Tourles offers suggestions to relieve stress, promote relaxation and to beautify every part of the body.

There are many books and resources available about crystals and practical techniques to use them for healing and harmony for your body, spirit and home.

> *Don't give up now. Chances are your best kiss, your hardest*
> *laugh, and your greatest day are still yet to come.*
>
> Atticus, Poet

13. Made to Measure

A strategy designed to maintain your spiritual boundaries.

Useful for: Not allowing others to drain your energy.

Future proofing: 'What else can my energy allow me to do and explore?'

This strategy is about your energetic boundaries. They are guidelines or limits that you create. They are useful to identify what are reasonable, safe ways to regulate the flow of intuitive information inside you and from outside yourself. These borders are a way for you to pay attention to messages and energies from the subtle realms. At the same time they protect you from harmful energies, information and sources.

How this strategy offers you an alternate coping approach

You have a light body that surrounds your physical body and extends beyond the body to interact with our external environment. It is a protective atmosphere that envelops you and keeps your body and mind alive and healthy. It is a natural boundary that filters out many of the energies you come across, and pulls in other energy that you need. The best-known energy body is the aura which consists of layers of light that manage the energy outside your physical body.

Energy medicine pioneer Donna Eden explains, 'The health of your aura reflects the health of your body; the health of your body reflects the health of your aura.' Have you noticed that when you are happy, joyful and light, it is as though your energy fills the entire room. The opposite is true when you are sad, lonely and despondent your energy crashes in on you.

Maintaining and enhancing our energy boundaries is an essential aspect of health, personal integrity and energetic strength. Boundaries that are soft, spongy or rigid are a sure way to cause energy leakage. A person with soft boundaries merges with the boundaries of others, making them disposed towards being manipulated. A person with spongy boundaries is unsure of what is let in and what stays out. They are prone to being overwhelmed by other people's negative energy. In contrast, a person with rigid boundaries is closed or walled off to others and energetically contracted.

This is how you can delight and enjoy its benefits

This technique can be used when you are feeling closed in by too many intruding energies. Slowly open your palms and face them slightly away from your body. If you can feel into the energy against your hands and imagine that you are pushing it away from your body. You can add a colour into the energy like gold or white as this is very protective. If you go slowly enough you may feel the pressure of your energy field as you push on it. Try applying this practice in the times when you are having difficulty claiming your space in the world or are feeling sad, small or squashed.

Alternatively, you can imagine yourself surrounded by energy in the shape of an egg-shell – this is called your 'aura.' Exhale slowly, push it away from you with your hands, begin about five centimetres from your body and out about an arm's length. Try feeling for any energetic resistance, force or tingling against your hands. Moving the energy out from your body will give you more breathing room, energetically and emotionally.

This is how I optimise it and gain the most value from it

Energetically, I can notice when my aura is overloaded with external energies or other people's energetic hooks, usually created by emotions and dramas. Part of my practice for energy hygiene, is to regularly use a learned technique from the medium James Van Praagh while attending one of his workshops at *Celebrate Your Life* in Phoenix, USA. It is called *Psychic Vacuum Cleaner* and is used to suck up energy that does not belong in my energy field. If you would like to try this technique it is easy and fun.

First, imagine your version of the psychic vacuum cleaner – its shape, colour and size (mine is shiny rose gold). Next, place your attention on the area around your body, about an arm's length. Using your awareness allow your intuitive sense to pick up any area where it feels heavy, dull, dark, blocked or dense. Doing this is easier than you think if you keep your critical mind out of the way. Direct the vacuum cleaner there and visualise it sucking up these lower frequency energies. If you are frustrated that you are not seeing it just make the intention that it is happening and it is done. Once captured inside the vacuum cleaner these unwanted energies are converted into gold particles. Then imagine the vacuum cleaner opening and sending the converted gold sparkles back out into the universe.

Where you can discover more

If you seek more ways to protect your energy, in the book *The Empath's Survival Guide* Psychiatrist and Empath Dr. Judith Orloff shares ways to nurture your empathy skills and how to protect yourself from individuals who exude negative energy that drains you when you are in their presence.

In the book, *Energy Medicine: How to Use Your Body's Energies for Optimum Health and Vitality*, healer and teacher, Donna Eden shares ways to take care of your energy and to keep your aura strong and healthy.

Remember, it's your own body, your own brain. You're not a victim of the universe, you are the universe.

Richard Bandler, Author and Trainer in self-help

14. Pleated Folds

A strategy designed to deal with unpleasant dramas.

Useful for: Finding what is the reason behind another's stressful energy.

Future proofing: 'What has to be here for this to be so?'

This strategy is about dealing with the push and pull of other people's energies. It shows you ways to go beneath what appears on the surface of someone's energy pattern and to find the source of unfolding drama. Like the pleated folds of a curtain we do not always notice what is folded behind the curtain or sits within the pleat. Initially, we may not know what is going on with someone's energy. In dealing with what we find pleasant or unpleasant there is a natural tendency to personalise the experience. This technique takes the personal interpretation away and treats energy as energy, rather than positive or negative. In doing so, you can mirror it back onto the person and be less affected and influenced by it.

How this strategy offers you an alternate coping approach

If you are constantly connecting to other people's energies it can become very tiring, so you probably don't want to be doing this all the time. By marking out what is yours and not yours more often you can hold your own equilibrium. This helps to keep your own spirit alive in stressful or tense situations.

If most of the energy you come across is 'stress energy,' it will involve someone else's ego. Typically these individuals are picking up the available energy to use in driving what they are want. If you do nothing to protect yourself then you are passive and they will more than likely take your energy. If you avoid them they have achieved a powerful position before they have even begun engaging with you. Either way they use your energy to achieve their purpose.

In tense and emotionally charged situations most often people capitulate with unwelcome demands. A different approach involves getting into rapport with the energy and not the person. This way you can de-personalise enough as a way to create emotional distance. Once you have created some space you can make choices about how you want to engage.

This is how you can delight and enjoy its benefits

The technique to create energetic space is called 'mirroring.' It involves becoming a reflector and reversing the energy back to the person. Whatever is coming to you or around you, be like a mirror so you can come towards it, curve it off and bounce it off.

For example, when you first meet the charged energy there will be a palpable tension. It could be experienced as a strong push back or resistance or be a pulling sensation. Using a mirror metaphor, the mirror doesn't take what is coming towards it but instead it will bounce the energy back. Once you become aware of the tension de-personalise from it. The way to do this is by using your own personal space as a shield. Ask 'What is going on here?' rather than 'What did I do wrong?' or 'How can I solve it and make it better?'

Intuitive Psychiatrist Dr. Judith Orloff talks about the importance of holding our centre rather than getting caught up in energetic dramas. She proposes:

> 'We have two choices when things pile up at work or we're surrounded by energy vampires who leave us feeling depleted. We can get frantic, hyperventilate, shut down, and become reactive. Needless to say, these responses to stress just make us more stressed. Surrendered people have the ability to pause, take a deep breath, and observe. Sustaining silence and circumspection are two behaviours that lead to better, healthier outcomes.'

By taking the 'I' out of the interpretation you can create some space and relieve yourself of the need to take responsibility for fixing it. Just like the mirror what you experience at the surface level is what you reflect back to them. Curve it off, bounce it off, move it away. Rather than wasting energy avoiding it, just reflect it.

This is how I optimise it and gain the most value from it

I practice de-personalising myself with energies that are not compelling. Forceful energies are not beautiful energies. The first thing I do is to notice my body reaction and internal dialogue – what am I saying on the inside? Usually my energy contracts and pulls in. If I can catch it quickly enough I can put my reaction off to the side and get back in touch with my own spirit.

If the energy is pushing me away or pulling me away I make a choice. It is about my willingness to engage with this energy. If it is not an energy I want to dwell in I deflect it off myself and reflect this back onto the person. For example, if someone is tense, stressed and charging with energy I will use mirroring and 'call' their state of being and say 'You're appearing stressed. You're not making your best decisions while you are in this state. What can you do right now to move yourself into a more resourceful state?'

Where you can discover more

Both the fields of NLP and Hypnosis offer information and training in mirroring and matching as techniques to gain and then improve rapport.

In *Dodging Energy Vampires: An Empath's Guide to Evading Relationships that Drain You and Restoring Your Health and Power*, Dr. Christiane Northrup shares strategies for taking care of your energy and warding off unwanted energies.

> *How people treat you is their karma; how you react is yours.*
>
> Wayne Dyer, Philosopher

15. Off the Cuff

A strategy designed to harness your intuitive vibrations.

Useful for: Seeking out spontaneous moments of joy.

Future proofing: 'I am curious about knowing what else I can enjoy today?'

This technique explores your spontaneous and intuitive vibe. It is not something that you can create or plan because that, in and of itself (*planned spontaneity*) would be an oxymoron. Rather, it is to avail yourself of those moments when you notice something different and then actively go with it and see where it takes you. Fascination and joy, invariably occur within the moment, when something captures or captivates our senses. The unexpected sparkles our spirit for it offers something different, a distraction which is informative or asks a question we had not even considered.

How this strategy offers you an alternate coping approach

Place yourself in new situations or different experiences as it fuels these two spirited aspects of yourself; intuitive spontaneity. You invite it in by stepping outside your character or its norm. In doing so you give yourself permission to go with life's flow without over-thinking it as a judgement – either good or bad. It is a gentler way to allow yourself to follow, and more importantly, to trust in your spirit, your intuition.

Spiritual teacher Gregg Braden explains that with intuitive experiences in our lives we discover two universal themes relating to our impulse to connect: first it is generally not a conscious thought; and second it happens spontaneously when we least expect it.

Have you ever had the impulse to call a friend and she says 'I was just thinking about you!' No surprise that your telepathic communication is working well. The key to our intuition is to notice when it appears and if needed to take some action. It can happen so fast, like a flickering signal in the energy field. If we are not in the present moment it can slip past us.

In these spontaneous moments there is freedom from meaning and a need to understand 'why.' There is so much of daily life which is about being measured or having logical reasons to follow. In a creative and spontaneous flow, it is about being open to where the energy takes you. Here you most likely will find your joy because you have stepped outside of yourself. It is not about expectations and being overly concerned about what people think of you. This is an opportunity to show more aspects of yourself. You are more than an automaton that runs off a set of programs. You can go beyond the expectations of others and live your own moments.

This is how you can delight and enjoy its benefits

As you go through your day, practice detecting your impulses, hunches, hints, knowingness, or 'gut' feelings. This is your intuitive intelligence in action. Your awareness is spontaneously tuning in and sending you information about unconscious opportunities.

For instance, when someone pops into your thoughts or you pick up a feeling about a friend honour that feeling by reaching out. Observe what is present when you make contact. Another way is to quietly say the things that pop into your mind without a need to search for why. You may ponder a question and hear a song on the radio and the lyrics grab your attention and give you an answer. Feel when you are being pulled towards a certain place that doesn't make sense. Go anyway and see what happens. Trust when you are being pushed from something or someone, rather than rationalising or giving yourself a hard time. Instead follow the flow, back away and notice how you feel.

This is how I optimise it and gain the most value from it

I talk to strangers! I actually approach them and start a conversation. For me this can happen anywhere – in a lift, getting on or off an aircraft, standing in a queue, shopping, walking down the street or travelling into unfamiliar places. I follow my spontaneity to make a connection and in those micro moments magic happens. Everyone has an interesting story and to listen to others invites something different into my world.

I also enjoy people watching! This can happen in any public space but usually happens in airports because I spend a lot of time there. It is interesting to pick up on peoples' idiosyncrasies as they go about their day. My curiosity is naturally drawn towards people who are different from me, particularly those who have a quirkiness about them. This pastime transports me spontaneously beyond my own world and into someone else's story.

Where you can discover more

Trust your Vibes by Sonia Choquette offers ways to train your attention and awareness so you can pick up on your intuitive vibes and gather information from them.

Intuitive by Craigh Wilson shows ways to access, develop and trust your intuition.

> *Our physical senses give us feet and keep us earthbound, while our sixth sense gives us wings and teaches us to soar.*

> Sonia Choquette, Intuitive

16. Heart on Sleeve

A strategy designed to make empathic connection.

Useful for: Staying vulnerable within the moment.

Future proofing: 'What else outside of my immediate surrounds do I need to track?'

This strategy is about living with an empathic essence of vulnerability, being open enough to engage and then reduce another's issues. Empathy involves grasping what an experience means for them, rather than ourselves. It is the ability to entail and openly extend what you are feeling as a person, while distinguishing what is yours and not yours. It is having the sensitivity to discern being present with the other person not becoming caught up in their feelings and losing touch with your own.

How this strategy offers you an alternate coping approach

Social connection is as important to us emotionally as water is to our physical body. We have a universal need to interact, be connected and have experiences of caring for others. Studies by Social Psychologist Roy Baumeister found that to belong is a crucial component of emotional health. We have a need to feel closely connected with others and to care, along with affectionate bonds that come from close relationships which are a major part of our spirited fabric.

In our brains we have mirror neurons which enable us to duplicate the emotional or sensory state of another's mind and body. What is happening in someone else gets transferred onto us as if we are having the same experience. We feel what they feel. Our capacity for empathy is innate and wired into our social brains. When we pay attention to someone else, and put our 'heart on our sleeve' we activate empathy and compassion. It is a key part of fostering loving relationships with others. If we personalise it as most do we lose our capacity to be present with another. In doing so we get caught up in their feelings while simultaneously losing touch with our own.

Empathy is to be in-tune and then to subtly shift someone's state for the better so they can then best resource themselves. Your energetic response affects those around you so rather than you becoming overwhelmed, step back and assist them to do likewise.

Holding your judgement is about tuning into what the story means for you and how you feel about it. Notice if you find yourself having a reaction. If you are, more than likely, you have been taken into the energy of the experience. Rather than getting swept up in the groundswell of the emotion and the circumstance, take a breath and quietly detach yourself. Sometimes, however this can be difficult particularly if there are strong emotions present such as loss, grief and anger as these can create powerful surges of energy.

This is how you can delight and enjoy its benefits

The key to being 'empathically open' is to differentiate what belongs with you and what belongs with another. This includes your thoughts, perceptions, sensations, feelings and any other awareness that is there for you. Holding a space for someone's vulnerability is the ability to be present with their thoughts, emotions and direct experiences without personalising it or relating it through your own filter or life experience. It is imperative that you manage their energies so your own feelings don't swing backwards and forwards.

One of the hooks that will move you away from empathy is to personalise what is happening to the other person and to turn it into your own story. This can happen suddenly and can cause you to lose your reality thereby creating changes in your emotional state. For example, if someone is telling you a story and you burst into tears, it is no longer about being open with them as you have brought your reaction into it. The skill is to gently untether your internal responses to another's story. Otherwise you could have the tendency to put your own baggage onto the situation.

This is how I optimise it and gain the most value from it

When hooked into a story I remind myself 'This is not about me,' and respect the other person's process and degree of emotional expression. This helps me separate my emotions from the other person. When someone is vulnerable I pay attention with how my presence makes their processing easier. Being empathically open requires the ability to step outside my past and future, to stay present and to send compassion towards the other person. I have become more aware of when I shift from empathy and compassion into either sympathy or pity. This is a sign that I have become embroiled within someone else's emotions and can leave me wiped out.

Intuitive healer Cyndi Dale suggests a way to figure out whether you are receiving empathic information or manipulative empathy is to notice the quality of the information that you are receiving. Empathic information will come from outside you and has a tone that is dissimilar with that of your own thoughts, feelings and sensations. Manipulative empathy will draw you into fixing the problem (pity) getting caught in the emotion or personalising it by concentrating only on your own reactions.

Where you can discover more

To learn more about energetic empathy *The Spiritual Power of Empathy* by Cyndi Dale describes that we each have empathic gifts and the key to develop them is knowing which ones you have. The book has a questionnaire on intuitive gifts.

Empathy is about standing in someone else's shoes, feeling his or her heart, seeing with his or her eyes. Not only is empathy hard to outsource and automate, but it makes the world a better place.

Daniel Pink, Author

17. Coloured Threads

A strategy designed to make intuitive connections.

Useful for: Reading energy and accepting difference.

Future proofing: 'What surrounding vibration do I need for myself?'

This strategy focuses on your relationships and belonging at a soul level and uses energy in the form of coloured threads to make and sustain these connections. The emphasis is to perceive energy in the form of colours and then create your own colour palette that suits you. It starts out by identifying the colours you are drawn towards and that you love. Then, go into the world with the intention to find more of those colours. Attached to the colour will be the people you are looking for and hopefully you will be able to make a connection with them. It is about knowing the colour you are taking out with you (your 'true colours') and seeking the same in the world.

How this strategy offers you an alternate coping approach

Across cultures and mythology there are different ways to describe how we are threaded to each other with a certain knowing of having met someone before.

In Chinese culture the colour red corresponds to the element of fire and symbolises good fortune and joy. An Ancient Chinese myth says the Gods have tied a red thread around every one of our ankles and attached it onto all the people whose lives we are destined to touch. This thread may stretch or tangle but it will never break – it has been pre-destined. Greek mythology describes a golden thread that is a guiding light and symbol of inspiration. When we recognise and follow this strand of gold it connects us to our true selves – our 'beloveds' and deepens a sense of belonging.

Understanding that there is a pattern behind the weave of our significant relationships can not only help us to function in healthier ways, it can be used to find those connections, bonds and clues for future friendships.

This is how you can delight and enjoy its benefits

Colour is one of the biggest descriptions of energy. Distinct colours resonate with different vibrations on a wave spectrum. Violet has the shortest wavelength and the highest frequency of the visible colours of light. In contrast, red has the longest wavelength and the lowest frequency of the visible colours of light. The range of shortest to longest wavelengths are: violet, indigo, blue, cyan, green, yellow, orange and red.

Understanding your own colours, the ones you resonate energetically with can be part of your intuitive guidance. Colouring your world and building a colour palette that works for you can be a cue to find your soul tribe. At a spirited level, it is a coloured thread that represents people we easily connect with.

When you meet someone who you instantly click with or feel like you have known before give this connection a colour, say gold, one which for you describes the energy you have together. Repeat this process with everyone you meet colour-coding their energy. Now you know what colours you may need to connect with or avoid depending upon your own energy needs. Also, keep seeking out different shades or variations by finding different colourful energies. Remember these are the basis of your dynamic. Notice how they differ with different contexts such as the differences between work, pastimes and family events.

If you love the colour of 'rose gold' go out into the world and search for rose gold 'threads.' Start looking and connecting with others who also enjoy this. Through meeting them you will discover more about what you are unconsciously connecting to. By exploring how they view this same colour it will give you a nuance of difference, enabling you to expand your colour palette.

This is how I optimise it and gain the most value from it

Quirky people fascinate me with their ability to appear at ease with their own uniqueness. They are not fazed by another's judgements or in following acceptable ways of fitting in. When I come across this self-actualising energy pattern it appears with a purple hue, some more mottled with pinkish hues depending upon the strength of their eccentricity.

After a while, most people I meet will tend to self-sort onto my colour palette. Of course a context or mood might alter their initial energetic colouring, but on closer inspection their deeper intent shines through. Unless they go through a significant life change watching these energetic shifts are colourful expressions.

As an energetic healer I have with experience correlated some of these surface colours and attributed them to either maladies they might face or moods they find themselves caught within. Common ones include being stressed, sadness, grief, boredom, playfulness and curiosity. Some appear as whole colours while most appear more transient with spots, splotches, streaks and speckles overlaying their true vibrational colours.

Where you can discover more

The Colour Healing Manual: The Complete Colour Therapy Programme Revised Edition by Pauline Wills describes the healing properties of colour and light that have been recognised since ancient times.

> *Friendship ... is born at the moment when one man says to another*
> *'What! You too? I thought that no one but myself could be ...'*

C. S. Lewis, Poet

18. Design Statements

A strategy designed to read another's energy or graceful ability to be intimate.

Useful for: Observing intention and contribution.

Future proofing: 'How do they contribute and add further to our shared dynamic?'

This strategy is about reading other people's energy and making decisions about when and how you engage with it. It includes being clear on the quality of energy exchange you are wanting to experience in your life. We are energetic beings and our energy emanates in such a way that it can either add or detract from a shared space. We perceive this sensation as a tangible ambience or atmosphere one which can profoundly influence us by dampening or inspiring our own internal charge.

How this strategy offers you an alternate coping approach

Some individuals readily give more, while others just take, drawing us down, resulting in weariness, sucking the life out of an interplay. While this is appropriate at times, when supporting another, some just know of no other way, other than using your energy to pick themselves up at your expense.

Quietly observe both their behaviours and input in your interactions. How do they leave you feeling? Is there an exchange of energy and do your relationships rise above the sum of your shared contribution? If someone needs a therapist recommend one. Notice what they contain within their personal space and how are they flowing with themselves before engaging.

Their energy can be seen by those who have the ability to see subtle energy. As mentioned previously it is called an aura, your personal field of energy that surrounds your body. Its function is to protect you and be an interplay between your physical body and lighter energetic body. Most of us can be aware of its effects even if we do not see its radiant colours. Stay with non-verbal cues, notice the pace and direction of their gestures and posture. Observe the communication and then colour code differences as a starting point to see their energy. We know when we are in the presence of someone who has a sublime grace or a major drama. Gather and build different insights into their mood and state.

This is how you can delight and enjoy its benefits

Giving someone the 'benefit of the doubt' would state that their desire to drain you of your energy is not a conscious one, rather it is more a habit of filling up their own energy needs. However this type of situation is probably one in which evoking your protection is necessary. You can deliberately conserve your own energy by containing it within your personal space. When someone reaches out and connects with you the shift will be felt in your own space. What is their intention? Are they connecting to share with you or to bolster their own need? How does their energy add or detract from you?

In dynamic relationships there is usually a profound respect to leave the other a better person from your interaction. See if and what it takes to make them glow or resonate in vibration. Notice if they are really interested in you and your well-being or just talking about themselves. If they are interested invite them in with questions about something you can both share in – a joint discovery, pastime or adventure. Energy dynamism takes on difference not in a need to prove, but in a curious, learning way.

When we become closer friends, we tend towards an open intimacy that is vulnerably shared almost knowing what the others are thinking and feeling before they can disclose and share. It is in this state of being fully open that we can energetically leave our physical form and any of its woes behind. Moments of transcendence occur within great conversations, where time disappears and you are left positively altered by your exchange. I call this energetic state 'love.' Not an in-love process, more one of a respectful gratitude for sharing in another's take on the world. How would it be to have more of these moments repeated in your life?

This is how I optimise it and gain the most value from it

For me, the best exchanges are those filled with a dynamic exchange of energy, a synergistic connection of caring and intrigue. I have developed my intuitive sight sufficiently and can see their energy as colours. My own learning has driven me towards seeking a balance. Pain and hurt are more obvious and give a strong pull for connection. However, I am missing out on their joyful play. When someone pointed this out to me, rather than directing my empathic abilities to just care by wrapping them in a caress, I could also energise myself from relishing their moments of happiness and pleasure.

Over time I have noticed when discussing certain topics our energetic colours will co-mingle or seemingly dance to a combined delight. I have put this down to 'moments of being touched and touching acceptance.' Three things add to this spirited dance: our intentions of goodwill, generosity of spirit and giving the benefit of our doubt. Combined, they work to reduce any judgements and offer a welcome acceptance of any differences we might have.

For me a spirited life is about tapping into your own spirit and those of others who playfully wish to share and discover.

Where you can discover more

Hands of Light by Barbara Brennan presents an in-depth study of the human energy field for people seeking happiness, health and their full potential.

> *My heart is so small it's almost invisible.*
> *How can you place such big sorrows and joys in it?*
> *'Look, He answered, your eyes are even smaller, yet they behold the world.'*

Jalaluddin Mevlana Rumi, Poet

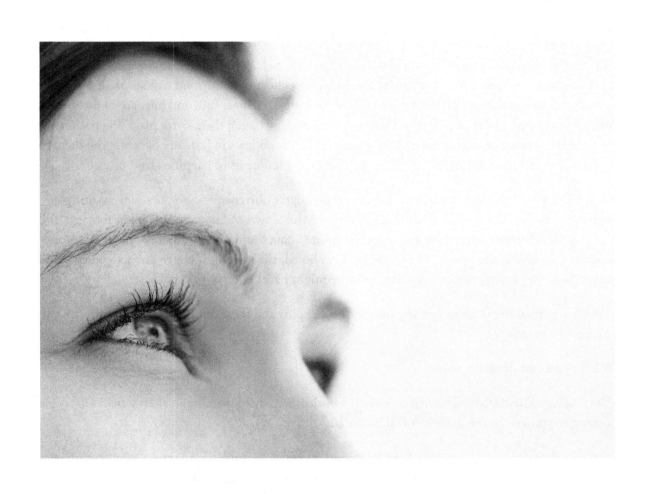

CHAPTER SIX

A spirited Way – own your exception

Yet the ancients know something which we seem to have forgotten. All means prove but a blunt instrument if they have not behind them a living spirit.

Albert Einstein

My purpose in writing this book is to offer you a range of strategies so you can re-shape and enhance your essential energy to live a spirited life. Over the years I have been fortunate enough to meet and engage with some charming characters who care about serving something larger. They view life as an accumulation of what is useful to ease suffering and to progress possibility. For them, each life is a living gift – one unravelled as a shared joy.

Finding Your Exception

Being your exception is about living into your character's breadth and depth. It is about finding your personal difference, your energy signature that describes 'Who you are.' Your energy configuration in the world has vibrancy that resonates a unique harmonic. It is what makes you exceptional. Finding your exception will give you gravitas and confidence to own who you are, from the inside out. Living fully this way becomes the intimate dance found nestled between your passionate verve expressed and your gentler sway caressed. Accepting who you are and being kinder with who you could become.

However, more and more we are subtly asked to blend in and follow the crowd where difference is frowned upon and not celebrated. All too often we can stereotype and 'box' people as this or that which can reduce and deny them the chance to live authentically. We now even sort and dismiss by referring to generations as X, Y, Z and millennials rather than focusing on how they are showing up in this lifetime with their distinctiveness. Acceptance and approval has the tendency to reduce what matters within our relationships. Being authentic with yourself is significant to stand out, yet we also enjoy being liked. Rather than just agreeing as a way of compliance, this can be readily achieved by offering a contribution, no matter how small. This is your exception in action.

You are 'Who you are.' In every facet of your life you are an exception, there is no one like you with your genetics, relationships, attitude and the choices you make. When you start combining all these differences your uniqueness grows exponentially. Knowing what makes you different is the key to find your joy, where you best relate both in the world (passionate verve) and with whom (your intimate sway).

Within each of the energy strategies you will find a connection point with your energetic spirit, your own unique expression. Some of them have been focused on how you get your own self out of the way so you can achieve your own exception. By this, I mean overcoming a lifetime of programs, habits and beliefs that have conditioned in you a response in certain unconscious ways often to the detriment of your own spirit.

Ask yourself the following question:

Are you living the life you wish, one that ensures the opportunity to have daily joy?

It only takes a single moment of joy to make a day enjoyable, and yes, there are many sound reasons for you not to do so. Most of these you are tired of hearing yet you still find yourself adhering to them. That is part of our challenge of being human. Risk, change and ego can get in the way of becoming you. The truism 'Life is short,' and 'You only have this lifetime once,' and 'You are always counting towards your life's last breath.' What will your last breath be? A wanted contented sigh or an exasperated regret? None of us know what it will be, but we do have a choice with all our intervening breaths. As with the breathing strategies within this book, sitting still and altering one's breath can affect your being, a simple yet wondrous state change, available to you whenever you wish. Every life change or risk ever taken started out with a first step and a single breath, one which can alter your mind's clarity, your emotional state and physical attitude to awaken your dreams.

How do you wish to show up and be recognised and loved for who you are?

There is no single way or solution as it depends upon your unique configuration. How many times have you heard 'Take this, do this, this is the solution, the research says this is the answer to the problem.' And then, the science discovers that is no longer true and a new truth emerges.

This book is about connecting you with your unique energy signature. By knowing your own frequency, you will attract and be attracted to similar frequencies, what some might describe as chemistry. After finding the 'what' of your dreams it is then 'how' you show up and 'where' most excuses line up and thwart your dreams. As you consider the following questions what sparks of insights are there for you?

How do I embrace and live fully my exception?

How do I live my joy?

How do I give more spirit to fully living my life?

Not all the answers for these questions readily exist in the now. Sometimes it requires a deep self-belief in your exception and then a leap of faith to just start. A single breath and step are all you need and then to be open enough to receive your answers already waiting on you to show up and discover them in the future.

What does it mean to live a spirited life?

I'm a generalist, deeply fascinated by so many aspects of life. My journey has been to discover how to live and flourish as an intuitive, taking pleasure in my frequency and energy signature. More importantly, my passage has been based around how I activate fully my own exception; by living my promise with a willingness to breathe in fully and then to embrace joyful difference. Some days, achieving this is more difficult than others when it all seems to flow. Yet I keep going, telling myself that tomorrow is another day and another re-take.

The challenge for me has been to live a resourceful and self-directed life. The more I have moved away from my spirit, the harder it has been for me to do this for myself. I would look for outside guidance and direction. While this has been useful at times, I have found it can be mis-directing in attempting to find my spirited self. For many years I have found a usefulness from the self-help movement but also realised that I needed to take charge of my own energy. While it has provided a path of reassurance, at times, I became more self-absorbed and meaning focused. Those of us who walk along this path have been asking comparable questions, 'How can I be my best self?' 'How can I fix the gaps that make me less than?' 'What can I improve and develop so I can be a better me?' 'How can I live a more meaningful life?' There is no guarantee that we can find the ready-made answers or a nifty solution, but for me I have been fortunate to find like-minded people who have assisted with my journey of personal discovery.

As spirited beings we are not separate, we exist in an interconnected dynamic field. We are human beings having a spiritual existence on this earthly plane. Dr. Lisa Rankin calls the spirit, the Divine spark in each of us. She says 'Your Inner Pilot Light is that ever-radiant, always-sparkly, 100% authentic, totally effervescent spark that lies at the core of you. Call it your essential self, your divine spark, your Christ consciousness, your Buddha nature, your higher self, your soul, your wise self, your intuition, or your inner healer.'

Living a spirited life is the journey to follow your joy, not to fix yourself. It invites you to follow the spark within you, to support others in being their authentic selves, honouring what connects us and what is unique. Cyndi Dale explains the spirit as, 'Your core-essence or self, that part of you that expresses a unique and well-defined spiritual truth.' She further states:

'It's your job to express this truth through all that you do, in order to create more heaven on earth. This expression is your destiny … Your spirit, is always connected to the Divine, retains a pristine picture of destiny no matter what happens to the other parts of you.'

For many of us this can be the simple truth of 'self-acceptance,' 'self-worth' and having a strong sense of purpose: What we are put on this earth to 'do,' and more importantly 'be,' for the short time we are here.

Our spirit is an expression and connection with something larger, that universal force that is part of every living thing on this planet. It is our life-force, our energy. When we are born our spirit starts out open and creative to move across realms. At this point anything is possible. Then as we go through life, depending on our context, we are taught to contain our spirit, conform to cultural expectations, common sense, familial and social norms. A spirited life means to escape your constraints and to become your exception.

This happens by challenging your limitations and releasing restricting programs and patterns. For example, running a strong approval pattern in your life can suffocate your spirited self. While as social beings living and working together we need a sensitivity to others and the ability to get along. An extended need for approval leads towards increased anxiety by basing our self-worth on another's approval.

The other way is to follow your spirited energy. What opens you up, lifts you, gives joy and offers a deep sense of connection to yourself and the larger collective on this planet?

Paying attention to the yearning of your body, heart and spirit is a useful guide as your logical mind often doesn't have all the answers. What are you creating and stepping into for the next chapter of your life? Where are your desires and the whispers from your spirit wanting an exploration and different experiences? Where do you wish for change in your life? Within this book the strategies can assist you to challenge limitations, and to strengthen your resolve and bolster your energy so you can be your exceptional self.

My own onward passage, a personal reflection, awaiting discovery …

My present developmental challenge is a spirited transition towards mid-life and growing older, a transition faced by us all. For parents it is a time when your children are moving into an adult life, going to university, leaving home, travelling overseas or getting their first job. It can also be a time when elderly parents are down-sizing into a smaller home or care facility. Often these life changes can come in clusters. What are your turning points?

In the Western world, with high divorce rates, many of us find that we are single and have not re-married. My women friends who have dedicated themselves to provide a comforting nest for their children in their thirties, forties and early fifties while running their businesses or careers, are now in a life transition towards the second half of their lives. During the first part of their lives at times there was little room or energy left to have a social life, let alone to find a new relationship. Now with an empty nest, they are facing the reality of dating and re-engaging in a broader social life. Those friends who have stayed married are looking at their relationship and asking whether they want to spend the second half of their life with their partner or not. It's a bit daunting.

While I am not able to speak as clearly for men, what do we, as women, want? Personally, I wish to feel loved, passionate, empowered, valued, wanted, safe and relevant; all the things promised by having the secure home, marriage, career and lifestyle. Many of us have expended vast amounts of energy on this family nest and now we must think about the next forty years without it and the emergence of our second nest. While it is important to plan for a future life that has sufficient security to feel safe it can also be a trap. It puts pressure on us and we end up feeling fearful that we lack and do not have enough to live. We are getting out of one nest and straight into the second nest without really considering what else is possible for a meaningful life.

The promise of our golden years is proving to be elusive as many women must work and save for retirement, thus creating more choices. At present in Australia the average superannuation payment for women is a third of the payment for men. It is the 'go-olden years' that women worry about. Will there be enough money? Will I be able to take care of myself? The research shows that for many women most of the time it's lonely and they spend a substantial proportion of their time worrying about their families, parents and own future. Neuropsychologist Dr. Mario Martinez offers sound advice for living a spirited life. From his studies of longevity the power rests with stepping out of the cultural portal called 'ageing' to defy the norms and beliefs of what it means to grow older. This means choosing a life that suits us, not what society deems as appropriate, conventional or safe.

For many women, menopause is a pattern interruption, a change-maker as hormones shift which lead towards changes in the body and brain. It can be a physically and emotionally challenging time with hot flashes, weight gain and low energy. If we help our body through this massive adjustment with herbs, diet and bioidentical hormones it opens us up towards engaging psychologically with opportunities of a new way of being.

In talking about menopause, Dr. Christiane Northrup explains it as:

> 'A natural transition in a woman's life. We're meant to begin life anew around the biological markers of our last menstrual cycle. Our bodies know it, even if our minds don't.'

Even if we are not paying attention, the awareness of our dreams and desires to make changes can sneak up. Christiane offers the advice 'Pay attention with this yearning and its subsequent questions "What am I going to create for the next chapter of my life? What am I changing into or becoming if I wish?"'

For those of you on the journey in the second half of your life I'm walking beside you in my endeavour to live a spirited life. I have noticed that my spirit is guiding me towards becoming more present with my vulnerability and owning my intuition and wisdom. The learning is not to second-guess myself, rather to trust in this inherent knowing. The other shift is to take larger steps into the world with an inner courage and boldness to live life without the constraint of fear – owning my exception. I wholeheartedly wish the same for you.

For those of you in the first half of your life, the strategies contained within this book offer you a way to embrace your exception earlier and not to wait with impatience for the second half of your life. You, my spirited friends, can fully do it now!

My energetic inner voice whispers its encouragement …

*Exhale your past fully breathing in your future promise, all the way in, expanding
your lungs and inner courage to take the first step to live a spirited life.*

*An eye is meant to see things.
The soul is here for its own joy.
A head has one use: For loving a true love.
Feet: To chase after.
Love is for vanishing into the sky. The mind,
for learning what humans have done and tried to do.
Mysteries are not to be solved: The eye goes blind
when it only wants to see why.*

Jalaluddin Mevlana Rumi

BIBLIOGRAPHY / RESOURCES

Books/Publications

Aggarwal, B. & Yost, D., *Healing Spices: How to Use 50 Everyday and Exotic Spices to Boost Health and Beat Disease,* Sterling Publishing Company, 2011.

Bandler, Dr. R., Thomson, G., *The Secrets of Being Happy: The Technology of Hope, Health, and Harmony,* IM Press, 2011.

Benson, H., *The Relaxation Response,* New York, Harper Collins Publishers, 2011.

Benson, H and Proctor, W., *The Science and Genetics of Mind Body Healing,* New York, Scribner 2010.

Blackburn, E. and Elissa, E., *The Telomere Effect: A Revolutionary Approach to Living Younger, Healthier, Longer,* Kindle.

Braden, G., *Human by Design: From Evolution by Chance to Transformation by Choice,* (Hay House, Kindle, 2017).

Brennan, B., *Hands of Light,* United Kingdom, Hay House, 1994.

Breuning, L., *Habits of a Happy Brain: Retrain Your Brain to Boost Your Serotonin, Dopamine, Oxytocin and Endorphin Levels,* Kindle, 2015.

Brown, B., *Rising Strong,* Vermillon, London, Kindle 2015.

Brown, B., *Braving the Wilderness: The Quest for True Belonging and the Courage to Stand Alone,* Ebury Digital, Kindle, 2017.

Byrne, R., *The Magic,* Simon & Schuster, USA, 2012.

Childre, D. & Rozman, D., *Transforming Anxiety: The HeartMath® Solution for Overcoming Fear and Worry,* New Harbinger Publications, Inc. Oakland, CA, 2006.

Childre, D. & Rozman, D., *Transforming Anger: The HeartMath® Solution for Letting Go of Rage, Frustration and Irritation,* New Harbinger Publications, Inc. Oakland, CA, 2003.

Chopra, D., &R E., Tanzi. *The Healing Self: A Revolutionary New Plan to Supercharge Your Immunity and Stay Well For Life,* Ebury Digital, Kindle, 2018.

Choquette, S., *Trust your Vibes: Secret Tools for Six-Sensory Living,* Hay House Inc., USA 2004.

Clifford, A., *A Little Handbook of Shinrin-Yoku,* Conari Press, USA, 2018.

Cooke, C., *Find Your Inner Gold: A Gold Medal Paralympian's secrets to Success,* Carol Cooke, USA, 2017.

Cuddy, A., *Presence: Bringing Your Boldest Self to Your Biggest Challenges,* Little, Brown and Company, 2015.

Dalai Lama, Tutu, D. & Abrams, D., *The Book of Joy,* Cornerstone, Great Britain, 2016.

Dale, C., *The Intuition Guidebook: How to Safely and Wisely Use Your Sixth Sense,* Deeper Well Publishing, 2011.

Dale, C., *The Spiritual Power of Empathy: Develop Your Intuitive Gifts for Compassionate Connection,* Llewellyn Publications, USA, 2014.

Davidji, *Secrets of Meditation: A Practical Guide to Inner Peace and Personal Transformation,* Hay House, United Kingdom, 2012.

Davidson, R. & Begley, S., *The Emotional Life of Your Brain: How Its Unique Patterns Affect the Way You Think, Feel and Live – and How You Can Change them,* Penguin Group, Kindle, 2012.

Dean, C., The *Magnesium Miracle: Discover the Missing Link to Total Health,* Penguin, Patnam Inc., USA, 2017.

Dennis, R., *And Breathe: The complete guide to conscious breathing – the key to health, well-being and happiness,* Orion Publishing Co., Great Britain, 2016.

Dispenza, Dr. J., *Evolve Your Brain: The Science of Changing Your Mind,* Health Communications Inc., Deerfield Beach, Florida, 2008.

Dispenza, Dr. J., *Breaking the Habit of Being Yourself: How to Lose Your Mind and Create a New One,* Hay House Inc., USA, 2012.

Dossey, L., *Prayer Is Good Medicine,* Harper, San Francisco, USA, 1997.

Dweck, C.S., *Mindset: The New Psychology of Success,* Random House, USA, 2008.

Eden, D., *Energy Medicine: How to Use Your Body's Energies for Optimum Health and Vitality,* Little Brown Book Group, USA, 2009.

Emmons, R., *Thanks!* Houghton Mifflan, USA, 2008.

Emoto, M., *The Healing Power of Water,* Hay House Inc., USA, 2007.

Epstein, G., *Healing visualizations: Creating health through imagery,* Bantam New Age Books, USA, Kindle, 1989.

Esfahani Smith, E., *The Power of Meaning: The True Route to Happiness.* Ebury Publishing, Great Britain, 2018.

Feinstein, D., Eden, D. & Craig, G., *The Promise of Energy Psychology: Revolutionary Tools for Dramatic Personal Change,* Tarcher Jeremy Publishers, USA, 2005.

Field, T., *Touch,* M.I.T Press, USA, 2014.

Fraser, A., *The Third Space: Using Life's Little Transitions to find Balance and Happiness,* Random House, Australia, 2012.

Frederickson, B., *Positivity: Top-Notch Research Reveals the Upward Spiral That Will Change Your Life,* Three Rivers Press, USA, 2009

Fredrickson, B., *Love 2.0: Creating Happiness and Health in Moments of Connection,* Penguin Putnam Inc., USA, Kindle, 2013.

Gerber, R., *Vibrational Medicine: The #1 Handbook of Subtle-Energy Therapies,* Bear & Company, Vermont, USA, 2011.

Gilman, S., *Transform Your Boundaries,* Island Bound Publishing, 2014.

Goldstein, E., *The Now Effect: How this Moment Can Change the Rest of Your Life,* Simon & Schuster, New York, 2012.

Greer, B., *Super Natural Home: Improve Your Health, Home, and Planet-One Room at a Time,* Rodale Inc. New York, 2009.

Gutman, R., *Smile: The Astonishing Powers of a Simple Act.* TED Book, Kindle, 2011.

Hanh, T.N., *How to Love: Choosing Well at Every Stage of Life,* Parallax Press, USA, 2014.

Hanson, R., *Hardwiring Happiness: The Practical Science of Re-shaping Your Brain – and Your Life,* Ubury Publishing, Great Britain, 2015.

Harris, R., *The Happiness Trap: Stop Struggling, Start Living,* Exile Publishing, Kindle, 2013.

Hay, L.L. & Kessler, D., *You Can Heal Your Heart,* Hay House Inc., USA, 2014.

Hay, L.L. & Schulz, M.L., *All is Well: Heal Your Body with Medicine, Affirmations, and Intuition,* Hay House Inc., USA, 2013.

Hofstede, G., *Cultures Consequences: Comparing Values, Behaviours, Institutions and Organizations Across Nations,* Sage Publications Inc., CA, 2001.

Hofstede, G., *Cultures and Organisations: Software of the Mind,* McGraw-Hill Education, USA, 2010.

Hougaard, R., Carter, J., & Coutts, G., *One Second Ahead: Enhance your Performance at Work with Mindfulness,* Palgrave McMillian, USA, 2016.

Huffington, A., *The Sleep Revolution: Transforming Your Life, One Night at a Time,* Virgin Digital. Kindle, 2014.

Ibarra, H., *Act Like a Leader, Think Like a Leader,* Harvard Business School Publishing. *USA, 2015.*

Jackson, M., *Lunar and Biodynamic Gardening: Planting your biodynamic garden by the phases of the moon,* Ryland, Peter and Small Ltd, Great Britain, 2015.

Kashdan, T., & Biswas-Diener, R., *The Upside of Your Downside: Why Being Your Whole Self--Not Just Your "good" Self - Drives Success and Fulfillment,* Plume Books, 2015.

Kaufman, S. & Gregoire, C. (n.d.). *Wired to Create: Unravelling the Mysteries of the Creative Mind,* Penguin Random House, LLC, New York, 2016.

Keltner, D., *Hands on Research: The Science of Touch. Greater Good Magazine,* Greater Good Science Centre, UCLA Berkley, 2010.

Kingston, K., *Creating Sacred Space with Feng Shui,* Little, Brown Book Group, United Kingdom, 1996.

La France, M., *Why Smile: The Science Behind Facial Expressions,* W.W. Norton, USA, 2013.

Lama, D., Holiness & Tutu, Archbishop D, *The Book of Joy: Lasting Happiness in a Changing World* (with Douglas Abrams), Avery Publishing Group, USA, 2016.

Lammers, W., *Self-Coaching with Logosynthesis: How the Power of Words Can Change Your Life,* Institute for Logosynthesis, Mainfeld, 2015.

Lawless, J., *Aromatherapy and the Mind,* Thorsons, Great Britain, 1994.

Lieberman, M., *Social: Why Our Brains Are Wired to Connect,* Broadway Books, USA, 2014.

Lindon, D. *The Science of Hand, Heart and Mind,* Viking, 2015.

Linn, D., *Space Clearing: How to Purify and Create Harmony in your Home,* McGraw Hill Contemporary, 2000.

Lipton, B., *The Biology of Belief: Unleashing the Power of Consciousness, Matter and Miracles,* Hay House, Kindle, 2015.

Lyubomirsky, S., *The Myths of Happiness: What Should Make You Happy, but Doesn't, What Shouldn't Make You Happy, but Does,* Penguin Books, New York, 2013.

Mann, S., *The Upside of Downtime: Why Boredom is Good,* Little Brown Group, London, 2016.

Marshall, L., *The Body Speaks: Performance and Physical Expression,* Methuen Drama, Kindle, 2008.

Martin, M., *The Chatter That Matters - Your Words Are Your Power,* Balboa Press, Bloomington, IL., 2012.

Martinez, M, *The Mind Body Code: How to Change the Beliefs that Limit Your Health, Longevity, and Success,* Sounds True, Boulder, Colorado, 2014.

McKenzie, S. & Hassed, C., *Mindfulness for Life,* City Exile Publishing, Kindle, 2012.

McQuaid, M.L. & Lawn, E., *Your Strengths Blueprint: How to be Engaged, Energized and Happy at Work,* Published by Michelle McQuaid, Australia, 2014.

Mednick, S. & Ehrman, M., *Take a Nap! Change Your Life,* Workman Publishing Company Inc., New York, Kindle, 2006.

Mohr, T., *Playing Big – A Practical Guide for Brilliant Women Like You,* Cornerstone, Great Britain, 2015.

Molesley, M., *The Clever Guts Diet: How to Revolutionise Your Body from the Inside Out,* Simon and Schuster, Australia, Kindle, 2017.

Molesley, M., *The 8-Week Blood Sugar Diet: Lose Weight Fast and Reprogramme Your Body for Life,* Short Books Limited, London, 2016.

Morjani, A., *In Dying to be Me: My Journey from Cancer to Near Death, to True Healing,* Hay House United Kingdom, 2013.

Mosely, Dr. M. & Bee, P., *Fast Exercise: The Secret to High Intensity Exercise,* Short Books Limited, Great Britain, 2013.

Mosley, Dr. M., *The 8-week Blood Sugar Diet: Lose Weight Fast and Re-program Your Body,* Simon & Schuster Australia, 2015.

Neff, K., *Self-Compassion: The Power of Being Kind to Yourself,* Harper Collins Publishers Inc., USA, 2015.

Neff, K., *Self-Compassion: Stop Beating Yourself Up and Leave Insecurity Behind,* Hodder Stoughton, Great Britain, 2011.

Nelson, Dr. B., *The Emotion Code: How to Release Your Trapped Emotions for Abundant Health, Love and Happiness,* Wellness Unmasked Publishing, USA, 2007.

Newman, M. & Berkowitz, B., *How to be Your Own Best Friend*, Ballantine Books, USA, 2016.

Northrup, C., *Dodging Energy Vampires: An Empath's Guide to Evading Relationships that Drain You and Restoring Your Health and Power*, Hay House Inc., USA, 2018.

Northrup, C., *Goddesses Never Age: The Secret Prescription for Radiance, Vitality and Wellbeing*, Hay House, United Kingdom, 2015.

Ober, C., Sinatra, S. & Zuker, M., *Earthing: The Most Important Discovery Yet?* Basic Health Publications Inc., Laguna Beach, CA, 2010.

Orloff, Dr. J., *The Empath's Survival Guide: Life Strategies for Sensitive People.* Sounds True Inc., USA, 2017.

Orloff, J., *The Power of Surrender: Let Go and Energise Your Relationships, Success and Well-being*, Harmony Books, New York, 2015.

Pennick, N., *The Pagan Book of Days: A Guide to the Festivals, Traditions, and Sacred Days of the Year*, Destiny Books, USA, 2001.

Pert, C., *The Molecules of Emotion: Why You Feel the Way You Feel*, Simon & Schuster, United Kingdom, 2012.

Peterson, C. & Seligman, M. E. P. (Eds.), *Character strengths and virtues: A handbook and classification*, Oxford University Press, New York, 2004.

Petrovich, K., *Elemental Energy: Crystal and Gemstone Rituals for a Beautiful Life*, Harper One, Kindle, 2016.

Provine, R. R., *Laughter: A Scientific Investigation*, Penguin Books, Kindle, 2001.

Rock, D., *Your Brain at Work: Strategies for Overcoming Distraction, Regaining Focus, and Working Smarter All Day Long*, Harper Business, New York, USA, 2009.

Rubin, G., *Better than Before: What I Learned About Making and Breaking Habits - to Sleep More, Quit Sugar, Procrastinate Less, and Generally Build a Happier Life*, Hodder & Stoughton, Great Britain, 2016.

Rudd, S., *Food as Medicine: Cooking for Your Best Health*, Novella Distribution, Australia, 2016.

Schulz, M.L., *The Intuitive Advisor: A Psychic Doctor Teaches You How to Solve Your Most Pressing Health Problems*, Hay House, USA, 2009.

Schwartz, T., *The Way We're Working isn't Working: The Four Forgotten Needs that Energise Your Performance*, Simon & Schuster, Great Britain, 2016.

Segal, I., *The Secret Language of Your Body: The Essential Guide to Healing*, Beyond World Publishing, USA, 2010.

Seppala, E., *Happiness Track: How to Apply the Science of Happiness to Accelerate Your Success*, Little Brown Book Club, London, United Kingdom, 2017.

Silver, T., *Outrageous Openness: Letting the Divine Take the Lead*, Atria Books, Kindle, 2014.

Silverstone, M., *Blinded by Science*, Lloyds World Publishing, 2011.

Sinek, S., *Find Your Why: A Practical Guide for Discovering Purpose for You and Your Team*, Penguin, United Kingdom, 2017.

Soojung-Kim Pang, A, *Rest: Why You Get More Done When You Work Less*, Penguin Books, Great Britain, 2017.

The Energy Project and Harvard Business Review, White Paper: *Human Era @ Work*, Harvard Business Review, 2014.

Thomas, L. & Obry, C., *The Encyclopedia of Energy Medicine*, Fairview Press, Minnesota, USA, 2010.

Yardley. G. & Kelly K., *7 Days to Effective People Management*, Times Publishing, Singapore, 1996.

Toleman, D., *Farmacist Desk Reference of Wholefood Medicine*, Vol. 1, Trideca Publishing, USA, 2008.

Toleman, D., *Top of Form*

Farmacist Desk Reference Ebook 12, Whole Foods and topics that Start with the Letters T thru Z: Farmacist Desk Reference E book series. YNOT EDUK8 Inc. eBook.

Tourles, S., *50 Simple Ways to Pamper Yourself*, Storey Books, Vermont, USA, 1999.

Berkowitz, G., *UCLA Researchers Identify Key Biobehavioral Pattern Used by Women to Manage Stress*, ScienceDaily, University of California, Los Angeles, 2000.

Vernikos, J., *Sitting Kills, Moving Heals: How Everyday Movement Will Extend Your Life and Exercise Alone Won't*, Quill Driver Books, Fresno, CA, Kindle, 2011.

Walker, M., *Why We Sleep: Unlocking the Power of Sleep and Dreams*, Simon & Schuster, Kindle, 2017.

Walters, J., *My Secret to a Healthy Lifestyle: Intuitive Eating*, Life Wellness, Huffington Post, 2013.

Warrell, M., *Make Your Mark: A Guidebook for the Brave Hearted*, John Wiley & Sons, Australia, 2017.

Wells, S., *100% YES! – The Energy of Success Release Your Resistance Align Your Values Go for Your Goals Using Simple Energy Techniques (SET)*, Waterford Publishing, Inglewood, Australia, 2016.

William, A., *Medical Medium Life-Changing Foods: Save Yourself and the Ones You love with the Hidden Powers of Fruits & Vegetables*, Hay House, Kindle, USA, 2016.

Wills, P., *The Colour Healing Manual: The Complete Colour Therapy Programme Revised Edition,* Judy Piatku Publishers Ltd, London, 2013.

Wilson, C., *Intuitive: How to Access and Use Your Birth-Given Intuition,* Michael Hanrahan, Australia, 2017.

Wilson, S., *First, We Make the Beast Beautiful: A New Story About Anxiety,* Macmillan Australia, Kindle, 2017.

Worwood, V.A., *The Complete Book of Essential Oils and Aromatherapy Your Body Language Shapes Who You Are: Over 800 Natural, Nontoxic, and Fragrant Recipes to Create Health, Beauty, and Safe Home and Work Environments,* New World Library, California, 2016.

Yardley, G., *A Delicious Life, One Moment at a Time,* Austin & Macauley Publishers, Great Britain, 2018.

Websites

Act Mindfully – Acceptance & Commitment Therapy Workshops www.actmindfully.com.au/

Andrew Weil M.D. www.drweil.com

Authentic Happiness Resources www.authentichappiness.sas.upenn.edu/

Barefoot healing – Earthing products www.barefoot.com.au/

Bioptron Light Systems - Asia Pacific Distributors: Kate and Stephen White https://www.lightfrequency.com.au

Binaural beat music www.I-doser.com

Clifton Strengths Finder 2.0 www.gallupstrengthscenter.com

Elektra: Magnesium products www.nourishedlife.com.au

Faster EFT Practitioner, Judy Timperon www.findingfreedom.com.au\

Grain Fields: Fermented prebiotic foods www.agmfoods.com/

'Jiyo': Internet of Wellbeing www.jiyo.com

Janesce: Organic Skin Care and Pure Essential Oils www.janesce.com.au

Lifeflow Meditation Centre www.Lifeflow.com.au

Loving Kindness Meditation downloads www.positivityresonance.com/meditations.html

Lumosity: Brain Training https://www.lumosity.com

Mercola: Natural health information https://www.mercola.com/

Microba: Gut testing https://www.microba.com

Orgon Effects Australia: Electromagnetic harmonising products www.orgoneffectsaustralia.com.au/

Probono Australia: Volunteer Match Program www.probonoaustralia.com.au/volunteer

'The Grounded' movie www.mygroundedmovie.com

VIA Character Survey www.viacharacter.org/www/character-strengths-survey

Programs, DVDs, Music and Apps

The Compassionate Life: Walking the Path of Kindness. (2018). [DVD], Barasch, MI.

Colquhoun, J., & Laurentine, T.B., *Food Matters: Prevent Illness, Reverse Disease, Maintain Optimal Health – Naturally.* DVD.

Insight Timer: Meditation App

Pert. C., *Healing the Hurting, Shining the Light: A Chakra Meditation for All Your Body Minds.* Music CD.

Pzizz: Sleep App

Smiling Mind: Mindfulness App

Events

Healthy Ageing Conference, Adelaide (2017).

World Street Food Congress http://wsfcongress.com/

TED Talks

Buettner, D., Sept 2009. *How to Live to 100+,* TEDxTC
https://www.ted.com/talks/dan_buettner_how_to_live_to_be_100?language=en

Cuddy. A. 2012. *Your Body Language Shapes Who You Are.* TED Global.
https://www.ted.com/talks/amy_cuddy_your_body_language_shapes_who_you_are?language=en

Fraser, A. 2015. *Three simple steps not to take a bad day home.* TEDX QUT. https://www.youtube.com/watch?v=4GRIxwBUCfU

Gilman, S., Dec 2015. TEDx talk, *Good Boundaries Free You*, TEDx.

Mednick, S., June 2013, Give it Up for the Down State. *TEDxUCRSalon.* https://www.youtube.com/watch?v=MklZJprP5F0

People

AdiShakti, Lifeforce Consultant and Practitioner
https://www.starlightpraana.com/

Arylo, Christine, Transformational Teacher
www.christinearylo.com

Auliq-Ice, Oscar, Singer, Author, Social Investor https://www.linkedin.com/in/auliqice/

Axe, Josh, Doctor of Natural Medicine, Chiropractor, Clinical Nutritionist
https://draxe.com/

Bandler, Richard, Author, Trainer in Self-help
https://richardbandler.com/

Baumeister, Dr. Roy, F. Social Psychologist
http://www.roybaumeister.com/

Benson, Dr. Herbert, Harvard Cardiologist, Pioneer in Mind Body Medicine
https://www.bensonhenryinstitute.org/about-us-dr-herbert-benson/

Bligh, Anna – Former Queensland Premier, CEO Australian Bankers Association
https://www.linkedin.com/pulse/anna-bligh-chief-executive-officer-australian-bankers-cathy-bryson/

Bliss, Remedy, Pioneer in Fermented and Raw Foods
http://www.remedybliss.com/

Bogo, Hiro, Mentor, Guide for Visionary Entrepreneurs
https://hiroboga.com/

Bolte, Dr. Jill Taylor, Neuroanatomist, Author
http://drjilltaylor.com/

Braco, Faith healer
http://www.braco.me/en/

Braden, Gregg, Author
https://www.greggbraden.com/about-gregg-braden/

Brown, Dr. Brene, Researcher, Author
https://brenebrown.com/

Brown, Stuart, Founder of National Institute for Play
http://www.nifplay.org/

Burston, John, Meditation Teacher
https://lifeflow.com.au/teachers/john-burston/

Campbell, Rebecca, Spiritual teacher
www.rebeccacampbell.me/

Carr, Kris, Author, Wellness Activist
www.kriscarr.com

Cherry, Kendra Child Psychologist, Author
www.explorepsychology.com/

Childre, Doc, Founder of the HeartMath Institute, Author
www.heartmath.org/about-us/team/founder-and-executives/

Chopra, Dr. Deepak, Spiritual Teacher, Wellbeing Activist, Author
www.deepakchopra.com/

Choquette, Sonja, Spiritual Teacher, Author
soniachoquette.net/

Cuddy, Dr. Amy, Social Psychologist, Author
www.linkedin.com/in/amy-cuddy-3654034/

Dale, Cyndi, Author, Intuitive, Healer
cyndidale.com/

David, Dr. Susan, Psychologist, Author
www.susandavid.com/

Davidson, Dr. Richie, Founder and Chair of Centre for Healthy Minds
www.richardjdavidson.com/

Deida, David, Author, Spiritual Teacher
https://deida.info/

Dement, Professor William, World Expert in Sleep Research, Author
https://profiles.stanford.edu/william-dement

Disney, Walt, Innovator, Story Teller, Entertainer
www.waltdisney.org/walt-disney

Dossey, Dr. Larry, Integrative Medical Physician, Author
www.dosseydossey.com

Duggan, Dr. William – Author, Senior Lecturer Columbia University
www8.gsb.columbia.edu/cbs-directory/detail/wrd3

Dyer, Dr. Wayne W., Philosopher, Author
www.drwaynedyer.com/

Eden, Donna, Energy Medicine Teacher, Author
www.edenenergymedicine.com

Einstein, Professor Albert, Physicist, Free Thinker
www.biographyonline.net/scientists/albert-einstein.html

Erickson, Milton, Psychiatrist, Hypnotherapist
https://www.erickson-foundation.org/biography/

Frederickson, Professor Barbara, Researcher, Author
http://www.positivityresonance.com/

Gates, Donna, Author, Wellbeing Advocate
https://bodyecology.com/

Gilman, Sarri, Psychotherapist, Author
www.sarrigilman.com

Graham, Martha, Choreographer, Author
www.marthagraham.org

Hagen, Walter, Golfer
www.worldgolfhalloffame.org/walter-hagen/

Hanson, Dr. Rick, Psychologist, Author
www.rickhanson.com

Hassed, Dr. Craig, Author, Mindfulness Expert
https://www.monash.edu/medicine/spahc/general-practice/about/staff-students/hassed

Hofstede, Geert, Social Psychologist, Author
www.geerthofstede.com

Huffington, Arianna, CEO, Huffington Post
www.ariannahuffington.com

Hyman, Dr. Mark, Physician, Author
www.drhyman.com

James, Dr. William, Psychologist, Philosopher
https://psychology.fas.harvard.edu/people/william-james

Kashdan, Dr. Todd, Scientist, Professor of Psychology, Author
www.toddkashdan.com

Keltner, Dr. Dacher, Professor of Psychology, Author
https://psychology.berkeley.edu/people/dacher-keltner

Kerr, Dr. Fiona, Scientist, Researcher, Author
www.fiona-kerr.com

Kettering, Charles, Engineer, Inventor
http://lemelson.mit.edu/resources/charles-f-kettering

Kleiner, Dr. Susan, Scientist, Nutritionist
http://drskleiner.com/

Kleitman, Dr. Nathaniel, Sleep researcher, Physiologist
https://www.smithsonianmag.com/science-nature/
the-stubborn-scientist-who-unraveled-a-mystery-of-the-night-91514538/

La France, Dr. Marianne, Professor of Psychology, Author
http://mariannelafrance.com/

Lack, Professor Leon, Clinical Psychologist, Sleep researcher
http://www.adelaidesleephealth.org.au/staff/view/16

Lama, Dalai, Spiritual Leader
www.dalailama.com

Lazar, Sara, Neuroscientist, Researcher
https://scholar.harvard.edu/sara_lazar/home

Lewis, C. S., Poet, Novelist
www.cslewis.com

Lisieux, Saint Therese, Carmelite Nunwww.littleflower.org

Maas, Dr. James, Sleep authority, Researcher
www.jamesmass.com

Mahlab, Karen, CEO Probono Australia
www.probonoaustralia.com.au

Marcellino, Dr. Frank, Chiropractor, Teacher
www.marcellinohealthcentre.com.au

Martinez, Dr. Mario, Neuropsychologist, Author
www.biocognitive.com

McCraty, Rollin, Director of Research Heart Math Institute
www.heartmath.org

Mednick, Dr. Sara, Sleep Researcher
www.saramednick.com

Mercola, Dr. Joseph, Alternative Medicine Proponent, Author
www.mercola.com

Muir, John, Naturalist, Conservationist, Author
www.smithsonianmag.com

Myss, Dr. Caroline, Spiritual Teacher, Author
www.myss.com

Neff, Dr. Kristen, Researcher, Author
www/self-compassion.org

Niemiec, Dr. Ryan, Psychologist
www.ryanniemiec.com

Northrup, Dr. Christiane, Women's Health Advocate, Author
www.drnorthrup.com

Oliver, Mary, Poet
www.poetryfoundation.org/poets/mary-oliver

Oz, Dr. Mehmet, TV Personality, Cardiac Surgeon
https://www.doctoroz.com/

Pert, Dr. Candace, Scientist, Author
www.candacepert.com

Peru, Elizabeth, Australian Astrologer
www.elizabethperu.com

Pink, Daniel, Author
www.danpink.com

Provine, Dr. Robert, Neuroscientist
www.provine.umbc.edu

Rankin, Dr. Lissa, Mind-Body Physician, Author
http://lissarankin.com/about

Rife, Dr. Royal, Scientist, Inventor
www.royal-rife-machine.com

Robbins, Tony, Author, Life Coach
www.tonyrobbins.com

Sandberg, Sheryl, Chief Operating Office of Facebook, Author
https://www.facebook.com/sheryl

Sandburg, Carl, Poet
https://www.poetryfoundation.org/poets/carl-sandburg

Satir, Virginia, Psychotherapist
http://www.satiraustralia.com/virginia_satir.asp

Schulz, Dr. Mona Lisa, Medical Intuitive
https://www.drmonalisa.com/

Schwartz, Tony, CEO, The Energy Project
www.theenergyproject.com.au

Seligman, Professor Martin, Director Penn Positive Psychology Centre
https://www.authentichappiness.sas.upenn.edu/faculty-profile/profile-dr-martin-seligman

Seppala, Dr. Emma, Author, Research Scientist
https://emmaseppala.com/about/

Shahar, Tal Ben, Author, Lecturer in Positive Psychology
http://www.talbenshahar.com/

Silver, Tosha, Poet, Author
https://toshasilver.com/

Snyder, Kimberley, Nutritionist
https://kimberlysnyder.com/

Tainio, Dr. Bruce, Plant Breeder, Microbiologist
http://www.tainio.com/about/

Tesla, Nikola, Inventor, Engineer
https://www.smithsonianmag.com/innovation/extraordinary-life-nikola-tesla-180967758/

Turner, Dr. Kelly, Author, Screenwriter, Producer
https://kelly-turner.com/

Tutu, Archbishop Desmond, Theologian, Civil Rights Activist
https://www.britannica.com/biography/Desmond-Tutu

Van Praagh, James, Evidential Psychic Medium, Author
http://www.vanpraagh.com/

Vernikos, Dr. Joan, Expert in Stress and Healthy Ageing
http://www.joanvernikos.com/

Vinogradov, Mikhail, Scientist
http://zapaliizgrada.rs/dendrotherapy/

Walker, Professor Matt, Neuroscientist, Sleep Diplomat
https://www.sleepdiplomat.com/professor

Walter, Jennipher, Pioneer of Body Positive Movement
https://fitbottomedgirls.com/

Warrell, Maggie, Author, Speaker, Media Commentator
https://margiewarrell.com/

Watson, Emma, Psychologist and Energy Practitioner
https://psychologicalservicesbunbury.com.au/

Webster, Richard, Psychic, Author
http://www.richardwebster.co.nz/

Weil, Dr. Andrew, Practitioner and Teacher of Integrative Medicine
https://www.drweil.com/

Wells, Steve, Author, Practitioner in Energy Psychology
http://www.eftdownunder.com/about-us/

Wilson, Sarah, Author, Minimalist, Entrepreneur
http://www.sarahwilson.com/

Winfrey, Oprah, Media Entrepreneur, Actor, Philanthropist
http://www.oprah.com/index.html

Wong, Ali, Stand-Up Comedian, Writer, Actress
https://www.aliwong.com/

Wood, Dr. John, Executive Coach, Consultant
http://www.leadershipsolutions.com.au/

Yardley, Gary, Author
http://www.ipips.com/content/about-us/people-of-pips/gary-yardley

Other Resources

Ancient Indian medicine (Ayurveda)
https://www.ayurvedanama.org/history-of-ayurveda/
https://www.kamalaya.com/holistic-therapy.htm

Barefoot Healing – Earthing Specialists
www.barefoothealing.com.au

Orgon Effects Australia – Electromagnetic Harmonising Products
https://www.orgoneffectsaustralia.com.au/

Chinese Feng Shui
https://fengshuiaustralia.com/
https://www.fengshuiliving.com.au/about-us/

Native American herbal cleansing rituals
https://www.wolfwalkercollection.com/blogs/news/
quick-reference-guide-to-native-american-and-other-ceremonial-herbs-resins

Emotional Freedom Techniques (EFT)
http://www.bradyates.net/eft.html

Forest Bathing (*Shinrin-yoku*)
http://www.shinrin-yoku.org/shinrin-yoku.html
https://www.conservationsa.org.au/forest_bathing

Franklin Covey Institute, Global Consultancy on Performance
https://www.franklincovey.com/

Greater Good Sciences Centre at the University of California, Berkeley
https://greatergood.berkeley.edu/

Harvard T.H. Chan School of Public Health
https://www.hsph.harvard.edu/

HeartMath Institute in the USA
https://www.heartmath.com/

Ikigai – The Japanese Philosophy to a Long and Happy Life
https://www.sloww.co/ikigai-book/

In-conversation' with Richard Fidler on the Australian radio station ABC
http://www.abc.net.au/radio/programs/conversations/

Iris Institute, CA for life long learning and deepening of awareness
http://www.irisinstitute.net/about.html

Kundalini Yoga – Gaia TV offers a range of videos
https://www.gaia.com

London School of Economics
http://www.lse.ac.uk/

Loving Kindness meditation
http://www.positivityresonance.com/meditations.html

Mayo Clinic – Integrated Clinical Practice and Research Centre
https://www.mayoclinic.org/

Om-Harmonics, Mind-valley – Meditation and Self Improvement
http://www.omharmonics.com/

Mosley, M. and Ahsan, S. *Trust Me, I'm a Doctor* Season 6.
https://www.bbc.co.uk/programmes/b08d6ctl

Safe Cosmetics Australia – *Toxic Free List*
https://www.safecosmeticsaustralia.com.au/toxic-free-list

Global Centre for Modern Ageing
http://www.gcma.net.au/

ABOUT THE AUTHOR

Known for her sensitivity and skill in inspiring people to connect more with their heart, mind and spirit, Sally J. Rundle is a thought leader in intuition, energy medicine and contemporary well-being practices.

As a coach and mentor, she educates and inspires people to discover their natural gifts, talents and strengths and in this way, she helps to empower and transform both individuals and organisations.

Sally has great curiosity for the latest developments in mindfulness, energy medicine, energy psychology, healing, relationship dynamics and metaphysics. She has a certificate in Energy Medicine, PhD in international management, Masters in Education and Bachelor of Science, with a major in Psychology.

As a coach with the HeartMath Institute USA – she uses world leading scientific tools to help people bridge the connection between their hearts and minds. Coupled with her training in Emotional Freedom Therapy (EFT), Hypnosis, Past Life Regression, Reiki and Dream analysis, Sally is able to support people intellectually, emotionally and energetically so they can achieve their full potential.

Printed in the United States
By Bookmasters